What A Life...

Things My Children Don't Know About Their Mother

Karen McKenzieSmith

DEDICATION

I dedicate this Memoir to the people that have prompted and inspired me to write this book as well as those that helped in many ways. You know who you are and I send prayers of blessings your way. I believe people are put in our lives for a reason and time therefore neither, GOOD or BAD. In no way, shape or form is this book meant to disrespect or dishonour any person mentioned.

Thanks to Kathleen Mailer for teaching me how to write, market and publish this book. Thanks also to my intrepid Editor, Coralie Banks of Leaping Cowgirl™ Productions Ltd. for patiently helping me extract this 90,000 word book from a manuscript that was 279,000 words. Finally, thanks to Maegan Neufeld, also of Leaping Cowgirl for taking amazing pictures for my platform.

It takes a village to write a good book, and I hope that you the reader enjoy all of our efforts!

TABLE OF CONTENTS

Preface 1

Chapter 1:   Before Conception I Was Cursed 3

Chapter 2:   Thank Heavens For Knot Holes In The Barn Wall 5

Chapter 3:   Animal Connection 21

Chapter 4:   Never To See Life The Same Again 25

Chapter 5:   A Higher Level Of Competition 29

Chapter 6:   Silent Danger For They Don't Scream, I Do! 35

Chapter 7:   "To Be Or Not To Be" 45

Chapter 8:   Starting Over 53

Chapter 9:   How I Met My Ex-Husband 57

Chapter 10: The Boss 63

Chapter 11: I Am Done! 69

Chapter 12: My Teaching Debut 75

Chapter 13: Aside From Teaching 85

Chapter 14: Gone Is The Jet-Set, Welcome Wet-Set! 95

Chapter 15: Stay At Home Mom 109

Chapter 16: Respect 119

Chapter 17: Divorce! 127

Chapter 18: Suicide 139

Chapter 19: Carried 161

Chapter 20: Mercy Me (1994-2000) 167

Chapter 21: Unbelievable Experiences 183

Chapter 22: My Crusades And Travels 225

Chapter 23: Weird & Miraculous 273

Chapter 24: Where I'm At Now 281

PREFACE

My dear children, all these years you have chosen not to let me into your lives, nor to be a part of my life. And yet I carried you in my body and cared for you with such love. I want you to know me, and who I really am. So, I wrote this book for you, and anyone else who might enjoy my "slice of life."

One thing is for certain, this is my truth. There are no lies nor do I seek revenge, or to slander anyone. I know that you may think I am crazy. What I have to say may not match what you have been told. Please provide your grace for me, for some of what I have written has been hard to share.

You the reader may also think I am telling a tall tale. Especially the part about the vampire I met. Trust me it is not a lie. I have Catholic friends that often suggest or get me books on the Saints and Mystics, due to the fact that I have similar life stories to write. I am fortunate to be of this lifetime. For once Mystics were burned at the stake.

Anyhow, it has been very cathartic to write down my story. I hope that it inspires you, and helps too.

CHAPTER 1:

BEFORE CONCEPTION I WAS CURSED

I am in my hospital bassinet struggling and screaming, exhausted from trying to get attention. There are sharp and steely spears hanging down from the ceiling over my head. Where's my Mom? As I wrote this vision down in October 1999, my adult-self begins to cry. I don't know if the baby-me sees the frightening spears or not, but they are there in my vision.

The vision abruptly switches to the ranch. I see myself being tossed and swung around. Who is hurting me? She is a witch! She looks nasty and evil, lacking in remorse as she tortures me constantly. I am amazed I lived throughout those months that never seemed to end.

My adult-self, in real life in October 1999, is crying harder than ever. It nauseates me, and I run to throw up but all I can do is dry-heave. I feel the sharp pinches and the way she would carry me, sometimes by one leg, or just grabbing me by an elbow. I want the vision to stop. "No more, no more," I cry as I see only her and that mocking evil look again in her eyes.

The vision finally fades.

I was cursed before I was even conceived. My family tree stems from a long line of Masons and Scottish Druids. Whether this CURSE comes from that background, I don't know. All I know is a relative of the family put a CURSE on my mother regarding childbearing. And guess who she had next after the spell was put in to action? Me!

When I was born my mother went into a Post-Toxic condition immediately in the delivery room. She nearly died because of it. She definitely would have, were it not for her doctor having just got back from a conference where he had heard of this previously undiagnosed condition.

I saw this as a GOD thing. Good news for my mom but not for me in the immediate term. She was whisked away one direction, and I another with my "nurse"/that witch, and neither of us got any time at all to bond. She wasn't even given a second to hold or even look at me.

My mom also told me that she had me when she was two months short of her 42nd birthday. Older mothers have a far higher risk of serious birth defects. The fact that I was born totally healthy, whole, and with above average intellect in that day and age, was a miracle in itself.

Ever since I found out from her about the curse it made sense. I had always felt like a "walking target" that had gone through so many near death experiences. You will see as you read on the number of times I was nearly killed, or attempts on my life were made to no avail. You will also find out why I could never die.

The remaining fact, though, is this curse prevailed for over 46 years. It caused an awful lot of commotion in my life, and my mother's. I felt taunted over the decades, as if I was a big bulls-eye and being hit from all angles.

Of course you can tell by the very fact that I am still alive to write this book that the curse lost its power! Besides talking to my mom and asking her about my birth, I also asked the Lord to reveal what was going on and why I felt I was a target. It took some years to zero in on, but I was able to break the curse from having any more effect on me.

CHAPTER 2:

THANK HEAVENS FOR KNOT HOLES IN THE BARN WALL

I was born on a hot and sultry afternoon late in June to Forest and Vivian Smith. In a small Saskatchewan town just across the border from Alberta, Canada and Montana, USA. In the very southwest corner of the province in the sand hills and Cypress Hills region. In good ole Maple Creek.

Our ranch, the Sand Valley Hereford Ranch, was huge. I found this out years later. The Smith family ranch covered 7 sections of land. We also had one section of leased Crown Land plus the use of a large swath of Saskatchewan Provincial Community Pasture Land. We grazed about 10,000 head of cattle as I recall.

It was a real treat to have Dad scoop me up into the saddle in front of him to go check the stock. One of my Cowboy Poetry poems I wrote years later was about "Riding the Range." The poem starts off with me saying:

"Riding the range at such a young age in the huge, huge saddle, next to my Dad!

With the smell of weather, wet sage and the leather…"

You might say my dad was a tad on the old-fashioned side. Farm work was not something my dad thought women and children should have to deal with. Dad felt my sister, two years younger, and I should be in the house with our mother doing the housework. Of course that only made us all the more want to be down at the barn or shop where he was instead.

We did get to milk the cows and feed the kittens. They would all line up when we were milking. It was so cute! All of them would try to lick up every drop from their faces. There was enough to spend all morning licking up.

There were other small jobs we were allowed to do but the nitty-gritty farm work was left to Dad, my brother and the hired help.

Do you know all those years on the ranch and farm we girls never got to see a calf being born unless we could watch through the crack in the barn wall? Much of what I picked up about my father and about farm life was through those knot holes in the barn.

HOW MUCH DO WE KNOW ABOUT OUR PARENTS?

From casual conversations with my brother and others that knew my dad, I found out that he had been in the army. I also found out that he could roll a cigarette at a full gallop. I saw him shoot a rabid cat right between the eyes from some 30 feet. Of course he did not see me watching. It was another one of the many observations made through knot-holes in the barn wall.

I learned from my dad the balance between life and death on the ranch and farm. At times dad had to put animals down to protect us and other animals from disease. Plus he would not let an animal suffer either, when nothing could be done for it.

There were other times too when we would run short of meat in the winter and dad would go out and hunt an animal or fowl for food for us. I learned from him NOT to hunt for sport but rather out of necessity. Although my sister and brother hunt and are quite good at it, I am afraid I just did not care for it. That does not mean I can't shoot if I have to. My sister showed me how one time. Though the rifle and shotgun were rough on my shoulder, I did seem to manage the handgun well enough.

My dad wasn't much for being the lovey-dovey kind. Nor was he much for buying gifts for us kids. However there were a couple of times that stand out as the BEST ever gifts from my dad. He put together an entire swing set in our new basement playroom for a

Christmas gift to my sister and me when I was only 8 or 9 years old. That had to be the best ever Christmas gift from my dad.

Then when I was in Junior High for my 13th birthday, Dad was unbelievably awesome! He sent me on a scavenger hunt through the store to find my very own set of suitcases. It was a beautiful blue set of Samsonite luggage; matching and everything! My dad had his moments all right!

Over the years with bull sales and the flow of liquor at them, my dad became an alcoholic. Unfortunately when he was drunk he would get nasty. I remember a time I could not have been more than 3 or 4 years old.

I am not sure where my brother or sister were for they were not around at the time. I somehow was right there in the sitting room when my dad started arguing with my mom and yelling at her.

He went to hit her and I ran in the middle to try to stop him by grabbing at him and crying out to him "STOP IT DAD! DON'T HURT MOMMY! STOP! STOP!" At the same time he took his other arm and scraped me away in his rage and I slammed into the wall off to the side behind him. That was it for me helping anymore.

I would beg Mom to leave him. I would even start packing a suitcase for her at times. She would not give up on the marriage. I concluded that she probably didn't think we could survive on our own. I don't know.

I do know one thing, having gone through something similar. We Mothers do the VERY best we can do for the lives involved. My mom did the very best she could at that time in our lives, just as I did in 1994.

When I was in High School, my dad eventually quit drinking. Well mostly: there were times when friends would bring a bottle into the store and draw him in for a holiday drink but that was short-lived.

Looking back now it dawns on me that I don't think I ever said to him how proud I was of him for quitting.

I WAS RUN OVER AND FROZEN

I was about four years old when another "near-death" experience happened. On the ranch we had a huge garden near the house. It was big enough to drive the tractor around up and down the rows to plough and plant. After the soil had been well ploughed up we had started planting.

My job was to sit on the side of the wagon. The wagon was made out of an old back end of a truck my dad converted into a pull-type wagon. It was full of seed potatoes. I had to drop them into the holes as we drove slowly up and down the rows. Somehow I fell off and under the back wheel of the wagon. It drove right over me before anything could be done. Another miracle occurred. My mom said there wasn't a scratch on me!

About the same time I was spared from a far greater force, the weather. My sister and I decided in the middle of winter to walk up the lane that was not ploughed out. The snow was very deep, wet, and heavy. The more steps we took the deeper we went, to the point that we no longer could get ourselves out as it started to cave in on us and it was getting dark.

An additional possible death experience may have happened, but our border collie was finally able to work his way out of the snow trap to go and get help. We were nearly cooked with boiling water by our mom in order to save us from pneumonia.

BULLYING

Grade one was traumatic enough since I had not gone to Kindergarten to aid in that adjustment period. On top of it was added the additional stress of being bullied by 3 or 4 grade six girls. Sheesh, what next! Maybe it was my stance against them that propelled them into a fit of persistence.

All I know is, when defending myself from them one day I accidentally broke the window in the stairwell of the playroom entrance to the girls' playroom. Now the silver lining part in ending up in the principal's office and paying for the window was, I wasn't the only one brought up to the office. Hence the bullying ended.

Paying for the repair of a window isn't common anymore. I know that because when I was teaching Food Sciences, a few students broke into the pantry and opened brand new packages of food. I sent them to the Vice Principal and requested that they pay for the items or replace them. He looked at me and actually asked if I would reconsider imposing a penalty!

Can you believe that? What a shame! As a teacher in this day and age, I do not see much accountability going on. I see this as a deterioration of society and an injustice to our students. They and society will suffer the consequences of it.

PERCEPTION PROPELS

Something happened in grade two that propelled things into motion for a pattern to become established in my life. This meant that the building of my actual character and very being were altered for the rest of my life. At least until I realized it years and years later after my divorce, and did something about it!

I was at the beginning of the line at the classroom door. We were going to the washroom and then gym. That's when my teacher exclaims nonchalantly, "Karen? Let Missy take your place and you come back here *because I know that you won't mind.*"

Most of the time I didn't mind and that is why she asked me in particular. It was just the way I was and still am for the most part.

But this time, I really DID mind! Can you see how that would maybe alter how I usually looked at things from there on in? It hit me that I do not like to be taken advantage of. It actually left things on a sour note for me. It was then that I developed a negative perception about such matters.

This thinking has a healthy aspect about it. But it can be quite unhealthy too. Here is the danger: getting jumpy about the whole thing and assuming that I am being taken advantage of all the time can be detrimental to my attitude and health. That is why keeping such assumptions in check matters. Therefore balance is key.

Later when I became an adult, I was able to put a finger on it. I began right away to deal with it and proceeded to make a healthy change.

If I do fall prey to the same ill-gotten thinking I try to notice it as soon as possible and repent of it by rendering my thoughts captive unto GOD, in order to set my thinking back on track.

Then I evaluate the whole scenario in order to determine whether or not I am being taken advantage of AND whether it matters and is a real issue worth being concerned about.

A perfect example may be when I am standing in a line-up and asked to let someone go ahead of me. I may say "Sure I don't mind," or I may have to say that I do mind because I am in a hurry.

CRASHING A BAR AT EIGHT

As I mentioned, my dad was an alcoholic. There was an incident one time, thank Heavens it only happened once, where Dad had two of us kids with him when he went into town. Once the business end of the trip was accomplished, my dad decided that he would stop in, "briefly," he said, at the local bar.

In Canada, anyone under the age of 18 is not allowed in drinking establishments. Consequently my sister and I, ages 6 and 8, were left alone in the car to wait for him.

Well, we waited all right. We waited and waited and waited. It was getting dark so I actually did something I wouldn't ever want to do again!

I told my sister stay in the car with the doors locked. Then I got out of that car and trounced across the street and into the bar.

I didn't, to my relief, have to go far to find him. He was sitting with a bunch of our neighbours at a few tables close to the entrance. I simply and firmly took my dad's hand and pulled on him until he came with me.

AWARDS

A totally opposite piece of information that is much more pleasant than the bar crashing scene, refers to church instead. I received the "Cross 'n Crown" for perfect attendance at Sunday School at the United Church in High River. I still have that perfect attendance pin in my collection of pins.

I guess you can say I was a bit of a tomboy. I now see this as my childhood way to get my dad to notice and be proud of me. It had its Pros and Cons! I received a number of awards as I tried to get his attention, which is good.

Yet it's not a healthy way to live out the rest of my life. For I realized that I could strive myself to death achieving all these awards and things, yet never get my dad to notice me. I finally discovered in my late teens that it was time to stop expecting to be noticed and to simply be content without his recognition or with whatever I got.

CIGARETTES

I wanted recognition from others too for different reasons. In so doing I found a sure-fire way to keep one from wanting to smoke. I smoked cigarettes on a dare. ALL of them! This was just to show the kids that had dared me to smoke how tough I was. The good news is, believe it or not, soon after I threw up around the corner. I never want to touch a cigarette again! See, good can come from bad. YEAH!

DUPED

I did a really stupid thing. All because I had a crush on my brother's friend! To impress him, I ran inside the house to put on my very best "Sunday-go-to-meet-in" western outfit. My Mom handmade made this really nice western suit for me. It was grey suit material made into a western jacket and matching pants. What was I thinking, but out I went to the barnyard to where my brother and his friend were. I let my brother dupe me into looking like a complete fool.

My brother had just roped a calf and laughingly asked me to hold the roped calf for him. I gullibly did. Only to have him turn and spook the calf, causing me to be pulled off my feet and dragged around the corral. In the muck and manure! I learned to take his laughing as a clue.

Oh no, was my mom going to be mad! But I liked the kind of mad Mom got. No spanking, no harsh words, just that look of disappointment that was plenty enough for me to feel grave remorse about it all.

I loved my brother dearly and looked up to him, and I still do! He was nevertheless the stereotypical older brother and a pain in the head. You know, the kind of brother that puts a garter snake down my neck!

It took me being a mother of boys and a science teacher to get over my fear of those slithery critters.

MY FRIEND THE WOLF

Do you know that kind of torture where a person can wrestle you down on the ground and spit on you if you don't say "UNCLE"? Well, my brother would do that to me all the time. It was impossible to ever get out of his hold! UNTIL… A Norwegian elkhound wandered into our yard one day.

That dog instantly took a real liking to me for some reason. He became my wing-man and my guard dog. My brother couldn't come within 10 feet of me. My newfound guard dog would jump in between us and growl like a wolf as well as look like one too.

If you know what Norwegian elkhounds look like, you will know what I am talking about. They look like a cross between a Husky dog and a wolf. My days of being picked on by my brother were over.

Because we lived 20 minutes outside of the city of Calgary, we often had stray animals that people from the city had abandoned. One of those animals, to everyone's complete shock was a purebred Hereford bull.

The first place my dad figured it came from was the Auction Market, but no bull was missing. My Dad even advertised in the local papers, the High River Times, the Calgary Herald and the Western Producer. No one claimed it, so we became the proud owners of a papered Hereford Bull. You see, papered animals such as this bull are more valuable because they are hybrids with quality sperm for breeding. That bull proved to be rather profitable as a stud for years and even when Dad sold it.

FIRE

My sister and I liked to play "Pioneers & Settlers." It was a game where we would pretended we were off on our own having to fend for ourselves and build from scratch on the land. One time we stole some bacon from the freezer and eggs from the chicken coop and took a bunch of matches. We set off for our secret spot in the woods along the overgrown, abandoned road allowance. There we set up and made a fire to cook our bacon and eggs on.

That went well until the campfire got away from us. The next thing you know the forest was on fire! We tried on our own to put it out but it just spread too fast! This was going to be something for which my mother could no longer protect us.

We feared getting the Razor Strap my dad had hung up as a constant disciplinary reminder. Instead, Dad gave us a spanking with his bare hand, and that was plenty good enough. I guess you could call this good news, for my dad never did use that Razor Strap on us, ever! It did its best work as a deterrent.

DEATH TRIES AGAIN

That same hand that gave me that spanking saved my life. With his bare hands. It was one of the times we were rounding up the cows and calves. I do not recall why I was on foot, but I was.

We had one cow that always was really mean. You had to watch your back with her at all times! I asked Mom why we even kept her. My mom told me that the cow always had twins. (This is not common among cows but very common among sheep.) So I can see why we kept her, that "Ole Meany!"

Somehow I ended up between her and her calves. This was enough to make the mildest cow get riled up and all upset. However this was not any cow. This was "Ole Meany" and she didn't just get upset. She began to charge at me like a Brahma Bull.

My dad yelled in his loudest voice ever, "RUN TO THE FENCE KAREN!" You betcha I ran, as fast as my little 8 year old legs could carry me, BUT it was not fast enough. I could feel her breath on my neck! Too close I knew, for she was closer than that fence and it was game over for me.

All of a sudden I felt my Dad's hand grab the back of my belt and pants and I became airborne! Whew! I was a goner until Dad rescued me out of the nostrils of death and scooped me up into his saddle in front of him! Saved again! I think I have more lives than a cat. The first few months of my life took up nine lives alone, and all this had already happened within the short timeframe of my first eight years of life.

MAKING THE BEST OF A BAD SITUATION

Four years later, we were living in Camrose, Alberta. Moving to Camrose changed everything for me! New friends, new math, new way of life and three new ways of living: first on a residential street; then in the back of the store; and finally in a trailer court.

By age 12, I had a new job as a store clerk, cashing out and stock taking. My very first job was back in High River running sales slips to the office from the auction ring. I had other jobs working for the school janitor and a paper route.

THERE ARE SOME PERKS

At any rate, my parents bought the corner candy store. The BEST part was, every kind of candy was now freely accessible. Umm!! However, my mom was a pretty smart mom. After moving into the back of the store, she told us we could have anything we wanted for a snack while watching TV before bed. With our eyes bugging out of our heads and our mouths' salivating, we dove in!

I took not a bag of potato chips, rather a BOX, not one but a whole BAG of red licorice and not a can of pop, but a whole litre bottle of pop. I also took my favourite chocolate bar along with two other kinds that I hadn't tried before. Heck no, why think small when you can go BIG!

Just as my mom suspected, in a matter of hours was I so sick! To this day I cannot finish a whole bag of chips at once, or a whole chocolate bar or a can of pop and definitely not a whole bag of licorice either. Mom never had to worry about us eating up all the stock and profit after that!

BREAKING FEMALE BARRIERS

As I took on further jobs I found I had to stand up for myself a number of times. Mostly because what I fought for were things that many in society did not understand. Not even other females got that I was fighting for them as well as myself.

I was the first female to ask for and get hired to deliver the local newspaper. I stood up for females to be able to enrol in Automotive and Shop in High School. I stood with other females to fight for ice time so girls could play hockey too.

I took all my Red Cross in one summer. Once I got my Bronze Medallion in Royal Life Saving at age 13, I was on my way to a career in Lifeguarding! This was an excellent choice as a good paying job for a female.

I was at that age where females were just breaking into the workforce where males had dominated for years. At the very beginning I was faced with having to stand up to my boss the Recreation Director for the City concerning equal pay. I was not getting the same pay as my male co-worker. We were hired the same time, we were the same age, and we had the same qualifications. The only difference was, you guessed it, that I was a female!

I was scared spit-less that I was going to get fired from my first professional job when I took a stance for my equal pay. Standing up for my rights along with a job of great responsibility, thrust me into maturity at the young age of 13. I am not one to back down when sticking up for fairness with all concerned. Hurrah! I got my raise for equal pay.

THE YARDSTICK

A life changing moment occurred in my grade five year. It happened during science class. What happened was awful, but it made for a positive career decision for me.

I found three things repulsive. So much so, that at one point I stomped home fuming. I declared to my mother that I never wanted to go back to school again! With this opening remark I burst into frustration and began rattling off what happened.

At any given point while teaching, if someone was talking or not paying attention, the teacher would throw pieces of chalk at them. Only the one the chalk was supposed to hit would duck or be missed. Inevitably the chalk would hit the person behind, catching them unawares. OUCH!

The greatest atrocity could only have occurred in those days when the strap and other forms of physical punishment were still allowed. It involved what the teacher did with the classroom yardstick. You need to know that the yardsticks were thicker and heavier because the wood was made of hardwood rather than softwood. They certainly were not these light balsa wood types of meter-sticks they have now. Not at all! Also, the yardstick came with metal corners, making them really sharp on the ends.

The student involved was a timid, reserved, somewhat insecure girl that rarely got into trouble over anything. I wish I could remember what angered this teacher to the point of doing what he did.

She was told to come up, to the front of the class. Then he told her to bend over. She was wearing a dress at the time, the kind that is tied in the back with a bow and the skirt part of the dress flares out from the waist. Bending over in front of the class was bad enough, but in a dress?

To add insult to injury he took the "yardstick" and started whacking her across the behind. On one of the hits, the yardstick broke in half! I was sick about how she was being humiliated as well as tortured. It was overkill to say the least.

As I spilled my guts out to Mom about what happened and not wanting to go back to school, she gave me some wise advice. Mom always had a philosophy for the way to deal with life. One was in relationship to us kids; she would say, "No news is good news."

The other is the one she shared with me then to help with the shock: "If you can't lick'em, then join'em and do better!"

After she said that I made a vow out loud to her, and more to myself, that I was going to be a Teacher and do better. I was never going to humiliate a student like that ever!

FAILING DUE TO AN ACCIDENT

The accident happened in High River, but its conclusion occurred in Camrose. It all began with my sister and her stubborn demands to hold Baby's reins when we were riding her out to take lunch to our dad in the field.

We made it as far as the top of the hill in the pasture. Then back in the corrals at the barn my brother's new stallion gave out a whinny. That was all it took for Baby to turn and high-tail it back to the barn and the stallion at a full gallop.

We were out of control, with me trying to reach around my sister for the reins that were impossible to grab because she had her hands in the air frantically waving them around. Then the unthinkable happened. She dropped them.

The reins were now flopping around on the ground in front of Baby. This could only result in a terrible crash. Sure enough Baby went down and lay there looking dead. I smashed straight down on my head. KABOOM! Into the rock hard pasture land. When I came to, all that was running through my mind was my dad's voice, ordering me to do what he always said to us kids: "You get bucked off! You get back on!"

That idea ran back and forth through my mind while my head kept throbbing. With no further thought to the matter, I crawled back to the horse, that was STILL lying down looking dead but thank God she wasn't. This allowed me the chance to crawl back on to the saddle before Baby stood up again. Otherwise I am not sure I could even stand up at that point.

I had no idea of the danger I put myself in. For that wasn't the end of it. Things were just going to get worse for me. The months that followed resulted in a rapid deterioration of both my facial muscle control into spasms and my school work.

It never occurred to anyone that it was due to the horse accident. Most likely it was because I had gotten back on the horse and sort of felt okay! No one really connected the horse accident to the subtle sequence of physical problems that appeared over a gradual period of time and started to take a serious turn. Along with the twitching drastically increasing I was failing grade five!

After these problems developed, my Mom started to take me to doctors all around the area to no avail. She even took me to a Hypnotist. That is when I discovered that I am not able to be hypnotized. This makes sense since I am not one to let someone control my mind in any way if I can help it.

This went on for a period of maybe two years with no results. In that time we moved from the farm to Camrose during my grade five year.

My dad had developed an allergy to grain dust, which was the reason we moved from years of rural life to the urban lifestyle. It was in our new place where my Mother finally found the care I needed. Friends suggested my Mom take me to a well-known Chiropractor right there in Camrose.

He took X-rays. It would be the most shocking X-ray I would ever see in my life. It showed me my upper neck area from the skull down to the middle of my backbone. The fourth and fifth vertebrae were barely attached and sticking out to the side - barely in place! This indicated how close I was to severing my spinal cord.

Right away the Chiropractor wrote out a note for all my coaches and teachers requesting that I cease all sports activities immediately! At the time, I was competing in figure skating, softball, diving and competitive swimming, as well as gymnastics at school. The Chiropractor said that if I had made a wrong move tumbling or hit the water too hard while diving, I would instantly have severed the nerves in my spine and become a quadriplegic. The curse couldn't injure me though, like it should have.

One wrong move and it could have been over for me. A wheelchair would become my way of life. I just can't imagine myself as a "Quad" in a wheelchair. I know one time in grade nine while playing basketball, I sprained my ankle. I ended up on crutches for several weeks. At that time, I thought it was the end of the world! So I would surely suck at being a quadriplegic!

It was explained to me by the Chiropractor that the twitching of my upper body muscles was one of the symptoms. That explained the spasms I was having, due to this constant tension in that area of my body. Also this resulted in faltering grades. These reasons, and the change in the Math programs by moving from High River to Camrose, resulted in me flunking grade five.

I can see now from a teacher's perspective that failing a grade isn't all that bad. The blessing is, had I not failed then I would probably have spent many of my school years struggling. And I would not have gone on to university to become a teacher!

CHAPTER 3:

ANIMAL CONNECTION

I have some sort of divine connection with animals. I've been referred to as "Saint Francis of Assisi" or an "Animal Whisperer." They have played a major role in the well-being of my life over the years.

God seems to provide them when I need them. They have come to my rescue in a number of unique ways. You read earlier that our border collie on the ranch saved my sister and me from a frozen grave. Then a stray Norwegian elkhound adopted us and became my instant body guard.

I can list numerous times when I have attracted animals of every kind. Wild kittens licked and healed my burnt hand, bunnies lay belly up for me to administer first aid, and I saved a gold fish by giving it CPR. A wild barn cat cuddled up to keep me company by purring in my ear. A cockatiel clung to me, taking 2 clerks to pull her off of me.

A Seeing Eye dog came to lay by me at night rather than stay with his master. A mother Husky and her pups curled up with me in my bed. Birds such as Canada jays and bald eagles, squirrels, wild rabbits and hares, deer and coyotes have all come up to me at different times. I will never forget the coyote that came up and stayed on the patio with me after my mom's funeral to help me get rid of my deep lonely sadness.

You might say, I am like the "Pied Piper of Pets", only I do not play any instrument when I attract them. I've drawn pets out of their yards by just walking by. Even when I delivered papers the dogs were calm and happy to see me. Especially the bigger dogs, oddly enough. I can't even get them to go away! I have to get mad at them and I sure don't like having to do that.

An animal I did not want to shoo away was a Norwegian elkhound that followed me one time. I wanted to keep him since he reminded me of my body-guard and buddy Kaiser, from the farm. Of course I couldn't keep him because he belonged to someone else. But I sure wanted to! I lingered as long I could before taking him back to his rightful owner.

I've brought animals home to save them from imminent death or cruelty. I remember saving 9 kittens all at once from drowning. I was delivering papers on my route when I came to a house where a little boy was sitting on the front step crying. I asked him what was wrong, he said between sobs that his daddy, when he got home from work that day, was going to take all those kittens he had on the step and drown them.

"OMG!" I blurted out, "He can't do that! Look, I will come back after I deliver all these papers and take them home." I never thought about what my dad would say when I brought nine kittens home to a FOOD store.

My dad insisted we not even bring George our cat from the ranch with us to live in the store for health reasons. So you can imagine his annoyance when I showed up just before supper with nine kittens in my bike carrier. He ordered me to go find homes for all of them and not to come home until I did!

Fortunately I managed to find homes for all but one kitten. Around 9:00 PM, I cautiously enter the back door of the store with the one kitten in hand. My dad was in the living room watching TV.

I came in and immediately but rather nonchalantly set the kitten down on the arm of the chair he was sitting in. Then I started to fill him in, taking my time to explain where each kitten had gone.

There was a method to my slow delivery, for sure enough the kitten had already stepped down on to my dad's lap and Dad had naturally started petting the kitty before I finished explaining.

"GREAT", I thought! "My plan is working!" I was hoping that Dad would take a liking to the cat so I could make a deal with him to maybe keep the kitten long enough for me to find a home for him. He said okay, and the kitten got named Tim after the store. As time passed, finding a home for Tim became history. We lived in the back of Tim's Grocery with "Tim" until I was in grade nine.

CHAPTER 4:

NEVER TO SEE LIFE THE SAME AGAIN

At the end of grade six I had a life-changing experience. I look back over my life up to that point and realize that I had been in the palm of God's hand right from before conception on! I needed Him at conception, again at birth and throughout that first year of my life for sure. And a number of times since, that are too numerous to count.

He was not letting anyone or anything take my life, that is for sure. I was definitely in God's care before I was even born. But coming to the Lord takes it to a whole new level. Now I am a Born Again Christian in two-way communication with God and the Trinity.

Mine was almost a romantic love story in many ways. During summer holidays, my sister and I would attend the Vacation Bible School at the Church of the Nazarene, across the street from our store.

Vacation Bible School taught me a lot about the love of Jesus for us. I had never heard my church speak of HIM in the same way that the Vacation Bible School leaders did.

The leaders of the summer school spoke about HIM as wanting to be a great friend! A very influential drawing card for me. After all, who can't do without more friends and great ones at that!

They told us that HE loved us so much, that HE died for each and every human being on this planet. That meant ME! HE also died so I could be free from DEATH and SIN.

All I had to do to receive this freedom that He graciously offered me, was to ask HIM into my life to be my personal Lord and Saviour. HIS friendship and unconditional love could be mine.

The messaged moved me so that I made a determined conscious move. I stopped one of the leaders on the way out as I was leaving on that last Thursday before the Bible School was over. I quizzed her on what it was I had to do to ask Jesus to be my friend? She made it sound so simple.

I told her that if HE was that loving and dearly desired my friendship, then I wanted to have HIS friendship! So she brought me into the sanctuary.

I recall it as if it were just yesterday. We sat down on the steps in front of the Pulpit. Above it was a huge painting of Jesus holding a child, with the little children at HIS feet. Don't you think that the setting with that particular painting was so appropriate for that moment in my life as a child? While sitting there the instructor answered my questions very assuredly.

Seeing my eagerness, she asked if I would like to ask Jesus into my life as a personal friend. I said yes so excitedly, without hesitation. For it just seemed like the perfect and right thing to do! To have HIM as my very own friend! So, right then and there I repeated what is referred to as the "Sinner's Prayer" or "Prayer of Salvation." It went like this:

Lord Jesus Christ? Please come into my life to be my Lord and Saviour and forgive me my sins.

I came as a young girl in love with someone by the name of Jesus that would give me that ideal, perfect love I relished. An unconditional love worth more than gold, I've often thought. Even when I think of that word now, "unconditional," I am moved to humble gratefulness to Him.

I did it! It was done. My instructor gave me a hug and off I ran home or should I say floated, maybe flew home would be better! I burst in the door of the store already with a mouthful of enthusiastic questions on the tip of my tongue. I could hardly wait as I blurted out to my mother the sixty-four dollar question that was first and foremost on my mind. "What do I do Mom? I am now a CHRISTIAN! Now what do I do?"

I told her what had just happened to me at the church across the road. So I wanted to know what I should do next if anything. She didn't know! However, she did suggest that I ask our Minister at the United Church and my Sunday School teacher and the other leaders. So at the first chance I got I did!

You will not believe what they said: "I don't know Karen." I must have asked a dozen or more people that I thought for sure would be able to answer my question on what to do after asking Jesus Christ into my life.

At some point while seeking an answer, the Lord spoke to me! Yes indeed HE did! HE spoke directly to me! I am NOT kidding! That was the very first time HE actually spoke to me directly! It was amazing!

HE told me not to worry about asking. For HE was going to be my coach and trainer. And added that HE would keep me under wraps. I felt HE did exactly that AND still is! Since I had lots of coaches, I find it interesting that HE would use these terms. HE knew full well that I would understand perfectly what HE meant by saying that HE would COACH me.

It seemed like HE took my lack of answers to my questions as the perfect opportunity to introduce HIMSELF to me by DIRECTLY intervening and becoming my own personal coach and trainer. HE became what I had asked for: My Best Friend.

#1 COACH, TEACHER, GUIDE

By the time I was thirteen, HE was showing me so much and teaching me a lot. HE would give me words for people long before I even knew what I was doing and before I said that prayer or even knew HIM.

I know it may seem strange to you, but as a child of no more than seven or eight years of age, it did not seem strange to me at all. To me it seemed to be a matter of urgency. Something from within me had the need to tell someone a certain bit of information whether I knew what that information meant or not. I didn't even see it as something coming directly from GOD at the time.

My dad had leaned more toward the idea that we kids were to be "seen and not heard." So if I got one of those urges that required telling him something, I would blurt it out and run to my room because he was going to be sending me there anyhow! Then, as I got much older, I realized I was giving people words of encouragement, knowledge and wisdom.

Interestingly however, there was one thing that always happened. Whomever I told my urgings to always seemed to use the information that I gave them, sooner or later.

Over the years and the older I got, the more I realized that whether I knew what the words meant or not, I had important information for people.

However, it became much harder to pull off blurting the words out and running as an adult. I was often looked at as weird or annoying, or worse yet as disruptive or even evil!

Just remember, Moses started out as a basket case
&
look how he turned out!

Although I was often misunderstood by some, it was very clear to the ones that received my information that I was right on.

Why would I be right on? Because HE gave me the words to say. They were not words I dreamed up myself. Most of the time I had no idea what the words meant at all until I gave them to someone, and they would always have an "AHA" moment. HE literally has been talking to me ever since and has never quit.

CHAPTER 5:

A HIGHER LEVEL OF COMPETITION

During grade ten we lived in a trailer park close to my high school. We had sold the corner store while I was in grade nine. Living in a trailer was something I thought I would never do. But it was more fun than I thought.

Added to that, I had a girlfriend next door that could drive and had a little convertible sports car we bombed around in. We would cruise into the drive-in to have root beers brought to the car window.

I kept very busy playing basketball and volleyball, and loved my gym classes. Badminton was another sport that I played well and competed in. I think I liked badminton the best.

Of course I kept up with my figure skating, then skiing and competitive swimming programs as well as tennis and my lifeguarding.

I began to golf in high school. I earned enough money caddying to buy my own clubs, and even competed, tying for third in the Provincial Golf Championship.

FRIENDLY FIGURES OF FACTUAL FABRICATION

While at High School I was involved in everything from sports, student council, drama, and the yearbook to writing in the school newspaper. That title above was the heading to my column in the school newspaper.

One time during Drama class, CBC came to the school to do a "staged" make-up session for us. They needed a few models to use for the demonstration. I was one of them that got picked. They did a gory wound on my one hand. It looked terrible!

I am surprised that I never caused my mother's hair to turn GREY. I never thought my pre-meditated pranks back then were so terrible. However now that I have been a mom I think I may have been a terrible daughter in some ways.

With Drama class at the end of the day I decided to go rushing home with my gory, "injured" hand. I acted like I had accidentally jammed it in the fire doors at school. So Mom gets all serious and grabs her purse and car keys as she orders me to get into the car.

We raced all the way downtown to the clinic. We ran in and all the way up to the nurse's desk with me still cradling my hand and grimacing with "pain" off and on. The nurse even gasped as she took a look at my hand.

Then I said to both my mom and the nurse: "Voila!" I peeled the wound right off my hand, holding it right up in the air in front of them so they could clearly see it was fake. "I am okay now! It is all better!" as I laughed gleefully.

My mom gave me that look that kills. The nurse offered up what I am sure my mom was thinking: "I'll help you kill her!"

BREAKING MORE BARRIERS

In high school we got to take a number of new courses. Home Economics was the option girls in grade 10 had. My Mom had already done a very good job of teaching me to do most of the things that were taught in Home Ec.

My thought was; why not take something I know very little about? So I went into the school office that very first week of grade ten and asked if I could take shop or automotive classes instead of Home Economics.

The office went pretty silent. Then it was diplomatically explained to me why I could not take those classes. Their reasons made no sense at all. It just wasn't done and no amount of insisting from my end worked at all to get them to change their mind for me.

However, GIRLS, it was all not in vain! For female students following in my footsteps finally got to take those courses. So never cease putting the sixty-four dollar questions out there like I have over the years. You never know how you may have changed the course of history.

THINGS ARE NOT AS THEY SEEM

Here's another barrier that you could say I broke, but for entirely different reasons of imminent danger and darkness. Eerie and, yes, very real. As teenagers, my friends and I played things that were really spooky but intriguing. We naively believed they were just silly childish games and not real.

But were they just games? I think not! I now see clearly that such games are truly harmful! Some of the games that fascinated us were Ouija Boards, séances, magic spells and levitation. There is a danger in playing these games. They can open the door or window a crack into the world of darkness. In so doing, one can welcome in evil.

I discovered long after the fact, that I had broken two barriers in playing these games. One way I did so was with the Ouija Board. It got so that my friends in Jr. High and High school did not want to play with me because I could control the board. I did not even have to be playing and I would still make the guide or rudder I guess you could call it, either go straight to the "YES" or right off the board!

Looking back now I see that to be a blessing. The reason was that I was not letting the board fully operate or be in control, therefore keeping it from opening any door to the dark world and any potential evil.

The other way that I broke a barrier was years later when I fully realized the seriousness of our silly games that were actually dark and potentially dangerous. I cut the danger off of me and my friends with a prayer to break any tie the games may have created between ourselves and evil. I prayed this in the power of the name of JESUS CHRIST of Nazareth.

You may think that I am just paranoid but if I were you I would search online for such topics as "curses" versus "cleansing prayers." I personally would rather err on the side of caution than not do anything about it. The truth is we can be cursed. We say cursing, damning words. Therefore we make satan our god.

Whether you believe such things or not, I do. I get rid of any potential danger right away. I honestly believe my world is a lot better for it too. After all, nothing of that curse has killed me yet. Upon discovering it I immediately dealt with it.

I have seen some of the dark side, proving it necessary for me to have taken action. I have used the WORD as a two-edged sword against it, resulting in casting out any power of darkness that could potentially take hold.

MOVING TO THE CRACKER BOX PARTY TOWN

My parents moved to Ponoka, a small town south of Camrose. This time my sister and I did not want to move with them. We wanted to stay with friends and finish the school year. As for me, I sure did not want to be known as a chick from Ponoka, where the "Cracker Box" is. (Now I am immune to heckling and retort with "I'm from Ponoka, what's your excuse?")

There is a mental facility there just south east of town that employs nearly everyone in town and keeps the town going strong. It is a huge institute up on the hill that you can actually see from the main highway.

My sister and I actually ended up moving to Ponoka sooner than we were going to. We had planned to stay back in Camrose while I finished grade eleven and twelve. It was important for me because I would be completing my last year of school. That would make or break my hopes and dreams of going to university to be a teacher.

All was going as planned until Easter of my grade eleven year. My sister and I went to Ponoka to visit our parents over the Easter holidays.

While in my mom and dad's store, three teenage girls came in. At first they were looking over at us and whispering a bunch between themselves with a few giggles here and there. I wrote them off as the typical catty girls that I just detest. However they had me "eating crow" almost as quickly as I thought that they were being catty.

They came over to actually talk to us. Wow, I didn't see that happening! They asked if we were new in town. We said we were here visiting our parents. After a bit more introduction they asked us if we wanted to come to a party that night.

WOW, shock of all shocks to get an invitation out of what I claimed was cattiness. OOPS, shame on me for making a premature conclusion that turned into a puny assumption. All because of past unfavourable experiences with cattiness. I think it might stem from my experience with those bullies way back in grade one.

I realized that I was dead wrong. I was condemning others. If I was to make such assumptions about everyone that looked my way and laughed, I would be the one to lose out. I would be the one that got hurt due to my wrongful thinking. Not the ones that were doing the laughing, and who were not necessarily laughing at me. Who was I to decide that ahead of time by assuming?

The epiphany was that I was putting a stereotypical label on ALL that behaved the way those bullies did to me way back in grade one! The way they would laugh and stare and sometimes point at me. Wow, I didn't realize I had been doing that!

I had made a judgement call that ANY laughter combined with looking and pointing directly at me was cattiness. Though the girls in the store had the same combination of actions, they carried an entirely different message than the girls from way back in grade one.

Once I get such revealing truths, I seek immediately to rid myself of the wrongful thinking in order to stay healthy in my thinking. The key is to spot it and squash it! So it won't become a nasty bad habit.

MY OLDER BOYFRIEND

I want to thank you Mom for understanding my reasons for dating a 28 year old in high school. I met him through friends of mine that were psychiatric nurses at the Ponoka Mental Hospital.

He was already well into his psych. career long before he met me. My mom of course was not impressed when she found out I was going out with a guy 11 years older than me.

I assured her that I would introduce her to him as soon as possible. I had a good reason: I told her that I felt safe with him as opposed to the high school jerks I went out with whom I would have to spend the bulk of a date fighting off. I'd come home more exhausted than having enjoyed the date.

He and I could talk for hours on the back step and get into really good existential conversations. Mom was okay with that.

I hope wherever he is, he's being blessed! He was transferred before I graduated. My Grad date was a Pre-Med student I knew. I even designed and made my own dress that I wore a number of times to formals at university after that.

CHAPTER 6:

SILENT DANGER FOR THEY DON'T SCREAM, I DO!

I did not plan it, but from that point on in my life on, I was no longer going to be living at home. What happened was drastically going to alter my direction in life and the places that I would live. It all started with an ever potential but SILENT DANGER!

It was a pretty big end-of-school pool rental making for very crowded conditions. The pool was a "T-shaped" pool. There were two of us guards hired to run the rental. I was guarding the deep end and my partner was guarding the shallow end on the other side of the pool, near the office.

I do not like pool rentals. Especially school-type rentals. You see, when classes rent the pool there is every range of swimmer. Some of them may NEVER have been in a swimming pool nor even swam for that matter.

As a matter of fact a lot in this case were non-swimmers! They weren't the usual "Pool Rats", with season passes, that hung out at the pool all summer. They were not even the ones that are there taking swim lessons.

So you can picture the two of us guarding a packed pool. A pool full of highly energized grade twos of all mixes of swimming ability. It made for a difficult job guarding them. As I mentioned, I was guarding the deep end. I had just spotted in the corner of my eye what looked like a non-swimmer crawling along the edge heading for the rope and the deep end water.

There was something about her that bothered me. I didn't have to wait for an answer from her to know she had never been in a swimming pool before. So I took my eyes off the diving boards for just a second to lean down and ask her if she could swim.

Sure enough after quizzing her, I was right! I proceeded to tell her that where she was heading was too deep for her. The water would be way over her head. I then told her to go back to where she came from so that she could stand up.

As she began to do as I said, I reverted my eyes quickly back to the diving boards just in time! At that very moment one of our regulars, a "Pool Rat," started horsing around on the high board! I quickly reprimanded him, so that I could turn to check on that little girl. I felt very strongly that I should keep an eye on her.

What the heck? I could not see her anywhere! I looked all over in every direction. In the shallow end where I had told her to go, by the bleachers, around the deck. She was nowhere to be seen! Where was she? There is no way she could have gotten to the dressing room in such a short time from where and when I last saw her.

At the same time my "gut" was saying that she had gone under! That she was on the bottom! Not that I hadn't looked there already, but I saw nothing!

It was unbelievable and I was getting scared of what I was thinking all along: I would have to call an emergency! However protocol requires a guard to NOT call an emergency unless they DO see someone on the bottom and know for SURE an emergency is necessary.

Well, of course you know already that my concern did NOT match that criteria. So what should I do? I could literally get fired for blowing the whistle! Match the criteria or NOT, I simply couldn't ignore that strong urge in me nor push it out of my mind and come up with a better conclusion.

You are just about to learn the MOST important KEY ever! If there is one thing I would hope you would get out of this book it would be this GOLD NUGGET right here!

I had to make a very SERIOUS decision over the whole matter. Should I follow my gut? Or follow protocol? I am here to tell you after all these years of similar experiences, AND because of what happened back then on that afternoon in late June: you should ALWAYS follow your GUT, not protocol!

Your gut feeling above ALL things is the best and the most accurate way to go! If you follow your gut, better known as your intuition or as in my case, your Holy Spirit, you can't go wrong. I can definitely say that my Holy Spirit has NEVER been wrong. So obviously I decided right then and there at the side of the swimming pool to call it an emergency. I blew one long blast on my whistle to announce an emergency. Then I jumped in!

Now here is the "Kodak Moment" shocker of all time for me as a Lifeguard. After all the training one can get as a lifeguard, I would never have thought this would be the case. It was much harder than I would ever imagine to find her body on the bottom of that swimming pool!

I still shake my head over it. I never thought in a million years that one could not see a body on the bottom of a swimming POOL! A lake or river, yes! Or an ocean with rip tides, but not a pool!

That's what made my gut response SO IMPORTANT! You see, as a lifeguard I would NEVER have jumped in first without seeing a body on the bottom. That is just it, I could not see one yet felt in my Spirit, that there was one. It turned out my gut/Holy Spirit was RIGHT as usual!

WHY I LIKE FLUORESCENT COLOURS

I had to feel my way along the bottom to find her. I must add that it did not help one bit that she had white blonde fair hair, like I did when I was her age. To make problems worse, she was wearing a pale faded blue bathing suit, making it even more difficult to see her because her bathing suit blended right in with the bottom of the pool and so did she, as she was already blue.

To this day, because of that, I LOVE bright fluorescent colours, in any sport for that matter. I like wearing brighter clothes too, they tend to brighten my spirits.

Finally I felt a leg! She had already slid most of the way down toward the deep end drain. I pulled her into me and moved her into a head lock hold to keep her neck as still as possible. With her tight against me all in one smooth move, I pushed her and me to the surface as fast I could go.

At the surface I started a modified version of a Tried Swimmer's Tow, only on my back, with her head held securely in between both my hands and forearms till I got over to the shallow end where I could stand up. I immediately start AR, (Artificial Resuscitation /Mouth to Mouth).

Now if that was not enough of a problem, I was to discover and have to deal with another BIG problem. The pool still had swimmers in it. Oh My Gosh! They were even still jumping off the boards the whole time her and I were down there and I was bringing her up to the surface of the deep end.

We could have been jumped on and both injured while I was retrieving her. So here I am with her in tow looking for the other guard.

Just imagine what I SAW? She was over where she had been guarding, all right but she was frozen stiff like a statue. Her eyes were bugging out of her head and her mouth was wide open. Oh NO! What was I going to do?

I promptly SCREAMED orders to the teachers on the bleachers as I pointed to each of them with a command: 1) "YOU, call emergency now!" 2) "The rest of you CLEAR the pool NOW!"

My colleague was still frozen. I kept giving AR as I slowly worked my way across to the shallow end. In between breaths, I continued to shout orders out to get extra help.

She was still NOT BREATHING. I was also wondering how I was going to get her out of the pool by myself with no one with the proper training to help me!

I managed, by putting my arms under her body in order to slide her off my arms on to the edge of the deck. I slid her off as straight and as carefully as possible, so as not to jerk her around. After all since I did not know how she got to the bottom of the pool, I would have to consider a spinal injury, hence the extra carefulness.

Then I got myself quickly out on deck to continue to give AR. Soon after she started to heave and vomit up water. That was a very GOOD sign that she was coming alive and could begin to breathe on her own. This allowed me to stop and turn her on her side to help her drain her lungs of any water.

In between breaths I had been giving instructions to the Teachers. I asked one to watch for the ambulance and another to get blankets while the others kept the students under control. I continued to help keep her passageway clear as she was vomiting up more water from her lungs and watched for any further problems and improvements.

To my great relief, my co-partner came to and was no longer a statue. So she took over the organizing for me while I was still dealing with my drowning victim. Shortly thereafter the medical help arrived. Off the little girl went to the hospital.

THE WORST 3 LIFEGUARDING DAYS OF MY LIFE

She would still be in danger so it became the worst three days of my lifeguarding career! Two things happened to me. One was not so good and one was really, really not good! The really bad thing was, I was not told for over three days how that little girl had fared.

I as a lifeguard knew very well the danger she faced. She had been without oxygen for at least two or three minutes, maybe even more. That meant that she could be a vegetable. Maybe I only revived her to live a life disabled and brain damaged or even brain

DEAD! All it takes for this to happen is for a person to go without oxygen for three minutes or more.

I was totally sick about it. It was hard to eat or sleep or think straight. Even calling the hospital didn't prove helpful. The staff there just kept me in limbo about it all.

Three days later to my elated sigh of relief, I found out that she was going to be just fine! Oh thank GOD, what a relief! Her future life flashed before me strangely enough. She could continue on into grade three; onward and upward to a long life ahead. I am sure she is doing something awesome with her life now.

THE OTHER BAD THING!

Once things settled, the other lifeguard and I sat down and began the long tedious job of writing out our own accident reports and forms.

Then two things happened. I am the type of person that deals with an emergency matter-of-factly with precision. Then I fall apart!

This incident gave confirmation of that for sure. You see a lifeguard can take all the training in the world, and pass everything with flying colours, but when it comes to the actual emergency we never know if we will respond or FREEZE or fall apart.

Which is exactly what happened in this incident. What a textbook moment! For both things occurred. Since I responded correctly, I now knew that I would be able to handle a crisis in the way I was trained. Definitely a good thing to know. It has come in handy on many an occasion since.

The other thing that happened was our supervisor showed up. I didn't like him very much as a supervisor because he would often make a mountain out of a molehill. He would get in a flap about things that he was not even involved in and didn't know anything about. Then he would blow them way out of portion.

Which is EXACTLY what he started to do the minute he showed up! Sheesh, how annoying! Here I am trying to recall the accident, detail by detail to write out in my report and he is yakking away at us bombarding us with questions, left right and centre and demanding immediate answers. Answers that he could get from our reports if he just left us alone to complete them.

Then of course I was starting to unravel myself from the ordeal. Hence, I was not in the best of shape to respond to this harassing interrogation to begin with.

So, to add insult to injury, I blurted out something I would most likely regret because it was not thought out well and could be very costly. However, I did not take that extra nano-second to think before opening my big mouth. Feeling under duress, I came right out with my rash retort in front of everyone.

I blurted out: "I quit!" Then I went completely numb. For I was then out of a seasonal job that is only open during the summer months!

The fact is that I said it and I wouldn't dare back-peddle over it either. It was just a matter of time before I would quit anyway. I have rarely continued in a job that I do not like.

It is probably long overdue to say, but a planned approach would have been a much better way. Sometimes when push comes to shove, I tend to blurt out a response as a defence mechanism. Looking back I can't say it has never served me well. Yet now I think I would take a different approach if at all possible.

DROWNING, GOOD OR BAD?

On my way home I was having flashbacks of the whole episode by evaluating and re-evaluating, over and over again. Now what? The damage had been done.

Here is a time that things actually worked in my favour. I had the good fortune to track down another lifeguarding position, in another small town. YEAH! It was a complete miracle!

It is virtually impossible to achieve a job in mid-season, as it is hard for a town recreation board to hire another guard mid-season. These jobs are snapped up in November and January. By February, Lifeguards know where they're working.

For this job to become available, it truly was a MIRACLE! Unfortunately it was at the expense of another lifeguard. Apparently this pool had a drowning and the Assistant Lifeguard in charge at the time had to take the heat.

It really was not his fault. The drowning happened due to the negligence of a Junior Guard on duty at the time. He however, was the person in overall charge at the time. Interesting how that works, isn't it? One loses a job and another is blessed by it.

FROM PONOKA TO?

All of a sudden my life was taking a right hand turn. I say RIGHT hand because it was actually going in the RIGHT direction to my delightful surprise! I had NEVER lived away from home before. A place was found to room and board with a family. It was just a couple of blocks from the pool.

The Supervisor picked me up at the bus stop on the edge of town. She introduced herself, using her nick-name "Maggot." She was not a local but an urbanite from the city. How could I tell all that from just meeting her, you might wonder?

Upon picking me up and driving me to my boarding house she began right away to tell me where she was from and how terribly boring it was in that "HICK" town where there was nothing to do! She went on and on about how small and dull it was. That I had better get a good thick novel from the drugstore to read to break up the boredom because there was nothing else to do.

By the time she dropped me off, I wanted nothing more than to run upstairs to my bedroom and cry my eyes out. What had I done? I bit my lip tight as I bolted up the stairs at the first opportunity to run for my bedroom. I flung myself on to my bed and began sobbing into my pillow. I thought, "Oh no, what have I done, what have I done? Have I made a huge mistake in coming here and leaving home?"

Once I was all cried out, I did exactly as she suggested. I dragged myself up off that bed and marched myself downtown to buy that novel. I still remember that book. It is probably the only novel of mine that I have never finished.

As I sat on my bed reading that first chapter of the book, I kept hearing my mother's voice speaking to me in my head. She was saying to me, "A place is what you make it Karen."

All of a sudden it dawned on me what she had taught me. This was as good a time as any to put it into practice. So I put the book down and picked myself up off that bed again and headed out the door. Each of my parents had a valuable message for me when I needed it most: "You get bucked off you get back on."

What happened after turned out to be the start of one of the best summers ever! Not that I am recommending to anyone to blurt out I QUIT anytime soon, but this sure worked out in my favour! It reminds me of Romans 8:28 in the Bible where it says: "HE will work all things out for those that believe unto HIM...."

I must say that is definitely reassuring to know HE can turn a BAD thing into a good thing for all those that believe in HIM. I made the place work out, and the job was so good I came back the next summer too! I decided that I would never finish that book and kept it in memory of that summer of '72!

CHAPTER 7:

"TO BE OR NOT TO BE"

After high school I enrolled in Red Deer College because it was much smaller than the other Post-Graduate facilities. I thought I would make the transition from high school to university smoother, plus it was a lot closer to home. Looking back, I don't think the adjustment to a smaller institution over a bigger one made much difference. It was just as high pressure as a bigger place and just as complicated.

The brand new student residences were cozy four-bedroom apartments. Since I knew no one, I simply put my name down to room with whomever. So I had three roommates whom I had never met before. The two girlfriends from Rocky Mountain House had two bedrooms at one end of the apartment. The other roommate from Sylvan Lake and I had the two bedrooms at the other end with a living room/kitchen in between.

The two from Rocky Mountain House seemed to have ulterior motives for living there. AND it was not for an education! I was not impressed when their boyfriends seem to live in a great deal of the time. That made for splitting the groceries up four ways impossible. To settle the problem, the two of them bought their own and the other girl and I bought ours together. That seemed to work well enough.

It was such an adjustment going from high school classes where we were spoon-fed, to post-graduate studies that were the total opposite. The Professors simply rambled on from the minute they got into class until the period ended. So I had to develop a short-hand to keep up with my note taking.

It was crazy, especially my Calculus course. The Prof. had a strong accent and I found it really hard to understand most of his lectures. Finally I got up enough courage to ask the guy across from me what the heck the Prof. was saying. It turns out he didn't know either, nor did the guy in front of him! So I got an idea then to form a study group after each class to get together and translate and decipher all that we had just heard in class.

The one roommate that had her bedroom next to mine, was nice and normal enough, I felt. We got along well and often socialized on week-ends together. I even went home with her a couple of times.

I will always remember her parents. When I first met them they owned a gas station on the main drag into Sylvan Lake. When they would pump gas for customers they wore Dutch shoes, referred to as wooden clogs!

I discovered clogs were actually very comfortable! I danced in them years later in 2009 at the "World Skills Games" that I volunteered for. The Dutch team brought their clogs to the dance, held at the end of the Games, to sell as a fundraiser. I gave them a try on the dance floor and found them comfortable but cumbersome.

Another interesting adventure we went on one weekend, was for coffee at the top of the Calgary Tower. We got there in a police car! Of course the tower was in Calgary and we were in Red Deer! My roommate had been in the Militia so she knew a number of officers and military police. Her boyfriend at the time was an officer. We double dated with a policeman friend of his.

Another time we went again to Calgary to a function at the Officers' Club in Calgary, at what was then the Curry Barracks. It is non-existent now, for I used to live in a condo complex built on what was the Military Base.

Isn't it interesting the overlap or full circle occurrences in our lives? To have visited the base in the 70's only to find myself living where it was 30 years later?

While at the Officers' Club something happened that totally caught me off guard and brought too much attention to me. On our double date I wore my corduroy blazer. It happened to have my Distinction Award pin for swimming pinned to the lapel.

Why you might wonder would a blazer draw attention to me? Well, you will laugh when you read what happened in the Officers Club at Curry Barracks in Calgary When I walked through the room that specific badge had everything to do with how I was received since it was visible for everyone to see.

Most of these awards I received from Royal Life Saving (RLSS) originated from within the military training courses. This was one such award and it was very challenging to earn, and the highest award achievable. At that time apparently, I was one of only 11 in Canada that had earned this award. Therefore it was highly recognized as such in the military. It also had identical markings as what the military's high ranking Officers wore. The only difference was the tiny wording on the badge.

Therefore when I went to walk into the Officer's Club, everyone stood at attention and saluted me! Can you just picture that? I sure wish now that we had camera phones back then to catch that rather official but over the top moment.

QUITTING COLLEGE

College life was short lived though. I had applied for a Government Student Loan in order to go to College. However, because I had put down that I was "Independent", rather than dependent on my parents, the loan was turned down.

I had this stupid idea that I was going to do this on my own. I was just plain stubborn and saw no other way to solve the dilemma. So I quit.

Instead of going back to Ponoka, I went straight to Calgary to get a job. Then and only then, did I tell my parents what I had done. The good news in the whole stupid mess was, I was able to stay with my godparents in northwest Calgary.

I got a job right away as well! I still have the light blue smock I wore as my work uniform. I use it now to paint in. This job was really an okay job but I was a bit lonely in the big city of Calgary.

I discovered how devastated my parents were with my news. I had really hurt them. Looking back I see how my stubbornness had not only cost me a full year of university but also disappointed others: my teacher; Miss Twiggy that put together a grant application for me; a nurse friend of mine; and of course my parents.

All of them stated after the fact that they would have contributed money toward my tuition in order to make sure that I went to school. I had no idea so many were my cheerleaders!

MEAT CLEAVERS

My parents felt it would be better if I returned to Ponoka for the rest of the year to save money. The plan was that I would re-enrol the following fall. Once home, I got a job at the "Cracker Box," in the kitchen department of the mental hospital.

One kitchen that I worked at had a snack bar that the patients ran. I assisted them at times. At a coffee break another women I worked with had the gall to tell me what one of the patients I worked with was in for. I tried to shut her down because I really didn't want to know such things about the patients, but that didn't stop her.

She proceeded to say that he had chopped his wife up into a bunch of pieces with a meat cleaver. Then she went on to say that one day in a fit of anger he had thrust an ordinary dull, butter knife at a staff member and impaled the counter just below where she was standing.

YIKES! Thanks a lot for sharing that with me, just the kind of thing I didn't want to know! From then on it made it difficult to work alongside him. That was the very reason I did not want to know why the patients were there. I was more than glad enough that we got along fine working together under the circumstances.

SOMEONE SHOCKED ME

Another shocking thing happened to me in that same kitchen. I was serving at the time this happened. As I greeted each patient that came up to my station, I inadvertently glanced further back in the line-up only to have my eyes fall on a person that made me start in shock. It was a guy I had gone to school with back in Camrose. I had a crush on his older brother and actually kind of liked him earlier on in junior high.

What was I going to do? I was frozen thinking about how to deal with this hugely awkward situation. I came up with the idea that I would pretend not to recognize him. That would be the polite thing and the most discrete. Just in time for he came up next in the line! I diverted my eyes down to the food I was serving to avoid eye contact as he was right there. What does he do? He enthusiastically said, "Hi" to me. I couldn't believe it! So I said "Hi" back in surprise.

It was his idea that the two of us met on my coffee break for a nice visit. He had admitted himself because of drugs. I was so pleased that he was of sound mind and not uncomfortable about me knowing about him in such a place. I pray that he is doing well now wherever he is.

SERIAL KILLERS

This hospital had underground tunnels or corridors running from the different Wards to the Kitchens. One of time in particular I remember delivering food via the tunnels to the Criminal "serial killer" Ward.

OH, it was creepy! The men sitting in the dining area all turned at the same time to watch me. It seemed like they were staring right through me. Yuck! I asked to never be sent back there. That ward is no longer housed in Ponoka.

While in the hospital job I discovered that I was lousy at shift work. I could not get my Biological Clock in sync with the shift changes kitchen staff faced.

So I gave my job up to a past classmate and picked up a new job with the Laundry Dept. The boss of the laundry happened to be the dad of a guy I graduated with in high school. We were in a lot of classes together and both were on the basketball teams.

The laundry was a fun place to work! Once I was promoted to the Shirt Press machines, I used to race against the clock. A few burns later I mastered the art. It was fun because I made it into a game, yet it was still monotonous enough to keep my desire to go to university alive and well.

Years later, as a Teacher, I occasionally suggested this line of work to parents that wanted their kids to go on to post-graduate studies. "Have them take on an assembly type job. Surely that will motivate them enough to go to university as soon as possible. They will be begging to be sent back to school."

I do admire people like the ones I worked with at the Ponoka Mental Hospital. Some of them had worked there for years already and planned on retiring from there.

God bless this type of worker. I always appreciate and thank people in such positions. For someone has to do them. I'm always praying that there are plenty to do those jobs and love the job they are in. It not something I was cut out for, that's for sure.

IMPALED

I volunteered a lot to occupy my time. Two places were in Geriatrics and in the Apollo Teen Drug Ward. I only volunteered once at the Geriatrics Ward. All it took was one nice little ole lady to scare me away for good!

I was talking to her while she was knitting, leaning over with my hand spread out flat on the arm of her big sitting chair. We were having what I thought was a nice cordial conversation.

Out of the blue with no warning whatsoever she stabs the sitting chair with her knitting needle right where my hand was. Unbelievable, to stare down at my hand with a knitting needle stuck in the arm of a chair between my fingers. I bet if a person were to do that a hundred times they wouldn't be able to do that again. That was the last time I volunteered there.

The Apollo Ward was mild compared to geriatrics. In fact it was rather depressing. One good thing about it was, it sure cured a person of the desire to take drugs of any kind! If you are reading this part and have someone in your life that is or is thinking about dabbling in drugs, maybe have them read this.

I met an eleven year old girl in the Apollo Ward who was a burned-out addict. Her brain was so fried that she was never going to remember her birthday let alone celebrate one again. Nor was she going to graduate from high school or get married, much less even know what these events represented.

ANOTHER NEAR DEATH EXPERIENCE

It was a beautiful day and the sun was just starting to shine on the lake. There was not a soul around that early in the morning, only me and the loons. I was about halfway back across the lake when it happened!

I swam right into a patch of weeds that were just below the surface so I couldn't see them ahead of time. In no time at all they had me tangled up and were already pulling me down under the surface of the water.

I was starting to PANIC! I couldn't believe I had lost my strength and the cognitive ability to save myself so quickly! I would not have thought in a million years, that I as a lifeguard, little "Miss

Fish", would be in so much trouble in the water that I could actually lose my life by drowning, of all things.

Yet the very second I panicked, I snapped out of it. I gave myself a pep-talk. I said: "Smarten up Karen! You know what to do! You're a Lifeguard! So do it!"

Since I was already zapped of my strength and short on air, I needed to recuperate first. I had to drown-proof until I got my strength back and at the same time I slowly moved the weeds off from being wrapped around my body and legs.

Once I got that done, I very carefully lay back on my back and did a very shallow and slow Elementary Backstroke out of the patch of weeds.

I made it! I was free and ALIVE! Whew! From then on I NEVER swam straight across a lake again. As a Lifeguard, what was I thinking?

I learned the hard way to swim parallel to the shoreline so I would be close enough to be helped if needed. Even be able to stand up if need be.

The wake up lesson as far as lifeguarding goes, was just how FAST a person can get tangled up in weeds and how fast they could pull you under. Those weeds felt like an Octopus had flung its tentacles around me in a death grip, then giving me a death roll like an alligator.

How many near DEATH experiences is that now? I've already lost count here and I quit counting years ago. You can count them if you like but I am not going to bother!

I have concluded that I couldn't die no matter how much I tried. For life is not over until GOD says so. Besides, the Rapture is apt to happen before that!

CHAPTER 8:

STARTING OVER

I went off to university again, this time with my parents' financial representation for my Student Loan. I was the only one of my parents' three children that went on to university so they were pretty excited.

BUT wait! I was flunking my very first semester. It was so hard to adjust to the demands for reams and reams of short essays and long paper assignments. I found my marks at Christmas were as close to a failing curve as I could get without actually failing. HELP-GULP! I was not prepared ahead of time for the shock of the way things are at university-level learning.

I quickly realized I had to come up with a different way to get better marks. Back in elementary school I loved cartooning. Over the years I had even earned some money cartooning. So I figured, why not see if some of the more reasonable Professors I had at the time would bend their rules to allow me to do some of my papers in "cartoon."

I had to write a paper on the Fur Trade, so one of the teachers that I asked was my History Prof. He was a bit hesitant, but won over by the fact a student would even ask, let alone suggest, such a never been done idea. So he said okay, but clarified that I was to bring my Comic Strip to him directly and not to the Teaching Assistants, or they would trash it.

Consequently I cartooned a comic strip and called it "The Skin Game." Guess what I got for a mark? My Prof. loved it and said he never laughed so hard over a subject such as the Fur Trade before!

It worked! I did something similar with my English Professor and again got an 'A+'.

Since I had competed in elementary school in Public Speaking, I decided to present my English Paper orally accompanied by a short outline. I was rewarded again. My English professor said it was a treat when she came to my paper out of the hundreds she had to mark. She could put her feet up, lay back with her headphones on and shut her eyes to listen to my paper.

As a result; by the time graduation arrived, I was able to achieve Distinction. So you see there are more ways to skin a cat then meets the eye.

University was the hardest part of my life so far. I was under so much pressure that I got internal aches, food poisoning and migraines while attending. I would actually have to study with gloves on so as not to scratch my face off.

All of which went away when I graduated. Once into my dream job, of teaching, I soared. It was such a joy and delight to teach. People said I lit up when I walked into a school! I even went on to teach Aides, parents and future teachers.

BUDDING PAINTER

In my 3rd year, the roommate situation was by far better. My roommate was an awesome girlfriend, and now teaches right here in Calgary. Because we had minimum finances, my roommate and I would come up with creative ways to eat on a shoe-string budget. One of those ways was eating Coyote Pancake Mix that can be made without eggs or milk, just water.

We also made what we called "Poor Man's Pizza." We used twenty-cent stale bread plus condiments that we got from the campus cafeteria. It actually was delicious; either that or we were just so hungry that it tasted good anyway.

All we did was spread ketchup on the bread and oven-toasted it. Maybe to add a bit of zest we put salt and pepper or a bit of relish, all from those little condiment packages that we picked up free from the cafeteria. Umm!

I also took up painting that year because our landlord was an artist. She let me have a go at it one weekend. The next thing you know she is my number one encourager. She even gave me some paint supplies and had me promise to never stop painting.

CHAPTER 9:

HOW I MET MY EX-HUSBAND

I met my husband to be in the spring of 1974. I had been skiing over Reading Week with the University Ski Club. A few weeks after our ski trip, we had a reunion to watch the video made of that week.

The party was to be held at a girlfriend's place off campus. She asked me since her and her roommate owed the two guys that lived upstairs a party, if she should invite them?

They had not come on the trip with us nor did they know any of us at all. In fact they didn't even ski. So my response to her question was, "Heck no! It wouldn't be fair to them and they'll feel out of place, having nothing in common with us."

She didn't follow my advice and invited them anyway. Sure enough, as I predicted, the two of them knew no one and spoke to no one nor did they care a thing about skiing. They just sat, literally right over in the far corner talking, and mingled with no one.

I thought it very strange and a bit pathetic. I should have taken that as a sign right then and there! However who at that age would be alerted by that?

Being the type of person that I am, I went over anyway to make conversation with them and help them to feel comfortable and welcome. Even their hostesses didn't really help them mingle much at all, to my surprise. They were introduced in the beginning but that was about it for further interaction with them and our group. Had I not spoken to them, I do not think they would have even stayed any longer.

My friend that invited them said sometime after the party, that they didn't like us or the party much. I could have said: "I told you so!" but I didn't. Here is the interesting part. I had run into the one fellow on campus a couple of times and said, "Hi" in passing.

Apparently he spoke to our mutual friend that hosted the party and asked about me! He even asked for my contact number and she actually gave him my phone number. I expressed my disapproval at her glibly giving out my phone number like that without asking!

It was so careless of her I thought. I was very particular about that sort of thing because of an earlier incident in residence. Something rather scary had happened to me the semester before Christmas that made me rather nervous about that sort of thing.

STALKING TO THE SECOND POWER

While living on campus in Residence, I became involved with the "We Care" Student Aid Program. A number of us volunteer students took shifts. We would be available to call or drop in on. Students could do so, anytime during after-hours in Res. It was a confidential way for students to confide in an impartial person if they were depressed or struggling in some way and just needed to talk to someone.

There seemed to be one student in particular that was always showing up when I was on shift. Somehow he would know my shifts. He even escalated to making phone calls directly to me in my room in Residence at all times of the night.

The situation should never have occurred since we were never to divulge our personal contact information. That meant one of my colleagues gave him MY phone number. Who would have been so careless as to do such a thing?

It stunned and appalled me to find out that it was a colleague that lived on my very floor in Res. I was quite surprised she would do such a thing. She didn't even seem to see what the big deal was until she found out the ramifications of having given my phone number to this guy.

She was shocked and scared for me when she found out I had suffered greatly, and not just from the lack of sleep I was getting as a result of his phone calls at four in the morning!

Missing my sleep was only a small part of the problem. He had become rather scary when he started following me as well. I reported this to the Administrator of "We Care." To my shock, this guy was not unknown to him. Nor was he to the Student Health Authorities.

Apparently he had stalked an ex-girlfriend shortly after they broke up. He had even threatened her with a knife.

The good news was that I had played it cool and neutral with him right from the start. I found out from the authorities that was a wise, good and safe attitude to maintain with him because he could have easily blow up if abruptly hung up on and rejected. Oh goodie, how lucky for me, what a winner of a guy!

I was relieved to be told to no longer have anything to do with him and to report any and all contacts he tried to make with me. I was asked to step out of the picture at "We Care" and the Authorities would step in along with this guy's Floor Chairman in Res.

What a relief when they took him in and I guess you would say, locked him up in the Psych. Ward for psychological testing.

THE RIGHT WAY DOESNT MEAN IT WILL WORK

Back to how I met my ex-husband. Shortly after getting my phone number from my so-called skiing friend, I got a phone call from him. The following weekend we went on our first date.

One of the reasons he said that he wanted to go out with me was because I was the only one that came over and talked to him and his roommate. We dated for a time until he started wanting me to drop my friends. I pretty much said I was not going to do that, hence, there's the door! It was over at that point. So how did we end up getting married then?

I am an objective person and think of things from all angles. Studying the brain was a favourite study of mine. I was tested on my brain power at one point when doing a personality test. I found out that I utilize all four quadrants of my brain.

In general we tend to use one side of the brain. Rarely are four quadrants involved in the human thinking process and all at the same time as well. However it also means that those four quadrants can, at times, argue between themselves and make it difficult to actually come to a consensus.

Once I manage them, they are a helpful advantage utilizing more brain cells and resources that help me stay objective. So for sure, I am not narrow-minded. Besides, I am not the type of person to quickly write someone off either. I think that like many women, I will give a man a second chance.

Due to my objectivity, when after a few weeks passed he came back with an apology and promise, I listened to him begging me to reconsider. He based it on the fact that he realized it was not right of him to tell me to give up my friends. Naturally as a reasonable and considerate person overall, I reconsidered.

I believe a couple need to discuss differences and resolve them in a peaceful, understanding and loving way. Consequently, I genuinely believed him. He even followed through on my suggestions. In fact he started walking to chemistry class with one of my friends as I suggested.

Another thing that made me think that it was really working out was that he was okay with us taking a semester class on marriage from the Catholic Church. It was a heavy commitment to take on with a full semester of classes. Especially when a person with his class load had all kinds of labs on top of his regular science classes.

I also felt I was handling the matter very well. I thought we were working things out the way couples should. For example, he would sometimes tell me that he thought I should wear something else when we went out. If I didn't agree, I simply stated so in a diplomatic manner and moved on.

I did not lose my esteem like some women might and therefore rush off to change the outfit. I never hid who I was as a person either. I would only state my disagreement in the assertive way of communicating. (Which is the best and healthiest way to communicate with another person, by the way.)

Unfortunately I was to find out that even though it is the right way to communicate it does not mean it succeeds. I spoke calmly and assertively and thought I was being heard. The shocking thing was, I was to find out years into the marriage I was not being heard.

By now we were dating regularly. So I sought a job lifeguarding in Lethbridge where he was during that summer of '74.

SUMMER OF '74 IN LETHBRIDGE

I had the good fortune to take a job in Lethbridge where my boyfriend's home and summer job were. I got along very well with my boyfriend's parents and two sisters.

It was an experiential summer. I got to lifeguard at the biggest pool in the City. I took on a live-in maid job for a while as a Nanny of a 5 year old little girl. The mother was very impressed with me because I could get their daughter to eat things they couldn't get her to eat before.

Then I moved into the Convent portion of St. Michael's Hospital. It used to be the nursing school's residences. Then it became only the residence for the Nuns at the hospital and a few elderly ladies. One of them became a good friend of mine a few years later. I tend to seek out an elderly wise woman wherever I can as a sort of mentor. They have a matured wisdom worth tapping into.

My ex had told me nothing about his dad until I met him. He was returning from his research projects in the US. We went to pick him up at the airport. So it came as a bit of a shock when I was introduced to him as Dr. McKenzie.

He was a Scientific Geneticist for the Federal Government. I discovered his name in the *Who's Who of Canada* for his development of Saw Fly Resistant Wheat and Wheat Genetic Alterations for production in developing countries.

Sadly enough he was killed in the summer of 1979 driving back from his research plots in Saskatchewan. I grew to admire him and sometimes miss his influential calming presence. He never did meet our three children.

CHAPTER 10:

THE BOSS

KISSING BOOTH

I was hired by the town of Fairview as a lifeguard. I was unsuccessful at convincing the Board that I needed more money for new life jackets, even when I brought the Treasurer, Chairman and any of the other Rec. Board members to my pool demonstration on how nicely the life jackets sank to the bottom of the pool. The K-Pox in them was rock hard.

This pool had been operating with some less than desirable or inoperable equipment. It is pretty hard to get money out of the Recreation Board when I had just persuaded them to up their insurance liability clause to a minimum of a million dollars. I did not go into this job expecting to have to continually request more money either. Every time I turned around, I saw things that needed to be prepared for the town's swimming pool opening the long weekend of May.

To my surprise they did eventually give me some money for the life jackets, but it was based on my ability to drum up money to match it. I figured out a way to do just that.

There was a Fair soon to be held in town that I took full advantage of, to not only gain more funds but in turn, to teach the public. I contacted the Fire Department in Grande Prairie which was the closest and biggest community around. I wanted to find out if they had a "Recussy-Annie" (resuscitation dummy) that I could borrow.

It turned out I was able to use one in in the Fair coming up. What I did then was, design and print fancy "Certificates of Accomplishment" to be given to every participant. Being a teacher at heart, I always like to make fun situations a learning experience if I can.

I decided to set up a KISSING BOOTH at the Fair. Up north, most young adults got married right out of high school. One of my lifeguards was proof of that. Therefore there were virtually no single women left in town older than 18 or 19 years of age.

It took no time at all for the eligible bachelors in the area to discover that I, single and female, had arrived in town for the summer. Apparently I was the only available single woman around for miles.

I figured that if I set up a Kissing Booth at the Fair I could capitalize on that. I would be able to make the money I needed for the pool and at the same time everyone would benefit from learning some first-aid as well. I would say it was a pretty good deal for a dollar, don't you think?

I was already teaching dugout water safety in the school Health and Physical Ed. classes. So it seemed like an equally good idea to give the average citizen the actual experience of breathing into a fake human simulator such as "Annie" to teach the basics of CPR and AR.

It was an amazing turn out, the line-up we got was so long that I think some joined in the lineup to see what was up! Even though they thought they were going to get a kiss from me, they did not seem to be disappointed when it turned out to be a chance to try something they have no idea is harder than it looks to do. So a great experience was had by all!

Whatever certificates were left over, I turned around and used the blank backs of to write and present my monthly report on for the Rec. Board. I thought I would show how I was being thrifty and recycling any excess paper by writing up my reports on the back of the unused papers.

My Director thought it was a superb idea and tactic. She and I got along fabulously right from the start. I often went to her place for supper. She was Caucasian, and her husband, a Veterinarian, was a Black Man. They had a Black lab that to my surprise, and interestingly enough, they called, "Nigger." I was impressed at his choice of name for their dog. I got a kick out of it whenever he called the dog.

I had the opportunity to help at the doc's vet clinic, so I jumped at the offer. I got to take part in seeing my first calf born without having to strain my eyes through a knot hole in the barn wall on the ranch.

CAST IN MATERNITY

Sometime near the end of July, I had to dive in again to rescue a drowning child. I was on the lifeguard chair guarding at the time. In order to get down really fast, I just leaped off the chair, landing straight on the hard cement. In one complete movement I went from the guard chair to deck edge and to the kid needing help.

By diving right at him from the deck I was able to use my body force to push him right to the surface; keeping him from sinking. With my adrenalin pumping, I really didn't feel a thing.

I simply, in a matter-of-fact way, went into emergency mode to retrieve the boy. He turned out to be just fine once rescued from the engulfing water, having only swallowed a few gulps himself. He was just a little shook up, that's all.

I was back in the office filling out the necessary accident forms was when everyone noticed. My cashier happened to notice it first. Everyone then looked at my leg in astonishment. Glancing down to see what all the commotion was, is when I discovered my problem. Instead of the little boy having to head off to the hospital, I was the one going.

The doctors shook their heads. They all decided to put a cast on though they really couldn't find the actual problem for my ballooned-out leg. I knew I was in trouble when I asked for a Fibreglass Cast and they didn't know what I was talking about.

I knew of these waterproof casts because of my previous semester working at the Strathcona Pool in Edmonton. The Olympic swim team trained there some of the time and one of the guys had a fibreglass cast on in order to still swim and keep up with his training. Of course I was not so fortunate so I had to continue life guarding with a large garbage bag taped over my plain old "plaster cast." Whoopee!

Now you must be wondering what Maternity has to do with my injury. Since the doctors were not sure of what the reason was for the swelling, they kept me in overnight. The only available room was in the Maternity Ward.

So, picture this. I am the only single women over 18 in this very small town, now placed in the Maternity Ward of the local hospital. Word of that would spread like wildfire before suppertime.So I decided I better call my mom to tell her what was up in case she found out second-hand from a friend of the family.

Occasionally I would pull a practical joke on my mom. So this one seemed like a convenient one to pull on her. From the phone in the hospital, I said, "Hi Mom! I am in the hospital in the Maternity Ward."

All I hear, is dead silence on the other end of the phone! "Mom are you there? Mom?" I hear a slight clearing of her throat and then a staggered response. "Well, I - guess - I - better - congratulate you on what 'IT' is?"

"Well, Mom, that is just it. The doctors do not know what 'IT' is!"

On that note I chose to clue her in. First I had to interject with a heartfelt thank you. I told my Mom, "Wow, I am proud of you for the way you reacted to the news of me being in Maternity."

I knew then that if I ever did come to my parents with that kind of news (being pregnant and unwed) I would not be disowned or thrown out of the home, unlike some I knew.

Then I got serious and told her the doctors really did not know what "IT" was. I had a cast on and my leg elevated overnight to relieve the swelling in my leg. AND of course I filled her in on the rest of the truth as to why I ended up in Maternity in the first place.

God love her, for she never, amazingly, got grey hair from raising us or at least me. She always remained a red head. Apparently, red heads rarely go grey if at all. Real blondes too are lucky, their grey hairs blend in with their light colour more so making them look blonde longer.

The one positive note about this silly unnecessary cast was that I got to do what I always wanted to do if ever I had a cast. I got to draw a zipper right down the front of it!

CHAPTER 11:

I AM DONE!

The start of this term was different because my fiancé had graduated the previous April and was now working for the Government in St. Paul, Alberta. Therefore he would only be in the city to visit every few weekends or so.

Absence does make the heart grow fonder. When I got back from working at that swimming pool up north and shortly after school started, he proposed to me one evening when we were out for dinner.

MARRIAGE PROPOSALS PLUS

I have had more than one marriage proposal. However, I do not think many people knew that until now. Nor did my ex-husband know that. Not that I was trying to keep it a secret from him or anyone. In fact, until not too long ago, I really had forgotten all about the first proposal. I guess mostly because I did not take it seriously. I brushed it off and pretty much lost almost all memory of it.

The proposal was one of two I received from a PRINCE. Again you may not believe me but I was proposed to by not one but two men of Royalty. The first was at university before I met my actual husband to be. This guy was an Egyptian Prince, here on an education leave.

I can't even remember how we met. I think I had a class with him and we got to know each other through that connection. For some reason we hit it off but he was such a tease all the time, which for me is not a good match. I always seem to miss the difference between a non-serious joke and a serious one. Therefore most of the time I seemed to be taken for a ride at my expense.

As it turns out though, that seemed to be what he liked about me and in one of our silly times he asked me to marry him. Like I said, since he was kidding around with me so often, I really could not tell if he was joking or not.

I just couldn't take him seriously so I brushed him off. Even though he would continually hound me about it, I really was not about to accept it regardless.

The second Prince was from Sudan and was living in Canada in exile. I met him years after my divorce when attending a Messianic Jewish Church service on Saturdays in Calgary. At first we were introduced by someone in authority that felt I could be of some political help to him. He was hoping that, because I knew Premier Manning as an acquaintance. He thought that I could approach him on his behalf. He also felt his country's people would warm up to and listen to me.

As we worked together on this, we FOUND that we enjoyed each other's company. Even though he was a "Born Again Christian" he also already had a wife that he introduced to me over dinner at his place. Though many cultures overseas do have multiple wives, it was not something I was game for at all. No way!

He often said that he could get me anything I wanted. I've heard that so many times I tend not to believe it. So I responded with: "Oh yeah sure! Then I would ask for something, "I want a Thompson Chain Bible." They are a very detailed Bible and expensive. I had had my eye on one for a long time, but because of the expense I could not justify buying it. Lo and behold, he got one for me. I still have it and he signed it as "Prince_____."

Since then I have been proposed to many times. In fact if I wanted to get married within the week I would just have to contact one of them that wanted to marry me. I recently asked one guy why he even sticks around. He said, "Well we men can always hope you change your mind."

AHHH NO SKIING

My second last year of university I was still lifeguarding with a full course load. On top of everything I was planning and preparing for my wedding.

I was an avid skier throughout university. It had to be really important for me to not ski during Reading Week.

In 1976, though, Reading/Ski Week was the week I set aside to make my wedding dress. I stayed with my Brother and Sister-in-law. I had recruited her to help me since she's a talented Dietitian and Home Economist. I knew she would be very resourceful and helpful for the task ahead.

I designed my own wedding dress and was able to complete it within the week. The sleeves were box shaped with lace daisies going up the sleeves. My neckline was the shape of a 'W' for Woman and upside down it became an "M" when I looked down at it. The "M" stood for my new married name.

The dress itself was cut in my favourite style, the Princess Line. What cost the most and took the most time was the lacework. I sewed each individual piece of the lace petals and flowers onto the front panel of the dress as well as a matching one on the train.

Then I took a hat that looked a bit like a cowboy hat and I covered it all with the lace to match. I sewed on a hat band with a homemade bow and crinoline netting cascading down the back from the hat. On the net I sewed little daisies all over here and there.

I wore that same wedding dress a few more times. I wore it for an "Evening of Murder" party while still married. Even after my divorce, I modelled it in a few fashion shows.

I had the good fortune to have my counsellor push for me to do my final practicum in Ponoka where the wedding would be. I even had a rather elegant tea party for a Wedding Shower so that all my grade six girls could enjoy dressing up and helping me make all the flowers to decorate the cars. We, along with my mom, had a blast!

My whole grade six class filled up several pews at the wedding. They ran up to me after the service to ask me for my autograph. I think they wanted to see if I would remember to sign my new name.

THINGS ARE DIFFERENT

My counsellor at the University of Alberta was able to use my marks to secure approval from the U. of A. Faculty to allow me to attend the University of Lethbridge my last year. That was a real plus, being newly married.

It would be the first summer I would not be lifeguarding in about 11 years! So I pounded the pavement. I walked from store to store through the Lethbridge Centre Mall. My feet were killing me when I got to the last store, a drug store.

When I inquired about a job, the owner of the drugstore asked when I could start work. I replied with optimism, "Anytime!"

I think the owner was testing my enthusiasm and seriousness, for a job because he answered back to my "Anytime,'" with "Then start right now!" So I did start working right then and there, sore feet and all. I sure didn't enjoy it nearly as much as the lifeguarding though.

I DID IT WITH DISTINCTION

Some awesome things happened when I graduated in April of 1977. First I achieved graduation with Distinction. Secondly, due to a friend's horrible experience, I kept my maiden name in order to not lose my graduation records.

Upon obtaining a job after graduation, I would be required to begin paying off my student loans. However a remarkable thing occurred after graduation. My supervising counsellor from U. of A. came through with a brilliant idea and it worked!

So brilliant that I did not have to pay my Student Loans! All I had to do was present a letter along with my marks to the U. of A. Board of Advisors and if they agreed I could get some of my loan dropped. Or as in my case a miracle occurred. My whole Student Loan was absolved. YEAH!

That was the end of university, but the beginning of a beautiful career. After all, I had been seeking it since grade five. I promised myself to do better and never humiliate a student like I had seen teachers do.

CHAPTER 12:

MY TEACHING DEBUT

SHOTGUNS & FREEZERS

My first year as a teacher I actually ended up with the ideal classroom. I only had nine students, YEAH! The things I could do with that size of class were phenomenal! Two of the students were twins that were so identical that I had to ask their mother every morning before class to tell me which was which. She always dressed them in the same outfits but in different colours so that I could tell them apart.

Not only did I have the most ideal students that all teachers dream of, but I had the most problematic student of all time as well. So it made for quite the class dynamics.

One family proved to be the most "socially-dyslexic" family of all my teaching career. I however was very fortunate to get on the good side of them. That wasn't a good deal either, but certainly the lesser of two evils. For if I was on their bad side I might get chased off the farmstead by shotgun, which is what happened to a Social Worker that had come calling.

I really didn't mind them that much. Everyone kept their distance from them, and since they liked me they tended to want to talk my ear off if they could. And the Mom sure did when she would phone me at home.

I was at the grocery store, rounding the corner at one end of the frozen food section with all the upright freezers. At the other end I could see Mrs. Talker at the end of the aisle. "Oh no", I thought "I can't run into her now! I just haven't got the time."

So I did the most ridiculous thing you can imagine. It was summer too. That meant I was not bundled up in a ski-jacket, toque and mitts either. I wish!

Can you just guess by that last sentence what I did? I dove into the upright frozen food freezer. There I stood inside this food freezer on a busy Saturday afternoon, while people shopping were walking slowly by.

I was just hoping no one would open the door to where I was hiding. Especially Mrs. Talker. Sure enough someone did open my door! I practically fell on them because I was squished up against the shelves. But I quickly responded with a "Shhhh," as the guy, in his late 20's, turned into a statue with only his arm moving as he simply shut the door and walked away. It was so funny! Saved by the freezer, as my student's over-talkative parents walked right on by me. Whew!

I did eventually figure out how to get rid of her if I could not talk any longer. I just went dead silent. I did not respond to anything, not even with a "yah," or an "a-hum" or anything. Absolutely not a peep and it worked!

Do you know how hard that is to do? After all the thinking and effort that went into coming up with and utilizing this approach, I am glad that it was so successful. I passed it on to my colleagues that wanted any idea I had that would work to keep the conversation to a minimum.

ATTEMPTED BLACKMAIL

In my first teaching job, at the Readymade School, I taught until Easter time. Then I resigned to take a temp position in Lethbridge. When I submitted my resignation, my boss attempted to blackmail me into staying.

She tried very hard to keep me by threatening to blackball me from ever teaching again. To make a long story short, she didn't want to let me go because the class enrolment had increased on the pretence that I was teaching there the next year.

I had every right to resign, though. Thank heavens I had an Early Childhood District Head that I went to immediately to get advice from. She advised me not to play into my boss's hand.

"Whatever you do, don't leave lessons plans," she said. "That might be seen as a sign of guilt. As if you feel you're doing something wrong. Which you aren't."

Then she added that she would make sure my teaching reputation would remain intact.

"Okay then" I thought, "good to know!" My whole career was already in jeopardy.

Can you imagine wanting to be a teacher since grade five, only to have it over in a flash like that? I honestly could not believe this was happening to me, and in my very first year! YIKES!

ANOTHER 1ST FOR TEACHERS

Regardless of whether I taught full time or not, I did speak at Teacher's Conventions and continued to Substitute Teach. It looked like I was not going to get my Permanent Teaching Certificate through the usual channels of having a full-time job. So I approached the President of the Southern Alberta Teachers' Association to request the ability to obtain a Permanent Certificate through Subbing as well. That was not something ever done before, and he said that he would have to look into it and get back to me.

To make a long story short, the policy was changed and I was able to pioneer another thing for all Teachers. From then on we could collect Sub Days to go towards our Permanent Certificate. AND not only that, but those same days collectively would go toward years of experience and increases in Grid Pay.

To obtain my permanent certificate, which was my primary goal, I had to collect 194 days of Substitute Teaching Days to collect a year's increment. I suspect that number was created to make it almost impossible to achieve in one school year. The average person does not realize what a feat that is to accomplish. You see there's just under 200 days in a school year. That meant we had to Sub pretty much the entire year to collect one year's increment.

Knowing how hard this was to do, I got busy and began campaigning for Sub jobs. When at a school I went all out networking for jobs. Since I got along well with pretty much all the teachers I got lots of bookings. I was able to know well in advance the jobs I had booked. As it turned out I got the number of days I needed to collect for a year's worth toward my Permanent Certificate! One of my best achievements up to then.

In 1978, I finally got a full time position teaching and again it was Kindergarten, this time in McGrath, Alberta. I was carpooled with four other teachers. I always said as long as I could get along with the Principal, the Secretary and the Janitor, I would be fine and could manage the rest.

It turned out that I had a great staff to work with though I was a bit leery going into the job. For I was going into uncharted waters where I was going to be a "token" Non-Mormon teacher. I made my stance plain at the very first staff meeting by getting a cup of coffee and planting it right down in front of my seat at the staff table. No one seem to comment on it or pressure me in any way about not drinking coffee or try to convert me to Mormonism.

If you recall, I became a "Born Again Christian" at age 12 so that could be a conflict of interest. Though I am not one to judge, I saw no reason for this job choice to interfere with them being one religion and me another.

It actually went very well considering a teacher friend of mine also got hired to teach in Cardston, further down the road from Lethbridge and McGrath. She was pressured a great deal. So I considered myself lucky and respected enough by the staff in my school to be left alone.

I taught two classes of Kindergarten each day. Due to my two Special Needs students, I required an Aide. One student was deaf, and the other had Down's syndrome. My Aide of course was invaluable to me. I eventually steered the parents of the Down's boy in the direction of the Special Olympics as a way of finding an avenue of interest for him.

With an Aide and a Volunteer Parent in each class, AM and PM, it allowed me to do some things most teachers couldn't. I had one-on-one time to familiarize myself with each child and find out how they ticked.

I took each child on a walk-about at the beginning of the school year to get to know them. It was a great asset.

I remember one child in particular being silent in class and not talking. He seemed rather withdrawn, considering his twin was the total opposite which maybe was why he was so quiet. (I came across the rambunctious twin while working at the World Women's Curling Championship, March of 2012. He is now a doctor in Lethbridge. I left a note of encouragement for him while there.)

While on our walk the quieter twin he didn't say much at all until a bird flew across the path. Then out it came, a whole exclamation on the bird, even the full Latin name of the bird and so on and so on.

Once back at the school I called the librarian to round up every Bird book at the Division One level. At the end of the day, I sorted through the trolley of books and created a file of fun exercises just for him to work on when he had finished the regular, other work required in the curriculum. He was set on fire to learn!

I did the same for a few other students with varying interests and degrees of intelligence. I couldn't get over how a little tweaking could make their learning such a success. It didn't matter how smart one was either.

I had one little slow learner that lapped it up when I put together his own personal work. I think the reason it went over so well, is the fact that it had no academic boundaries. All the students with files just knew that they were special and smart so they acted like it. From there they ran with it and accomplished lots. They also felt important, aiding their esteem, and hence their academic improvement. In my opinion that follows. I feel it's my job as a teacher to awaken their own expectations through building their esteem. Through promoting their esteem and their own potential, academics with follow.

I learned a lot from each of the children's individual walks. They each had their inabilities as well as their abilities. Equally as important, I learned bit about each of their uniqueness.

I believe in testing for certain things right from the very beginning of the school year. This again is where my Aide was of benefit. It freed me up to administer tests on student's sight and hearing. This is something in my opinion should be made compulsory for Kindergarten to Grade 3 at least so that any impairments can be caught at an early age. Thanks to my Aide and the Volunteer Parents for their assistance. It was because of them I was able to make a lot of things happen.

Volunteer Parents came in to every class to assist in any way possible and bring the snack for the day. I continually encouraged, hinted, coaxed and pressured the fathers into coming as much as possible. Their child and every other child responded so differently to having their Dad in the class for the day as opposed to the Mother.

With Mothers, the students tended to be on the whiny side. With the Fathers they were on their best behaviour and accomplished so much more by showing them all they could do to impress them. Even the other children would try to impress any father or male figure that was in that day. It was absolutely wonderful to have such volunteers and talented ones at that!

At the beginning of the year, I gave an Orientation Meeting to the parents before their children even entered the school. This was for many reasons, such as to brief them on how to bring their child to school and how to leave to minimize their child's chance of crying and help them adjust to being left.

I also had them fill out a questionnaire that mostly had them list areas where they could help. Some, for example, could play an instrument and could do so for the class. Others were worth their weight in gold by being able to cut out over fifty Pumpkins or Snowmen, or Christmas Trees, etc.

My favourite of all time gift was from a student. It was "Half a Bottle of Perfume" that I wore the rest of the year. It moved me so that it still brings tears to my eyes as well as a prayer, for all the children who were in my care as a teacher and a Mom.

At Christmas time I was in charge of putting a program together for the concert. Each class was required to play and sing a Christmas song. I was pressured by the other teachers to get a certain child to just play something and NOT SING!

I refused to succumb to the pressure to shut the child up. The singing was very bad, I must admit, but the child LOVED to sing! I just could not take that away from a child just because they didn't sound nice. Besides, it turned out that he stole the show! He made a joyful noise unto the Lord.

GONE IS MY SICK LEAVE

I was busy on a Friday after school, putting up my Valentine's Bulletin Board. I was very fortunate to have the grade six teacher still working in his room. Thank God he spotted me out of the corner of his eye, on the floor, clutching myself as I groaned away.

He got me to the staffroom and gave me some water to sip and a cloth to put on my head since I was feeling a bit faint. I lay in a fetal position on my less painful side. I eventually managed to get all the way back to Lethbridge when the pain subsided enough to move.

I went straight to the clinic and my doctor. After he saw me he said in a rather matter of fact monotone voice that I was to go home and pack for the hospital.

Once my husband got home, the two of us were to come back to the clinic after hours to speak with him.

He said nothing of the seriousness of it until we were both in his presence. In a matter fact tone he told us both that I had a tumour the size of a grapefruit in my ovary, with some smaller ones as well. He said I was to go to the hospital right away to be admitted for emergency surgery the next day.

The next day was Saturday. I knew that things were bad if the doctors were going to operate on a weekend. The other MORE startling things was my doctor said that he may have to take both ovaries in order to remove all of the tumours. This meant that I may not ever be able to have children.

No one knew this, but it was going to be my last year teaching. My husband had been asked to go back to the university to take his Masters in Soil Chemistry and I had gotten my Permanent Certificate. Therefore we planned the perfect time to start a family.

This just proves another way that the Lord can intervene and take over one's emotions in order to protect them from even themselves! After such shocking news that meant no children, I should have been a basket case!

Now here is the very BEST part! The surprising thing was I was NOT! I was completely calm emotionally, not rattled and quite matter-of-fact. I took in all that the doctor said and knew the severity of it all, but I did not fall apart, nor focus on the negative and impending danger I was facing.

It was probably the combination of my ability over the years to handle a crisis as well as the Lord stepping in to aid in carrying me through that trauma. It is hard to determine what percentage is which! Nevertheless I most appreciated GOD stepping in for me. That's something I wish I had more often!

Three days later when I was recovering in the hospital, my doctor came in with a bit of a smile on his face, which was a good sign since he rarely smiled. He had good news. The biopsy was benign and he was able to save both ovaries! As a result, my three beautiful, healthy children came later, partly due to his expertise. Thank you Doc!

HATFIELDS VERSUS MCCOYS

In addition to the surgery that used up all my sick leave, I was black-listed in June. One family accused me of beating their child and of course since everyone is either related to the Hatfields or the McCoys; half that town was against me, and the other half along with rest of the teachers were for me.

Again I came out of it with my reputation cleared and commended. In some ways I was sad to leave teaching at the end of that year but I had accomplished what I intended.

Now I was eager to have a baby. The timing was perfect. Although we told no one until the three month danger zone for miscarriage had passed, I was pregnant and due in the end of January of 1981. We were away at U. of A. living in Married Residence on campus at the time.

ABC'S OF GRADUATION

I seem to get most of my great ideas at night. I came up with an affective story for children complete with illustrations that turned out to look just like the parents of the women I helped work through issues around her father. It was truly prophetic! (Affective has to do with psychology, relating to one's feelings and the reasons for emotionally reacting.)

I came up with my entire Kindergarten graduation program that was a big hit! The kids came up on stage wearing their Dad's white dress shirt on backwards with graduation caps made out of black cardboard. Each recited what they learned in Kindergarten under their letter in the Alphabet. For example, "C" is for "Community" and how we are better off getting along rather than at war.

After finishing that little song about the ABC's they each came up to me to get a hug and their nice calligraphied diploma I handmade for each of them. I would trade it for their Alphabet letter, completed by a hand shake, accompanied by an encouraging word from me to each of them. I was so proud of all fifty-two of them!

Years later when they were graduating again only from grade twelve, I got up to give another word of encouragement to them. I read from a scribbler that I had my volunteer parents keep with special little memories on each of the children. I still have that coil scribbler jam-packed with memories.

CHAPTER 13:

ASIDE FROM TEACHING

FIRST SIGN OF DESTRUCTION

Between the close call with my first teaching job, and the troubles in my marriage, I was stressed and depressed. A lot transpired to add insult to injury. I was not getting the jobs that I was well suited for. Take for example, a job offer from the College to teach nine severely handicapped young adults. I did not take the job. I knew my capabilities and knew that since the children were not the kind that would ever achieve much progress, I couldn't enjoy that job.

Our marriage too was giving me grief. The first time I left my husband was four or five years into our marriage. I knew something was seriously wrong when he blew up over me buying "Crest" and not "Colgate" Toothpaste. It all ignited over a tube of toothpaste. YIKES.

It was like his blow-up unleashed everything that he had stuffed way down inside of himself all those years. He sure did a good job of stuffing because I had no idea whatsoever that he really had not agreed with my point of view about items such as there being no reason why I should drop all my friends just for him.

If anything, I hope you the reader get from this how unaware one can be. It just goes to show that one spouse can't always tell if the other spouse has genuinely resolved issues.

It was then that I realized that I was in a marriage trap! I was at a crossroads to my life. I did not believe in divorce but knew that I had to figure something out. But what?

Much later, I packed after another one of his blow-ups and left. I went out to the bus stop around the corner. I stood waiting there for a long time wondering what was taking the bus so long.

It is amazing how the slightest thing can divert a person's LIFE, altering their path! There apparently was no bus service on Sundays. Waiting all that time for nothing allowed for my ex's dad to show up at the bus stop and pick me up.

He was a very calm, wise man that I respected a lot. He talked me out of leaving and I agreed to give it another try.

I went back but stood my ground, so my husband knew that he could not explode like that again. Consequently, he didn't for years, although I got many a silent treatment with no resolve or end in sight. It made for a strained relationship.

I had to be very careful and pick my battles. Frequently I contemplated ways out, only to feel hopeless and done in.

A few years later when we had already bought a house I was more than ever feeling this way. I fell into quite a slump and did something I am not proud of.

With all the battles I had to face at home, and the corruption in the school system, I saw no end in sight. So I sat at our kitchen table with all the pills in the house that I could find. I swallowed over 300 pills of all sizes and strengths. It was a huge bottle that I kept for years as a reminder of my state of affairs.

Well, I found out that nothing I did would succeed in killing me. The bottle of pills had absolutely no effect on me whatsoever. That very same day only a few hours later, we attended a BBQ at a friend's place. I acted as if nothing had ever happened. I could not believe myself that I felt just fine having taken a whole large bottle of pills full of Aspirins, Tylenol and similar only a few hours before. (Keep in mind the CURSE on me is still active.)

ENTERTAINER

I loved entertaining, whether it was for my husband's staff or our annual "Evening of Murder" party. We frequently had guests over for a game of cards. Christmas was full of festive times. Every Christmas we went out as a family to chop a tree down.

Other times it gave me a good excuse to have a bunch of ladies over for a Christmas party. I hung little gifts on the tree for each of my guests. When we finished our treats and decorating, I would tell them to go retrieve their gift before heading home. Of course this was a perfect time to serve some Christmas cookies that I got from our annual Cookie Swap in late November. Twenty dozen cookies later of every description made me ready for any number of parties from Christmas to Easter.

Every year for my husband's birthday I made sure I planned something unique as he requested it not be tied in with Christmas Day. So I made sure we had beach parties in minus 30 degree weather, an "Evening of Murder", or a retro-party.

For Christmas gift giving to each other, we would plan a night out around the end of November. We would start by shopping together, checking out what we each had already staked out for each other to try on and pick. We then headed to a lovely place for dinner to finish off a great evening. In our Christmas outfits, we were now set for the holidays. This was a great way to keep the frustrations out of gift giving. Then we just gave each other something tiny wrapped under the tree for Christmas Day.

SPORTS ADJUSTMENT

I was proud of my husband for taking on the sports that I was involved in. He learned all of them from me, although we didn't necessarily keep active in all of the sports I introduced him to.

I drew cartoon characters of each of us from the time we met to the time we got married. Lots of the pictures depicted us playing sports activities together. One illustrates us portaging a canoe with him going one way under the canoe and me going the other way!

Another showed me accidentally bonking him on the head with a tennis ball. I think there was one of him skiing downhill with his skis crossed yelling out, H-E-L-P! All dramatized in cartoon, moments from the time we met right up to our wedding day. The one illustrating our wedding day, shows both of us dressed like little kids with big people's clothing draping around us. They were a big hit.

It was not until my divorce years that I virtually quit sports, due to a drastic cut in my finances. I did keep curling but I only spared. Had it not been for a good friend of mine that wanted to learn how to golf I may not have kept it up either.

I even parted with my antique clubs. But I couldn't part with my cart. Besides, clubs these days are fabulous, almost ecstasy to the touch. I have tried a few Demos and a lady lent me her Driver one time. It was called "BIG BERTHA." That was heaven to hold and a climax to drive! That one club alone costs about six hundred dollars. Wow!

That'll be the day I go and buy one those! For I never felt that good hitting with my ole wood driver, no way! Especially since BIG BERTHA increased my drive by 100 yards!

I no longer compete. My trophies only serve now as memories and motivation for me. I still enjoy volunteering at Opens, Links and Legends and PGA Tours. About all I do now as a stress reliever, is to go out and hit a bucket of balls occasionally.

BEETHOVEN'S 5TH

I had asked my ex to start going to church with me. We ended up back at the United Church that we both grew up in as children. This time around I had the miraculous opportunity to present the children's story every Sunday at the front of the church.

The United Church speaks very little on the topic of Salvation and being filled with the HOLY SPIRIT. It was miraculous because the LORD let me leave that church years earlier at 13 years of age. Now I was back and had the opportunity to teach the children and the whole congregation about Salvation and the Holy Spirit.

I also led Ladies Stitch'n Study, as well as an exercise study. Then at one point it was decided that the church would put on a Talent Night to show off the many talented people in the congregation. I was chosen to be the Master of Ceremonies. I decided to open the show with an act of my own. I did not take music lessons as a child. I did discover through my professor at U. of L. that I was musical.

I decided to get my neighbour, a Piano Teacher to teach me Beethoven's 5th. Yes, you read right. Even though I knew nothing about how to play. I asked if she could teach me. I added for her assurance, "Not the whole piece, just the beginning, please". It was so weird a request that she was game.

For the talent show I got all dressed up in my Tails and Tux. On that night I walked out to the centre of the stage to start the show. Without saying a word I did some stretches and then a few more. Then I walked over to the piano. Finally I stood in front of the piano next to the bench, again doing smaller stretches for my hands and fingers. I really played up the stretching and flexing like I was warming up to play the piano.

Finally for the big moment. I stepped in front of the bench and faced the keyboard. I did one more flex of my fingers just to add some further suspense. Then I made an exaggerated flip of the tails on my tuxedo high up in the air in order to sit down on the piano bench. Again I made two more flexing gestures with my fingers before I slammed them down onto the keyboard to begin Beethoven's Fifth!

I simply pounded out the first few lines of Beethoven's Fifth; then promptly stood up in front of the Bench with one hand firmly placed on the piano facing the audience. With my chin in the air, I stoically bowed stiffly before pivoting on my dress shoe heels and majestically walking off the stage. It was my first, last, and only, one-of-a-kind, piano recital.

♫ TA-DAAHH! ♫

Backstage I waited long enough for the audience to finish applauding first. Then I held back just a few more seconds so as to build a bit of tension. They were now wondering what was going to come next. On that cue, I walked back out onto the centre-stage again.

I bowed stiffly in a dignified manner, one more time before proceeding to emcee the rest of the talent show that evening. I can hardly believe that I did that!

FIRST SUSPICIOUS SIGNS OF THE END

Call it a wake-up call. Meager toothpaste was an alert, forming into a warning that I clearly noticed.

Boy did he get upset! That is what I took as a cautionary heads-up. It was just too much overboard to not be a yellow light for me.

From then on the yellow lights began to increase in number. In 1994 I finally left. Just to give you a fast flash forwards: The messy divorce went into 1999. I didn't even receive the settlement before I was served with a lawsuit by my ex. I spent, all together, seventeen years in and out of the courts burning up money I didn't have to burn. All because my ex was suing me over and over.

The first lawsuit lasted nearly seven years. To me this just spells ABUSE, loud and clear. Only this time it is done through the

courts LEGALLY. How can the legal system allow further abu
continue when everything is signed sealed and settled? I
APPALLED at the system!

My ex husband did not want me to have any of his Pension th
by LAW, had a legal right to. It was clearly agreed upon and settl
in the courts that I would receive what I was entitled to. M
question is, why would any lawyer take his case to sue after that?
do know that his two divorce lawyers would not.

When a person has a vendetta against another person they may get
away with it on a worldly level but on a Spiritual level they will
not! For the Spiritual world will set it right! Like, what some
people will refer to as Karma or "What-goes-around--comes-
around."

Scripture states it clearly, "What you sow you reap." Like, Pilate, I
washed my hands of this vindictive stuff. I have learned that the
easiest way through life is to stay away from trying to vindicate
myself on my own. It just careens out of control and into one big
headache.

But, I digress, back to where we were in the story.

I MADE LEMONADE OUT OF MY TUMOUR

I had felt a small pea size lump in my breast. I went to my family
doctor to check it out. He informed me that the lump was most
likely benign. Then he added that we could just keep an eye on it. I
said I did not want to just keep an eye on it! I can't believe that he
would say that when his own wife had just gotten out of the
hospital from having a mastectomy. All I could think of was, I
wanted it out as soon as possible!

I went to another doctor in the clinic, a specialist, to see if he
would take it out. He said the same thing. Worse, he simply took
my list of questions and sloughed them off! Sheesh! I don't like it
when doctors or anyone does that. I wonder what they would say if
it was them with the diagnosis?

ly I found a doctor that offered to take the lump out before I asked him to. In the meantime, throughout all this searching husband could not see what the big deal was. He sided with the r doctors and felt that I was making a mountain out of a ehill. In fact, I was making sure I was not making a mountain of a lump that was smaller than a molehill!

ong answer from my OWN husband! I thought husbands were pposed to be supportive of their wives. I tried to shrug it off but e whole thing put a bad taste in my mouth about our relationship ʒain.

he day I was to go in for day surgery to have it removed I took a ʒouple of supportive friends with me. Then we went out for lunch ιfter to celebrate! So I made lemonade out of a lemon that was pea size!

Scary health issues really put a timeline in perspective. We were glad that we took time for ourselves before tumours, teaching and children were to occupy our lives.

My husband and I traveled with his mom back to England to visit all our relatives "over the pond" as they say. We had a fabulous whole summer away in England, Wales and Scotland. Some of the relatives were dignitaries in government there, so we had a few special occasions to attend.

I got to play cricket and if you can call it that, I made a home run! I saw Land's End, and golfed at the first golf course ever called St Andrews. I loved Wales and Robin Hood's Bay. Oh and York was my favourite city, it is the most modern in some ways yet the tourist trap there is a narrow market place of tiny little Dickens's type shops, called the "Shambles."

Edinburg was nicer than London because the streets were like ours in cities in Canada: STRAIGHT!

In London I felt I was walking around in circles most of the time completely lost when we were on our own. Take it from me, if you are going to London, take a guided tour so that you don't spend the whole time walking in circles.

CHAPTER 14:

GONE IS THE JET-SET, WELCOME WET-SET!

Dear children: I have always loved each of you dearly and have always been extremely proud of each of you. I remember each of your births so clearly! They were planned and such wonderful, arrivals!

I somehow hope that all three of you can see what efforts I made to continue to be the best mom I was and could be. It just wouldn't be with your dad, unfortunately. What a shame.

THE BIRTHS OF OUR THREE CHILDREN

In February, we had our first child, a son, while living in the married Res. at U. of A. while my husband completed his Master's Degree. I had prayed months before for He/She to be a well behaved, quiet, content and happy baby. (I called all of my Babes-To-Be, "He/She" as in those days we did not know which we would have ahead of time.)

It was important for us to have a quiet baby so his dad could study undisturbed by too much crying. If not, we had decided ahead of time that our son and I would return home alone to Lethbridge.

My prayers were answered, for he was a great baby. In fact, he slept right through the first nights at home from the hospital.

This was a bit frightening for me, for there had been a few crib deaths at the time. So instead of enjoying a nice night's sleep while my son slept so well, I stayed up beside him all night watching for his chest to rise and fall, making sure that he was okay.

But back to being pregnant: I was overdue and feeling it. I looked like the "Great Pumpkin" in my bright orange ski jacket. After all I was expecting twins so I was pretty huge! I kept my swimming up, for it was the one time I could be on my stomach! AHH! I think our He/She liked that too, he sure was active in the womb when I swam.

I was getting awfully tired of being overdue and sure did not want a Caesarian. I was also into the "nesting phase" of my pregnancy, scrubbing, waxing and polishing my floors. I tried Murphy's Law and it worked. I had a party. That evening during the party, I was having what I thought were "Braxton Hicks" but were really CONTRACTIONS!

To be on the safe side, we said our goodbyes to our guests and went off to the hospital. Unfortunately nothing happened. I think He/She heard the annoying racket the nurse made when admitting us. She was going on about how I was not doing my breathing right. I'd never make it at that rate and so forth! So He/She decided not to come out into a world with all that racket! Smart thinking if I say so myself!

So He/She did the unimaginable and literally backed up! Once babies are ready to come into this world a tell-tale sign is their dropping down into the delivery canal. The staff were baffled to see that strangely enough He/She moved back up in my womb even with my water broken. I think He/She's mind was made up not to enter this world until that awful nurse left!

The nasty nurse had me so convinced that I was not going to make it. Between her and another women in labour screaming obscenities, I was beside myself demanding drugs of any kind and a Caesarian before I even got to the delivery room! A far cry from my visions of a natural birth!

Sure enough, morning came, along with a shift change at 7:00 AM and in walked this marvellous Jamaican nurse. She was the total opposite of that other nurse. She said that I was breathing just right and doing a superb job with my labour!

Well, listen to that will you! I must say, she was a breath of fresh air! I felt much more confident and ready to have He/She the natural way I wanted to. Encouragement is everything!

Obviously, He/She felt the same way too. The birth took under three hours and that is without transition! YEAH!

Our first son, literally squirted out like a watermelon seed. I almost jumped off the delivery table to catch him myself in case the doctor and intern were going to drop him. I told them they better not or else!

Afterwards the doctor, whose name I'll never forget, complimented me on having what he said, "was a textbook delivery" and he said, "It was a privilege to be a part of it." WOW!

There had also been a twin that didn't develop, that I gave birth to later.

SLEPT LIKE A BABY

I took my son everywhere because he was so well behaved and I wanted him to adjust to all kinds of environments. In fact he listened intently at symphonies and slept through Wayne Gretzky's record breaking assist goal when he broke Bobby Orr's assist record with the Oiler's hockey team in '81.

The crowd went wild for over 15 minutes, delaying the game. That, along with Crazy George the mascot making the Wave, didn't even wake our new son. When the game was over people were commenting: "Hey look, there's a baby that was here the whole time, Eh!" The fans couldn't get over the fact that he slept through it all!

MUSICAL BEFORE BIRTH

After six months, when our first baby had begun to sit up, we were visiting my brother and sister-in-law in Elk Point. I was chatting with my sister-in-law while he was sitting on my lap facing the piano keys. Suddenly, he began to play! I don't mean banging away on the keyboard either. I mean actually playing with each finger being used individually on each key individually. We both looked simultaneously in awe. This proved that he was musical.

The very first day after we brought him home from the hospital I turned on the classical music that I always played while I was pregnant. Immediately he began moving his baby hands in the air like a conductor of an orchestra. I remember it felt like he was doing the same thing in my womb, to the music.

We already knew what we wanted to call each of our children. We gave all of them Scottish names. We also wanted to give our 1st son his Grandfather's name for his middle name as he had been killed only a few months earlier.

In the first months of the pregnancy we kept He/She a secret. And there is something else we kept secret until He/She was born. You see, my husband's dad had researched their genealogy when in Edinburgh, Scotland. He found as far back as six generations that the Clan had all sons for their first born.

So we could very well have a first son also. Since we did, that made it now the 7th oldest son of the oldest son and we went on to have a second son as well. Now it will be up to our 1st to have a son for his first child so it will continue. I'm just saying, no pressure here.

I found out too some more interesting clan information. The castle on the Shortbread cookie tin was once a family Castle, sold to one clan that made it a prison for another clan.

This involved the Stewarts and the Campbells. When a prisoner was set free, they were simply pushed out of a window and would have to swim to shore for freedom.

ULTIMATUMS

That was the beginning of the 1980s for me. It was a great start for both of us. Seeing England, then my first full-time job as a teacher, and the safe removal of my tumour, then going off to school to obtain our Masters and have a baby at the same time.

Once back home, I was contacted by my past Early Childhood Coordinator at the College. She was asking if I would come back to teach Post-Graduate Studies.

I then asked for a couple of things that weren't done before in the jobs of working Moms. You could say that they were ultimatums because I really didn't need to go back to work. I asked first if I could work out of the home instead of having to go into an office on campus for an 8:00 to 4:30 type job. They agreed. I also asked "If I had to, could I take my baby to my lectures?"

I only did that once. I remember, it was too funny because my baby fell asleep pretty much right when I started the lecture. I recall saying to the class it was due to my boring lectures!

One last request was that I did not want to take these lectures out to outlying campuses which meant traveling during the winter. It is a good thing I did, because my courses were growing in popularity and outlying campuses were requesting me to come and teach them. I was willing to provide the material for them but not to go myself.

I taught a popular, "Big People/Little People" Series for parents to learn with their children fun ways to educate them at home. Some of the courses were called, "Kids'n Kitchens", "Kids'n Krafts", "Kids'n Carpentry" and others. Another I developed was "Parenting and Teaching the Gifted Child."

I also taught a "Discipline" course and then I taught an Early Childhood course to adults. I had a specialized background in the Montessori Method of teaching that lent itself well to the method of parenting that I designed my lectures around.

SON #2, AMBULANCE RIDE

Our second son was born within an hour, right on the stroke of Midnight on Remembrance Day. To solve the issue of an exact date the doctor decided to give him the birthdate of Nov. 12th, 1983. Since my babies came fast, my doctor had taught me how to do an emergency home birth delivery if need be.

I remember my water breaking on the floor in the bedroom about 11:00 PM. Nov. 11th/Remembrance Day! What an appropriate date! He/She's dad and I jumped into our little brown VW. Rabbit car, with me up on my knees in the front passenger seat facing backwards due to severe back labour.

We were about to stop at a red light on Mayor McGrath Dr. and 6th Ave. as I hastened to keep going. "What if a cop pulls us over?" he responded. I in turn said, "Then I'll talk to him." We barely made it into the elevator at the hospital before I began to deliver. Thank Heavens the nurse, when I said, "I am having this baby NOW!" didn't argue and whisked me off to the delivery room immediately where my doctor was waiting.

That was one anxious different kind of birth, I tell you. I had read that a women giving birth, if having to stop pushing when her body naturally wants to push, would be facing the hardest thing ever.

Within a few minutes on the delivery table that is exactly what I had to do. It seemed impossible until my doctor told me WHY! The cord was wound around my baby's neck so tightly that the doctor could not even get his fingers or scissors in under it to cut it away.

I gave it all that I had to NOT push. This was exceedingly difficult when compounded by the fact that I must stay very, very still too! That's next to impossible, but I did it for my child.

That allowed the doctor to carefully saw his way through the umbilical cord with a scalpel. Once the baby was saved, though all blue, the nurse was smart and kind enough to give me a nano second to hold him before rushing him away to ready him for the intensive care unit in ANOTHER hospital.

I jumped off the delivery table to follow right behind the nurse that was rushing our new son away. I was greatly relieved to hear my doctor state rather emphatically, "And she goes with him!" So the good news was, I wouldn't have to carry out "Plan B."

What a relief not to have to drive over to admit myself at the other hospital in order to be with our baby! I had heard that women were left behind when their baby was taken over to intensive care at the other hospital. I could never stand for that and had already planned for Plan B to go into effect if necessary.

I followed the nurse to where our son was put in a portable incubator while we waited for the ambulance drivers to pick us up. While waiting, I literally had to wring out my wool work socks. I had worked so hard to keep from pushing. All of the strength had drained out of me.

While next to my son's incubator, the nurse and I noted something pretty bright and intelligent about our 2nd son! Only a few minutes into his life and he responded to his name! As I reached in through the holes to touch him, I called out his name. He had been placed on his stomach facing the other way in his little oxygen helmet. Which, by the way was too small for him because he was 8 lbs. 5 oz. Those helmets were for preemies.

When I called out his name he lifted his head and turned to look at me! That is what the nurse and I were in awe of! A baby only a few minutes old can't do that yet! Their heads are too heavy and their necks not strong enough yet. Not to mention that he had one and a half collapsed lungs as well from the tight umbilical cord cutting his oxygen off.

We both knew right then and there that he was some pretty special baby! I could see how strong he was not only physically but in determination; not to mention he was acutely intelligent and recognized his name minutes after birth, and it was the first time I spoke it too. WOW!

I was glad that I knew the ambulance drivers. One was a Christian and right away I asked him to pray with me for the baby. Then asked him to get his wife to pray for us too when they could. (His wife and I had curled together.)

At the other hospital a specialist was waiting for us. He and I stayed up all night watching and waiting to see that the baby's second lung didn't completely collapse as well. If it did, an opening would need to be made from the outside in to the lung.

We were blessed, for by morning the baby's lungs were recovering fine and he was out of the danger zone. That didn't get him out of intensive care though. The nurses ALL loved him and all wanted to hold him ALL the time, since he weighed a healthy eight and a half pounds.

Most of the babies the nurses took care of weighed only a pound or two and were too awkwardly tiny to hold in the usual way. So our new baby was a welcome change and was spoiled! I had to almost fight with them to get my turn. It was usually not done in intensive care but he was a special case, so I persisted and was able to regularly feed him myself, thank God.

It wasn't even a year later when we were living in the married student residence on the U. of S. campus. His dad was completing his Doctorate at the time. I spent several all-nighters along with a Resident doctor whom lived across the hall. We were desperately trying to keep our son alive and nurse him back to health.

His dad and I were not even sure we should have his 2nd birthday party, given how weak he was. It was a blessing that we lived on campus and had access to one of the top pediatricians and Pediatric Research department in the world. Thank the Lord this leading pediatrician had gotten back from a Hutterite Colony where he diagnosed and dealt with something new called Beaver Fever.

He felt that after all the tests had been taken, the symptoms closely matched that of Beaver Fever. I thank you Lord; for just a few days before his birthday, he began to eat and feel better. So we went ahead and had a BIGGER than ever birthday party for him in the party room!

Onward and upward was his life from then on. Especially after he asked Christ into his life when he was five and sitting at the kitchen table wanting to talk about God with me. He prayed the sinner's prayer then.

SWIMMING WITH BABY

Once our second son arrived on the scene, I did decided to retire my teaching notes and handouts for total undivided Motherhood. I even had my last Art Showing that fall. I could see very clearly that once one has more than one lively, strong-willed boy, they are officially a parent! I didn't need the added stress of course loads so I officially retired.

I even had to go jogging now in the school yard instead of the lovely peaceful Henderson Lake a block away. I would put my three year old in the playground area, and begin my jog with his little baby brother in the pram, running the perimeter of the school grounds until either Baby Brother got restless, or my 3 year old got into trouble on the play gym. I would rescue him and we would head home. Some days I had a good jog and other days not so good, maybe none at all.

Shortly after that I started going to Aqua-fit instead. I would put my 3 yr. old in the wading pool to splash around, while Baby Brother watched in his car seat. Then I did my exercises in the pool next to the wading pool. The two of them were in their glory getting lots of attention from all the ladies in the Aqua-fit class.

The routine worked out really well and the baby was kept amused and remained content where he was and often he fell asleep. Sometimes I wanted to swim a mile or as much as I could after the Aqua-fit class, but did not want to leave Big Brother unattended in the wading pool.

So I would take one of the pool's floating doughnuts that had a seat to sit him in. Then I would push him along in front of me as I swam the lengths of the pool doing the Breast Stroke. It worked out just fine for both of us. Until Baby Brother let us know it was time to quit in no uncertain terms.

HOW CAN I MAKE BIRTHING/LABOUR LAST LONGER?

Along comes a baby sister. I was hoping to extend my labour for her. Under an hour was way too short a time to deliver a baby as had happened last time. I asked my Lamaze instructor if she knew or could find out for me how to make labour last longer. She was shocked and said, "You WHAT? No one has ever asked me that before! I am not sure you can," she said. "But I will see what I can find out for you."

It resulted in me managing to stretch my labour out to just under two hours by simply walking while singing. YEAH!

I sang my way through labour because I couldn't get the hang of the last level of breathing. So I sang really fast.

♫ *Oh the Lord is good to me and so I thank the Lord*

For giving me the things I need

The sun-and the-rain and-a ba-aa-bee

Oh the Lord is good to me-ee-ee. Hallelujah! ♫

The nurse said that she would never forget me: the one that sang her way through her delivery. After that I was asked to be a coach for other moms' deliveries.

I DELIVERED MY DAUGHTER MYSELF!

With a lifeguarding background and my doctor preparing me for a home birth during my second pregnancy and on, I was definitely ready for my third baby.

I had made it to the hospital in time but my doctor still asked me if I wanted to deliver He/She myself! I said, "You bet!" It was one of the most incredible things I could ever do in my life and I did it!

I delivered her into this world to become the awesome women she is. Her brothers were waiting outside with my mom, her Grandma.

When they came in to see little sister for the very first time, I had slipped a little present in beside her for each of them. Her younger brother saw them first and said, "Look! She gave us presents!"

They were buttons that said "V. I. B." It stands for, Very Important Brother! I had made them for her to give her brothers as a way to help the three of them to bond well. I am thinking now, years later, it went so well that it may have backfired on me.

I suspect her two brothers protected their sister so much they persuaded her not to let me give her diabetic shots. Hence, separation grew between her and me.

I did, though, have the good fortune to bring her to the Lord. She asked Christ into her life with me in my car after bringing her home from shopping. She was five years old.

I did everything to insure that each of my children were born with optimum health. I ate important foods for each trimester. Not one of them had ear infections or any childhood ailments. I nursed each of them for a full year and even froze my milk to extend it another year in order to fully build up their immune systems.

I did everything in my ability to in enhance their intelligence. I even ate sardines and liver, (YUCK!) in my first and third trimester for optimum brain development and it worked! All three have above average levels of intelligence.

LIFE IS POETRY OF ALL KINDS

I used to write a lot of poetry in my teen years and first year university. You may be surprised to know that I had one published that I won an award for. In fact I find it rather amusing, as a teacher, to have my poem pretty much in every high school in North America. The reason is, it is in *The Anthology of Literature,* which is a book that English classes often study.

Here is a poem that I put in my will for each of my children. I didn't write all the poem myself; I found it in a card and adapted it to my preference in order to express what's in my heart.

"IF TOMORROW STARTS WITHOUT ME"

If the sun should rise and find your eyes all filled with tears for me;
I wish so much you wouldn't cry away the day.
While thinking of the many things, we didn't get to say.

But when tomorrow starts without me, please try to understand,
that an angel came and called my name, and took me by the hand.

And said to me that my place was ready, in heaven above.
That I'd have to leave behind, all those I dearly love.

But as I turned to walk away, a tear fell from my eye.
For much of my life I missed having you three nearby.
I had so much to live for and much left to do. But I am satisfied.

I thought of all the yesterdays, all we shared and
all the fun we had, if just for a while.

If I could relive the last half of my life,
I would want to recapture my time with my daughter.
But now I pray good memories will take the place of me.

Now I walk through heaven's gate and feel so much at home.
God looked down and smiled at me for it was time to come home.
Today life for me on earth has passed.

Here in Heaven it starts anew!
There will be no longing for the past.
But you have been forgiven and now are free at last!

So when tomorrow starts without me,
don't think we're far apart my children.

For every time you think of me, HE & I,
are right here in Heaven and your hearts.

AND I want you to know how much HE above really loves you.
So answer the door of your heart, and let HIM in to start.

The most recent poetry I've written was in and around 1995 to '97. A cowboy poet got me started, writing cowboy poetry. Since I was wrangling at the time it seemed a good fit. Riding seemed to spur me on; pun intended. Yuck- Yuck- ! I volunteered at Pioneer Camps so my children could all go camping with me for free!

My middle son was the only one that actually did go camping with me. I still have a little note he left me in the craft room at camp. Another volunteer spotted it for me on our paper table cloth. I cut it out, and I've kept it all these years. It said: "Mom I love you!" This was at the time I was divorcing his dad and my sons weren't talking to me much at all. So that tiny little note was more precious than ever. It was the last bit of communication he and I had.

CHAPTER 15:

STAY AT HOME MOM

ANSWERED PRAYER

My two boys seemed to think I was weird for helping street people by leaving food for them, or in one case I gave a lady a dress of my mom's. They also seemed to side with their dad when it came to me praying about things all the time. One time in particular though, I sure hope they remember.

We were expecting our third child and looking for a bigger home Anyway, when coming home from downtown one day and stopped at a traffic light, I recall my son complaining about wanting to decorate his own bedroom.

Since I knew we were in hopes of finding a house soon with our third child on the way, I had been stalling our oldest son on the decorating. This time, however, he really pressed the issue on me. So while stopped at the light I prayed about it with the boys. We prayed that the Lord would find a new house for us really soon so that the boys could have new bedrooms to decorate for themselves.

Well, guess what? The prayer was answered that very night when we went to look at a house and liked it instantly. Since it was not on the market yet but soon would be, we put a bid in right then and there.

I think it was awesome how the LORD answered his personal prayer like that, and for both boys to witness how fast prayer can be answered. It was a real testimony of GOD's love for my sons to see. I hope that proved to the boys how valuable and powerful it is to have prayer as a resource.

GETTING RUN OVER AGAIN?

I liked that our boys had inquisitive minds, curiosity and such vigour. My parenting goal was to have them channel it in positive ways that were not harmful to themselves or others. And to surround them with plenty of prayer.

I must tell you of another very frightening near-death experience my oldest son and I had together. We had just left the Haig Clinic in Lethbridge on one of the main drags. It connected West Lethbridge to South Lethbridge so was very busy with traffic.

This particular afternoon, I was walking up to the corner with my son hand in hand to cross at the crosswalk lights. We waited for the cars to all yield to us even though the light showed we could go.

Then we stepped off the curb onto the crosswalk to proceed across the street to our car. My independent, rambunctious child wrenched his hand out from my grip and took off ahead of me!

I was alarmed and upset at him but figured all was okay until - Oh my GOD in Heaven! I saw it out of the corner of my eye. It was a van in the far lane of traffic coming up to the intersection. It didn't look like it was going to stop at all! I screamed at the top of my lungs for my son to "STOP!"

Thank GOD he froze. Just in time too, for the van sped past my son, missing him by inches!

Whew, that was close! So I took off after my son and scooted him and myself over to the curb. All we could do was hold each other as we stared at the road. We sat, white as ghosts and held each other as we shook. Kids have no idea what they put us through at times!

There was another time he took off on me. I forget exactly what the disagreement was, but he was going to pack to leave home. I learned the hard way to not call their bluffs. For I said to him when he turned on his heels and trotted off to his bedroom to pack to leave home, "Alright then, I will help you pack."

Unfortunately that didn't deter him one bit. Darn! Now what could I do since my bluff had been called? I ended up letting him stomp out the back door and all I could think of doing was wait a second and then follow him. I tried to keep way back out of sight but have him in my view at all times to make sure he didn't run into trouble anywhere.

I think about half an hour to forty-five minutes passed with him wandering up and down the alleys in the neighbourhood. Finally he must have realized he had no idea about what to do, so he turned around and headed back toward home.

OMG! He was coming straight toward me. I disappeared as quickly as I could to avoid him seeing me. I ran to get back home and make like I was there all the time.

A few minutes later the back door open and shut. I went to look and sure enough it was him. He had returned home safe and sound. WHEW! I didn't get after him, I just said I was very glad that he had changed his mind and made a good choice to come back home.

As a teacher I know very well that there is no good reason or helpful learning strategy in throwing back at a child a comment like: "I told you so!"

ESCAPED

I am still puzzled by this next story. To this day I do not know how our son at age three, got out of the house somewhere around the time of 5:30 to 6:30 AM one morning in June. We had deadbolts on both our doors plus the screen doors were locked. They were hard to unlatch because they stuck, especially the front door. I even struggled with it myself to open it. It completely baffles me how our son got out at that time of the morning.

We didn't even hear him. Neither one of us had any idea he was out and about. Not until our neighbour across the street knocked on our door at about 7:30 AM. She asked if we were missing someone, and she had our son in tow! I was so SHOCKED and totally dumfounded as to how the heck he got out.

Apparently he chose to visit our neighbour across the street that morning. He had a tendency to break out of the yard during the day and wander around looking for a handy neighbour to visit. He loved to help Mr. Cook in his garden and to help the Laundry's water their lawn. He would talk to the little old lady on her porch and of course visit Ms. Wendy the teacher and her little dog.

That is who he visited this particular morning. It sounds like she had a most intriguing and enjoyable chat with our boy. They walked the dog, had breakfast together and had a good visit before bringing him home before she had to go to work. He had been at her place for couple of hours!

I felt absolutely mortified to think we stayed asleep through the whole thing. He just thought he was helping everyone. Almost a regular "Dennis the Menace." I can't thank our neighbours enough for their enjoyable tolerance of our little son the wandering helper.

I got my son to agree to make it a game of adventure. He had to pick a neighbour on a map of the neighbourhood I had drawn on the fridge. Then he could pick one of those magnetic alphabet letters that matched the neighbour's name. Then he had to place the letter over the house on the map to match that particular neighbour. Then he could go there, with permission of course. We had no more incidents. Sheesh. Was that ever scary and embarrassing!

NOT A DULL MOMENT

I kept as active as I could even after having the kids. I usually did not do anything for myself unless it included the kids and was best for them. For example, if there was a Bible study I could go to, I only went if there was good childcare for the boys or I didn't go. I felt it was important to involve the kids in things I did in order to condition them to be okay in different settings.

When I was young, my family went most weekends to see my Uncle play at the Cypress Hills Community Hall. We kids often fell asleep on or under the church pews. Therefore I think we grew up feeling comfortable in any setting or situation.

I took the kids swimming, to the playground, church, curling rink, Bible Studies, volunteering, library, and Symphony lunches at the library and so on. I was involved in all of their field trips at school and was part of the PTA. The saddest thing I have to live with is, I only got to go on one of my daughter's field trips in Kindergarten.

We even took the boys golfing with us when they got older. I actually made nifty golf bags for each of them out of old jeans. Their dad and I were blessed to have his mom available at times to babysit for us. That gave the two of us opportunities to go out to functions together or with the boys.

I was on the executive of a few boards and went to the odd women's conference. Then I had the opportunity to go back and complete my second degree. Before I did though, I sat down with my family and asked if they would support me in going back to university. I clued them in to the fact that I would not be making many meals nor doing any extra things for them until I had finished my summer courses.

MOM'S ON STRIKE!

They all rallied behind me and started cheering, "Go MOM, go!" That gave me a boost in spirits knowing that they were behind me and not going to mind if they ate TV dinners for a while. Well that lasted about a week. Then they really realized what it meant when I said I was not going to be cooking meals. With all the complaining that went on, you would think the world was coming to an end. Sheesh!

It was only Summer School and it was not going to last for ever! Yet my two boys and their dad quickly grew tired of my class schedule and the support petered out. I felt quite choked at their disappointing show of support. So I went completely on strike. I hauled the picnic table out onto the front lawn. I got a thermos of coffee a snack, put my "On Strike" poster up and began to do my homework.

I did get my degree, with or without their support.

I camped out on our lawn one more time in May. We decided to build a double car garage on to the West side of the house and make the carport into a patio. I went and camped out over my flower bed and gave the workers homemade Black Forest Cake and coffee. That way they would treat my yard work with care and also do a better job on our renovations.

MCKENZIE CLAN COMICS

I was rather creative and "artsy-fartsy." (In fact, at my condo I still have a sign that says: *I would rather have a creative mess than tidy idleness.)* In our home I painted little angels in the corner of each room. I had each of the kids stick their hands in paint and put their little handprints all over the laundry window blind as a decoration to brighten up the laundry room. I got to stick their hand prints in the cement when the sidewalk out front on the street was being redone, complete with the date.

I was the kind of person that made birthday cakes from scratch and decorated them. I recall one in particular that I really enjoyed doing. I made a great big hockey rink complete with Oilers and Flames cupcake team players for each of the party guests. Another one was much similar only made of flowery colours for our daughter's christening party.

I would make homemade birthday cards and started handmade Christmas cards in November, completing them with some unique family picture taken earlier on in the year just for Christmas.

One time I had every one of us wear our royal blue polo shirts so we could drive out to a Canola crop where the field was covered with bright yellow flowers. The contrast between the blue shirts and the yellow flowers was perfect for a family photo. Another time I bought us all McKenzie Clan shirts. Even little sister got one. Her shirt was bigger than her!

She was only one and a half. The shirt looked very cute on her as the sleeves hung over her hands and draped down on my lap as we all sat as a family along the ledge in front of the lit fireplace. With the fire going and all of us cuddled together in our Clan tartan shirts, you couldn't have a gotten a better photo from a professional photographer.

I didn't just sign the Christmas cards, insert the photograph, and send them off without a note. The way I see it, people want to get a bit of news about your family at Christmas. I began the tradition of what was to be called the "McKenzie Clan Comics!" At first when the kids were too small to write in their own little "comic bubbles", I would put some little bits of news about each of them in the bubbles myself on their behalf.

As they got older, I drew a little cartoon figures for them and they filled in their own bubbles. They did not have to say much. They only had to put something in the bubbles that told something about what they were doing or what they achieved that year. Something short and sweet that was not too much to ask of the kids to do. It became a big hit with all the relatives at Christmas.

ONLY ONCE IS TOO MUCH

A mother never wants to hear this. But if they are going to hear it, the sooner the better. There was never any proof before or after. It was only the one time but I found out about it and took pictures for evidence. I was afraid to ask or nose around with my children on this topic so as not to alarm them in any way.

In early 1994 I had been out running errands. When I arrived home, I was dramatically greeted by my four and a half year old. She was all excited and had something to tell me. Bless her heart that she had enough sense to innocently blurt this terrible thing out to me or I may never have known.

She just blurted it out. Maybe it was only because it was a weird and crazy thing she had witnessed and therefore wanted to tell me about.

I was very glad that she did. For what she blurted out was unbelievable. She exclaimed that, "Daddy hurt Colin!"

Of course I was taken aback and in a bit in shock but I quickly gathered my faculties in order to not alarm her and her brother.

I asked for more information as to why. "What were they doing for him to get hurt?"

She explained in haste, "No! Daddy was just choking him!"

"Really?" Again without sounding alarmed.

"Yah!" She demonstrated with her hands.

"I see, when did this happen?"

"Just a little while ago" was her reply.

"Oh okay, thanks for telling me dear."

At that moment the son of my concern came upstairs and I actually saw his neck. Sure enough there was the proof on his neck about what she had told me.

I just calmly got out my camera. I asked both of them to help me with the camera. I pretended I needed to test it by taking a picture.

I created the fake problem in order to take pictures of his neck while the markings were still very visible. I did not even bring it up with him for fear of alarming him. It worked, neither of them were the least bit puzzled or suspicious as to why I was taking pictures.

Once it was all said and done, I went and did two things. I got the pictures developed at the one hour photo shop. Secondly I made appointments for both of them for their coughs, to see their doctor. I actually was going to take both of them anyway to the doctor to examine their sore throats. That way I could get them to the doctor without either child being suspicious as to the real reason.

At the clinic, I asked the doctor see me before going in to see them. That's when I pulled the doctor aside and I gave him the pictures, as I filled him in on the details. I also clued him in to the fact that I had not told the children why I was really bringing them to see him. Aside from the fact that I did of course want him to check their coughs. That was paramount.

I also told the doctor that I was reporting their dad to him for abuse towards Colin. He then informed me that he would have to report it to the authorities anyway. I agreed. Not long after, we received a phone call from Social Services.

They asked to come and see us. A time was arranged and they came. I was rather disappointed that he got no more than a slap on the wrist. I knew however that he got the message and I knew he would never do something like that again. Nonetheless I continued to be vigilant on this matter, however I truly felt no concern that there would be a reoccurrence.

On the other hand, I did bring the pictures forward in order to bring home to my husband that I was keeping said pictures. I felt that would insure he not ever do it again.

Certainly I did not leave it at that when I left. I contemplated what I could do for the best, under the circumstances, to assure my children's safety. So I arranged for three different families that my children had close friends in. One was just down the street and one across from the school and the third around the corner.

I either made lengthy phone calls or visited to discuss my concerns. I then asked if they would allow my child to come anytime day or night to them for help and or to be able to phone me from their place any time of day or night.

I gave them my contact information and then told each of my children that if they felt unsafe in anyway, they could go to such and such a friend's parents to get help and to contact me if they needed to.

Whether further down the road they chose to take my advice or not is another story. I tried as much as possible to lead them to water but I knew well enough that they had to choose to take that drink of that available water on their own. I really could not make them drink. I pray even now after all these years, that they make the necessary choices they need to heal of any wounds they took on over the mess of the divorce.

I have always known I have no influence if any. So I played my cards right and nonchalantly in a roundabout way brought up ideas. I was fortunate, for example, to establish the idea of friends' parents being a support if in an emergency of any kind. Had I done it later on after they decided not to have anything to do with me I probably would not get them listening in any way, whatsoever.

Thank God HE answers prayer! I had to trust they were in good hands and under the watchful eye of Jesus Christ. When I was leaving I prayed: "Lord, I have turned my kids over to YOU, not my ex-husband. Therefore I put my complete faith and trust in you to look after them and watch out for them as their father over and above their biological father."

CHAPTER 16:

RESPECT

My ex-husband was growing more and more difficult. He was questioning me as a person more than ever! I saw resentment more than respect for me in him and it appeared to be escalating. Did he ever feel respect for me, I wonder?

It seemed like I was entirely on my own yet still married. I was not involving him at all in my Spiritual life anymore, it was too risky. Since he was growing more and more resentful of the Spiritual part of me, I kept it more and more to myself. I felt that I was being a bit deceptive, but it became the lesser of the two evils. In reality it became a necessity for survival!

It got so that I could not share my accomplishments. Those were contentious issues as well. Instead I was sharing my accomplishments pretty much only with my Lord.

There was one time when my curling team had just won the "Lethbridge Open." After leaving the curling rink when finished with the Press and interviews I did not stay much longer for fear of upsetting him. It hit me that we achieved not only 1st Place but history as well! It was quite the feat, for we won every game, shaking hands EARLY! That had never been done before!

As I headed to our van talking to GOD about our victory, I wondered if I should scream out a big "Hurrah," or something? I needed to get my celebrating done before I got home. At that very moment the horn in the van started blaring away in different notes like Morse code or something. It meant to me that the Lord was celebrating with me!

Once I left my husband, such incidents occurred daily in my life. So stay tuned, for there is more where that came from!

I recall three times that I did something for myself. I completed my second degree when the family agreed to let me and originally supported me. Another time I went to a conference. Before I went I made sure I explained to the kids that letting me go was to their advantage. I asked them, "When Mom goes to these things, doesn't she come back a better Mom for you kids?" The answer was YES.

One other time I went for myself because it was an opportunity of a lifetime. It was pretty much the one only time I did something against my husband's will that he outright said "No" to. I chose to go to Japan to compete because I just couldn't give up that chance.

But, it didn't seem to matter what I did, he would show displeasure with his silent treatment regardless. He had a look of anger that reminded me of my Dad's look of anger when he didn't like what we kids had done. It was uncanny how much they were similar in actions and facial expressions. It was actually quite eerie at times. It was a look that made you want to tread softly and watch your back.

GOLD MEDAL

I was able to go in 1992 to compete in the Japanese Mixed Curling Championships. We were also going to represent Sports Canada as Ambassadors for the Sport of Curling to promote the sport becoming an Olympic event. In order for a sport to become an Olympic one, it has to be up and running in a minimum of twenty five countries, the more the better.

Japan was one of those countries new to the sport. Besides competing while in Japan, we were to hold a coaching clinic and leave the equipment behind because it's very expensive there. Going to Japan was one of those times I will never regret. Right down to the GOLD Medal and autographs.

I felt the LORD gave me a chance to get a peek at what I might have experienced had I chosen to aim for the Olympics, way back as a child. I had to make that decision when I was about age 11. I decided that I did not want to focus on just one sport because I liked them all so much.

I am glad that I did not aim for the Olympics. I realized from some of my friends, what a gruelling thing we put our bodies through. They seemed to torture their bodies for one thing and one thing alone. No offence to them but I didn't want to put my body through that.

One of my teacher friends competed in Ironman/Woman competitions so she really prepped her body and I remember her saying that she felt her body could not take it anymore. Consequently she decided to quit.

I also felt so sad for a couple I went to university with, that were heading for the Olympic Summer Games. That year Canada boycotted so my friends could not go. One was in Track and the other was in the Decathlon. Can you just imagine working so hard and in something as brutal as the big Decathlon to miss out on it, due to politics? Harsh, really harsh. I still cringe for them when I think of it.

Going to Japan allowed me the opportunity to experience something similar to the Olympics. We were given the Limousine and red carpet treatment. We were treated even better than if we were in the Olympics, for the Japanese really know how to be fabulous Hosts.

There were several things in particular that I will never forget, besides winning the Gold Medal and standing on the podium while their country raised our Canadian Flag as we sang "Oh Canada." I was moved so much that I still feel that butterfly excitement in my inner being whenever I hear our Canadian Anthem. I will never forget being treated like royalty.

I SENT SHOCK WAVES THROUGH JAPAN

Before we even went over to Japan, our whole team had to write up and send on ahead of us a Biography on each of our team members. My bio apparently sent some shock waves among the Japanese throughout parts of Northern Japan, in and around Obihiro.

It certainly was not my intention to cause a stir, but I guess that I was the only one on the team that was a housewife with little children at home. You see, in Japan, the cultural standard, traditionally, is for the wife to stay home and raise the children. The women in Japan traditionally would never have the opportunity to do what I had done. So it had a lot of women wanting to meet me when I got there. Off and on, I unintentionally created a few waves at some of the functions we attended.

Even now their Olympic women's teams are professional curlers and must be unmarried.

I WAS WRONG

Our marriage was working on many levels. There really only was one level that was not working at all! Unfortunately it was a major deal breaker! So much so that it boiled down to choosing one battle a day to confront.

Sometimes I would get my husband to see marriage counsellors. Also I continued on my own to see what I could do to solve this major issue between us.

I even took an "Assertive Communication" course. When that instructor finished describing Assertive Communication he looked right at me and asked, "What is wrong? You look white as a ghost!"

I was stung by his description of this type of communication, and I must have shown it on my face. I responded to his question with a question back. "I am pretty sure that is how I speak now, so what is wrong?"

He continued to look right at me with a slight change to empathy and sadness as he answered with, "You can say everything perfectly and still not be heard I'm afraid."

Right then and there I knew my marriage was over! I remember getting home and slumping down against the wall to the floor in the kitchen in tears. I was asking the Lord what to do if I'm not being heard? Where does one go from there? That was the sixty-four thousand dollar question I had for my Lord.

RALPH KLEIN BROKE OUR MARRIAGE UP

After that I simply asked the Lord to help me pick my battles each day. For my husband was growing tenser and tenser. Anything I tried to do to help him seemed to do the opposite. I felt caught between a rock and a hard place. This got particularly bad around the time Calgary Mayor Ralph Klein came into office as Premier of Alberta.

Premier Klein's first policy was to clean house. My husband would come home every day from work with a report on who got a "pink slip" that day. I kept assuring him that he would never be let go because he was the only one in government that did what he did. He saved farmers thousands of dollars and did so much for the farmers.

I even suggested he take a leave for a bit and I would go back to work. I was concerned for him and his health. I worried that maybe he would end up having a stroke or heart-attack.

His only comment to my suggestion was: "You, get a job? You couldn't get one!"

Little did he know that I had called up the college that same day and secured a job if need be. Since he was upset about my suggestion, I simply let it go.

When a person, controlling or not, sees the world around them squeeze in on them it can be foreboding. My ex was the kind of the person that needed to be in control of his world all the time. Otherwise he felt threatened. Mankind tends to go into a fight or flight mode when threatened.

In his case he would fight, mostly verbally. However, after divorcing him on the basis of abuse, I learned more about domestic abuse. I learned that a spouse DOES NOT HAVE TO HIT YOU TO BE PHYSICALLY ABUSIVE.

I thought that I was never physically abused and felt I could manage it. Especially since he tried to hit me one time. I blocked it, looked him right in the eye and said: "If you ever try that again you will wish you hadn't." I was wrong and realized, after the fact that I was being physically abused all along whether or not he hit me again.

Physical Abuse can and does consist of anything from murder to as much as blocking the door so the other cannot leave, or slamming a fist down on the table beside you, or kicking a hole in the wall beside you. These all are forms of abuse and physical to boot. All of these except murder, I had faced in any given moment in my marriage.

Emotional abuse and brainwashing can be so subtle that it can easily succeed in diminishing a person's esteem. So effective is this emotional abuse, a woman can actually believe that everything is their fault and that they are worth nothing more than a plug-nickel. 95% of domestic abuse occurs to women and 5% to men.

Sometimes I felt I might have been better understood if I did have a black eye and broken arm to prove abuse. Emotional abuse is not easily seen or believed.

YET I WASNT ALONE

I had almost everything one would want in a marriage. I had my dream home, great family outings, great kids, security in a reliable husband with a good income and fantastic friends! Yet I lacked appreciation and the respect from the main person that respect should come from. I was angry about dealing with singlehood. I did not want to start life all over again and alone! The good news was, I had Christ with me, thank God!

It was hard at times to spiritually see scriptures in action such as "with Christ, who can be against me..." (Romans 8:31). Then again I would see this same verse come alive in my life. HE did protect me and visibly showed HE was with me.

SECRETS REVEALED

When I left suddenly back in August of 1994, I found out a lot of things that I was not the least bit aware of during our marriage. I think the first thing said to me was "I can't believe you lasted that long with him."

One of his staff said that whenever I was recognized in the local paper for anything they were not sure they even wanted to go to work that day or even that week. They knew that my ex-husband, their boss, would be out of sorts and not the greatest to work with. This could last for a few minutes or a few days. There really was no way of telling.

A relative mentioned one time that they noticed something odd. When I had gotten that gold medal in Japan my brother and his family all came for a visit to see my winning medal. Everyone was gathered around the kitchen table asking me about it. Hubby was off by himself, and my relative noticed that he was on edge trying to get my brother drawn into a discussion of his own. This relative sensed that he did not like me getting all the attention.

There was also the time my brother told me how hard it was to get me from the back of the church on my wedding day. That immediately brought back for the first time ever the memory of when I could not say my vows during the wedding ceremony. That really glared at me as an obvious sign that I should never have married then.

Looking back, I realize that I had no clue about it until all these years later. So, my hunch is that the Lord took a not so good situation and turned it into a good one of which the end result was three bright and super children!

Whether they are in my life or not, they mean the world to me. So I don't see it all as a loss. There is a scripture verse that refers to this, Romans 8:28: "HE will work all things for good for those whom believe and love GOD and have been called according to HIS design and purpose."

CHAPTER 17:

DIVORCE!

HUSHA HUSHA, WE ALL FALL DOWN!

All kids need to know that, in general, parents don't do this deliberately to them and it is just as painful for the parents as it is for the children. I didn't like leaving the marriage any more than my kids liked it. It was not easy for me to make a drastic decision like that.

But I knew one important, determining factor. The fact was that it was inevitable that things would escalate and get even worse. Definitely this made it unsafe for me to stay. Statistics prove that abuse and controlling behaviours only intensify and they don't cease.

Also, the extent of the emotional abuse is perhaps more damaging than physical injury. After I left the marriage, two different relatives and a colleague at totally different times said, "Karen, you haven't laughed like that in years." This shocked me and clued me in to how emotional abuse had eaten away much more of me than I ever realized. It gave me further confirmation of how grave things had become.

The whole divorce felt like severe blows to my stomach. At times I felt so close to succumbing to the blackness that it threatened to suffocate me. I would get as faint as if I was going to pass out and at times I did pass out.

I had to stop it somehow. I was getting sick on my way down to Lethbridge before even arriving there. That was nonsense and I had to put a stop to it. It was a warning sign to change and prevent getting prematurely sick, perhaps with yet another tumour.

The first place I lived was a house sitting job for one of Anthony Robbin's assistants. He had all of Tony's tapes of course. So I would listen to them as I cleaned.

I remember a technique he advised using for just such a problem. Called an "Interrupter" I think. In order to stop worrying, I had to change my thoughts to pleasant ones.

Then as I changed thoughts, in the middle of it I was to start doing an odd movement. He suggested getting up and circling your chair. Since I was driving I couldn't do that, so I had to pick some strange movement with my hand while still safely driving. It worked!

My dad always emphasized the necessity for backbone, leaving me to thinking that I must fight back or I'll be walked over. My spiritual thinking has turned around so I now give the fight over to my LORD. Which does not mean that I chicken out or give up. It means I turn the other cheek, which in some ways takes more guts. It has become a relief actually to give my heavy yoke up to GOD.

Is it possible to feel wrung out like a wet dish cloth yet exhilaratingly okay, all at the same time? I have to say things were getting somewhat better! I want to see GOD's justice prevail and leave it to HIM to vindicate.

It took me a long time but I now see there really isn't worldly justice, only HIS justice will prevail.

THE HOLE IN THE DAM

I married into his circle of friends from university. They always met for a reunion every year on the long weekend of August. I often would stay up visiting around the campfire quite late. It would be the very last "reunion" campfire visit that I would have with them.

A certain thing occurred that I think was the catalyst that led to our divorce. I was going to retire from the campfire when one of his long-time friends said, "Wait, I will walk you back to your trailer." It was dark but he had a flashlight.

Part way along through the trees he pulled me over and up against a larger tree. He startled me by leaning down to give me a kiss. In reflex reaction I pushed him away as I said, "What are you doing? Your wife is a friend of mine!" He quickly backed off overflowing with apologies. So I pretty much felt the whole thing was dealt with.

Knowing the jealous state my husband could get into, I did not reveal this to him until the weekend was over and we were well on our way back home. Heading home with trailer in tow, when the kids were asleep, I began to share what had happened that night when I was coming back late from the campfire. I could tell right away that I had made a huge mistake in telling my husband.

There were two important reasons why I did though. Firstly, I believed in a marriage where there were no secrets from each other. Secondly, I thought that he would be proud of me, knowing I was hit on by one of Res's hottest guys and that I resisted and turned him down flat.

Not so though, for you could see the steam coming out of his ears as he drove. I can remember being cautious around that look. A look that could explode at any second with any amount of unpredictable violence. That is why I think he lost it and made such a bizarre suggestion as me having to stick by his side at functions.

Sure! Like that was going to work! If he is so worried about men being around me then me staying by his side around all the men at the BBQ isn't going to solve anything. It wasn't about me and distrusting me. It was about him not trusting other men around me.

I have no idea whether my ex knew of such attractions to me or not. It definitely came as a huge surprise to me. If any of these were known to him previously I would not have suspected.

Unfortunately that didn't help our relationship. It only put a wedge in it due to his hyped paranoia around his over the top jealousy. A week after the reunion at his BBQ, everything went sour. Only a few days after that, I was filing for divorce on the grounds of abuse.

While at the BBQ, he stated he wanted to go home. On that note, one of my colleagues made the comment: "Karen why don't you stay longer, you don't have to work in the morning and we'll give you a ride home!" I would not have minded staying longer. It was not often I got to visit with them. However, I glanced over in my husband's direction and saw that he was not impressed, so I declined and got up to follow him to our car.

To my shock he already had himself in the car with the kids! I couldn't believe it, he was just 10 or 20 steps ahead of me. How could he get in the car that fast with all the kids already rounded up? As I reached to open the car door he already had it locked so I couldn't get in!

I asked him nicely to unlock the door. He would not as he spouted off in swear words for me to go back to my F_ _ _ _ _ _ party! "To F_ _ _ off and get the H_ _ _ out of here and go away! Back to your party!"

My party? Since when was it my party? After all it was a BBQ put on by fellow scientists from his workplace. I tried to get him to calm down so that we could talk about it after we got the kids home and to bed. Of course I did not want to involve the kids by asking one of them to open my car door.

Our daughter was in the front seat crying her eyes out. The boys were frozen stiff in the back seat with their eyes bugging out of their heads. They looked to be in shock. That may have something to do with them blocking it out of their mind later on when they decided not to have anything to do with me.

A day later I sat all three of them all down. "You saw what Daddy did to Mommy yesterday?" They nodded yes, in silence. "Well, no Daddy should ever do anything like that to any Mommy. Now

Mommy has to make a very hard decision for the best for all of us." I added that "Reported evidence shows that things like this only get worse and I have to be concerned for my safety."

I then turned to look the boys right in their eyes and said, "If either of you treat your girlfriend or wife, like that, I am going to have to side with them." Then I turned to my daughter and concluded with "I'm doing this for you as well. By leaving your dad, I am showing you that it is not acceptable to be treated this way by any future boyfriend or husband of yours."

I told them I planned to see a lawyer and figure out what to do, then come get them. That I also wanted their dad to go with me to a Marriage Counsellor.

Nodding their heads made me think they understood completely and knew why I was leaving their daddy. However, looking back I think maybe they blocked the whole shocking incident out of their minds. I bet if you were to ask them to describe it now they would very likely have no recollection of any of it ever even happening!

This is the type of situation abused women often end up in. It is easier to forget, ignore the signs, blame the victim, etc. Plus, keep in mind many abused spouses stay in the relationship because leaving will always increase their spouse's anger, causing lives to perhaps be in danger.

A SURPRISING REALIZATION

Over the years a few individuals came forward with some surprising information on a need to know basis. There were one or two that did not work closely with my husband but for the most part, the majority did work with him, under him or in the same building.

This certain gentlemen came forward and explained that if he kept his distance from me, it was for no other reason than his personal attraction to me in one form or another. A few others mentioned similar. They were not keeping their distance because they disliked me. On the contrary. I was totally taken aback by their divulgence, but did appreciate their heads up consideration on my behalf.

Now that I am aware of other men having an interest in me that certainly fits with my ex acting over-possessive. I remember how jealous he could get. On that day in August, when others thought I had been set up, that could very well have been the case.

There were lots of things I was finding out after the fact that confirmed it was just a matter of time before divorce. I found this quote in my journal from just after I filed for divorce: "Gran and Dad were being rude about you Mom, in front of us kids." I wondered too if any letters of mine were getting to the kids. So I kept copies.

I was beginning to get the picture that this divorce was not going to be easy no matter how much I tried to make it go that way. I got that had to make sure I had witnesses with me to see that three of my phone calls, in a row, to home and the kids were not answered but instead hung up on.

Yet I am accused of not communicating. Speaking of communicating, here is a method I learned in my counselling that prevents others from pushing any vulnerable buttons. It is called the "Broken Record."

BROKEN RECORD

The Broken Record statement I made up and repeated back to my ex when confronted with his button pushing pressure was: "If we can't stick to the issue at hand, then I will have to hang up." I kept it written on a card in my pocket or purse to remind me to repeat it every time he tried to change the topic.

What a broken record does is eventually gets the other person to stop badgering you. Here's a good example: not wanting to lend someone car keys but they keep pressing in and hounding you to do so. You keep repeating the phrase over and over, one more time than they do. Hence, sounding like a "broken record."

It is important to say it in a neutral tone so it's not antagonistic. If not said in a neutral manner, it could escalate things and make matters worse and that's not your intention. It really does work on any gender of any age!

Each time you use it you will find that you repeat it less and less. The result will be, the person hounding for the keys will soon realize that pressure won't work and quit trying.

There is no point going in to the divorce settlement and divulging what terms were agreed upon, since much of what my ex was supposed to provide, he did not. I'm told that I could even sue him for it. That would be a whole other story.

Throughout my journals I noticed that several times I had stopped and asked the Lord to help and heal our marriage. "If not at least heal my children regardless Lord, since I turned them over to you to parent rather than their dad. I pray their hearts heal so they do not die full of the bitterness that is the root to psychosomatic diseases, such as cancer."

I saw numerous times throughout my journals from while I was married, statements such as, "He flew into a flap again." I figured out afterwards that my behaviour had only added fuel to the fire. How so? First of all a person that has to be in control does not want to relinquish a thing.

It just makes controllers angrier. It seemed, the calmer I was, the madder he got. I have news for anyone in an abusive relationship. You will not be able to solve it or deal with it. Even if your esteem stays intact as mine did, it still ends up a no win-win situation! A person in this kind of situation has to determine how safe they are. The level of safety decreases every time there is a blow-up.

The very next blow-up could be the lethal one. This kind of anger can escalate to the point of harm to one or more involved. No one can guess when that point will be reached. That is what makes any situation of this type dangerous and unsafe to stay around.

This was the case for me. I never did let him put a hand on me, but I experienced lots of emotional attacks, and was jolted by physical damage to objects around me that implied I could be next.

In a situation where a hole gets kicked in the wall, many women would scurry to fix it immediately. I didn't. I left it and hoped someone would pop in and see it there. It sure was one thing that got fixed really quickly.

Perception is a strong tool of destruction and I think unfortunately the kids see things the same way as my ex. When I would go for a walk or leave until he calmed down, he tended to interpret it as me not caring or even being negligent. I really was caring but knew prolonging the argument was futile at the time. Misunderstandings like that did not help the marriage at all.

PRISON LOOKS GOOD

I was in a second "Discovery" with my ex and his lawyers. I was sick and tired of discovery after discovery and being abused through the legal system. Given the way I was being talked to in these Discoveries, I informed my lawyer in no uncertain terms that if they were going to talk to me like that again, I was going to warn them. If they kept it up I was going to walk out.

Guess what my non-supportive lawyer said? She said if I did that I would be in contempt of court and put in jail. I turned, looked directly at her and said, "Then so be it, for prison looks pretty good about now! At least I will know where three square meals a day are coming from and I will have a roof over my head and even have TV!"

If not for my attitude of determination to keep going to get what I felt I needed and deserved out of the settlement, I would not have come out of it satisfied. For me the pension I deserved from my husband was more important than taking material things. After all, as a stay at home housewife, I would not have a retirement plan.

Attitude is more important than the past, facts, education, money, circumstances, failure or successes. More than what other people think or say or do. It is much more important than appearances. It makes or breaks a performance or company or home.

The remarkable thing is we have a choice every day regarding the attitude we will embrace for the day. We cannot change the fact that people will act in a certain way. We cannot change the inevitable. All we can do is chose an attitude. It is often said that life is 10% what happens to you and 90% how we react to it. I am therefore in charge of my attitude, and therefore I focus on trusting HIM daily.

DEAR JOHN

I am not really concerned much about anything my ex might have said. It is not my intention here to slander my ex. I am simply going to conclude this by saying he crossed a line that I had in my own personal boundaries. The LORD knew that I would not compromise my values on the boundary I had made regarding this abuse. When push came to shove, I had to leave. I am doing well because of God's provisions and trust HIS hand is in this all the way.

I have learned certain things since. Before I left, he had told another mutual friend of ours that I had stayed out all night at a party. In fact, he locked me out all night and I was taken in by mutual friends of ours. Quite a different truth and since it occurred to me, I think I had firsthand information on that.

Yes, he locked me out, even after three level-headed adults tried to talk him out of it. SO yes he is right, as usual. I was out all night. Only as usual, he leaves out the important facts! Such as what he SAID and DID to me! My very supportive friend, a colleague and her husband, took me in out of the pouring rain for that so called "all-nighter."

She was one of those level-headed adults that tried to reason with him and was, along with her husband, a primary witness to the whole thing. So my ex can talk and say whatever he wants, but there were others at that time that were witnesses.

After over 18 years of being whittled away at, it was time to save what was left of a once very bubbly happy person. I thank GOD I still had most of my esteem intact. Which probably helped me gather the courage to leave.

If you went ahead and picked a side without hearing my story please do not think I am taking this out on you when I write this part. I was only annoyed the more I heard how he was going about revealing the whole divorce thing.

No doubt he's kept from his own mother the reason I left and that I filed for divorce based on abuse. That is a bit of dirty laundry he surely does not want anyone ever to know.

I lost a lot a weight then and remember not eating much. Whenever I was in Lethbridge I suffered sleeplessness, headaches, a sore jaw, heaving and an upset stomach.

Did you know that a "sore jaw" is a psychosomatic symptom for not being able to say what you want to or need to? By the way, through the LORD's help, my counsellors and my own work toward healing, I have good news: no more sore jaws!

PAIN OF DIVORCE

After a fire in my first apartment, I finally moved into a townhouse near the family home. It was growing intensely painful to live around the corner from my kids, so close yet unable to see them! I hoped for them to come stay with me after school to make the transition as easy on them as possible. Then their dad could pick them up on his way home after work, since he had to go by my place anyway to get home.

My ex had decided to play hardball and the kids showed they were truly serious about leaving me out of their lives.

It was my mom that suggested that I get out of the fire, meaning Lethbridge and at least into the frying pan. I needed to create some distance in order to take care of myself.

I finally could not take it anymore. In the fall of '94 I had to leave Lethbridge for health and sanity's sake, as my mom suggested.

My own three kids had turned on me, and I was filled with great sadness. My kids hadn't got the facts nor was I free to give them the facts.

Though I left, the sadness came with me, only giving me brief breaks from the pressure building in the divorce battle. The Sadness was so gripping it was not allowing me to hold on to the peace and relief I first felt when I left my husband of nearly 19 years.

I left for the sake of safety but was suffering severely from three bleeding wounds coming from my heart and attacking my spirit. I was at the end of my rope and discussion with GOD on what to do.

I fully realized the horrible reality that my three wonderful children were really NOT going to have anything to do with me. It was too much at the time for me to take. My spirit had shut down. Nothing was working out. All the divorce seemed to be was sheer hell. My body had shut down in distress from crisis overload and my mind couldn't come up with any more solutions. Therefore the only solution I could come up with was to end my life.

BIZARRE

From here on in this book it is going to get pretty bizarre, if you hadn't thought so already! Maybe quoting a verse from scripture, will explain away some of the bizarreness. It declares that we who follow the TRINITY, Christians, are a peculiar people.

Just to make sure, I don't have you thinking that means crazy or weird, I want to clarify. We are not crazy, but "set apart" as in Deuteronomy 14:2 and 26:18. We are a people set apart from the world. I find this very prophetic in many ways.

CHAPTER 18:

SUICIDE

They won't know God's glory
If you don't tell your story.

BROKEN HEART

Something miraculous happened in October of '94, or I truly would have succeeded in killing myself! Due to the deepest despair, the only solution I could think of to bring an end to the pain was suicide. I didn't deserve all the hell that was happening to me.

I decided the safest way to die was quietly in a garage. So I drove around looking for a residential garage in High River to drive my truck into and wait peacefully to die. I finally found one in a newer area of town. It was already dark, thank Heavens.

I pulled in, got out of my running vehicle and went around to close the garage door. Once I had done so, I got back into my truck.

As I sat there in solitude and silence I prayed to the Lord for forgiveness for what I was about to do. I told Him that I couldn't go on, one-by-one listing off to HIM my lexicon of problems as I waited with my eyes shut, for the carbon-monoxide to take effect.

Maybe ten minutes passed. I realized that nothing had happened yet. I remember opening one eye to look at myself to see if I was still alive. What, I was! I asked the LORD GOD, how long should it take? (To die, I mean, of carbon-monoxide poisoning?)

As I was looking around after asking that question, I noticed out of one eye that the garage door was now open. Oddly enough, I don't even recall hearing it open. So I got back out to go around and shut the garage door again. I easily shut it and as I was about to climb into the truck again, the garage door opened!

Not again! What the heck? Good grief, as I stomp in frustration, back to shut the door again for the third and last time I hope! Can you just believe this? Picture me trying to kill myself and now the door decides not to shut! Though I STOMPED back in frustration to simply close the door again, it wouldn't! I literally jumped up and hung from it and it still did not budge! So I gave up and succumbed to the LORD's power.

Keep in mind as funny as this is story is, I was seriously trying to kill myself! I truly wanted to succeed. So I was mad and backed out of the garage, telling Him so. Yet here I am alive and well and plenty more to tell.

Take it from me, nothing is worth suicide especially if children are involved. Even though they weren't, it should not be an option. It really is a trick of the enemy to take us all out. Coincidentally, Halloween was the night I drove into that garage.

Promise me right now that if you ever get to that point in your life where the devil is pulling you under with suicidal thoughts, you won't do anything till you have opened up to someone you trust. Or vice versa you can ask someone to promise you the same. This is a helpful prevention technique. Usually if one does promise, it is very unlikely they will break such a promise.

Had I not remained alive I would not be traveling the world in ministry or have made an impact by pioneering policy-making for females and teachers. Or made a difference in thousands of children's lives rather than just my three. Pretty amazing when I think long enough about it.

Sure, after that attempt on my life things didn't suddenly turn rosy. I still had to deal with a divorce that went on for seventeen years including the three attempts by my ex to sue me. I even had similar slumps, but did not allow them to take me down so much as to attempt to die again. Partly due to the ability to shut satan down with the authority I have in Christ Jesus!

Dear Kids:

I am glad I did not die that October of 1994.

I pray that you see how much I love and pray for each one of you.

PERSECUTION

First of all a word on "persecution" or is it perception? I have heard this or similar numerous times: The ignorant only cast blame whereas the wise seek solutions. In my opinion, ignorance just breeds prejudices. Regardless, rest assured in Romans 8:31, it clearly says, "If God is for me who can be against me?" So persecute or perceive away but it's a waste of time. And, it may come back to bite you.

We need to keep negative perceptions from ruling our thoughts. The solution is in getting to know others, along with the use of wisdom and discernment. This allows us to free ourselves up to *see things from a knowledgeable perspective* uncontaminated by prejudice. For example I personally faced condemnation from fellow Christians. It happened so frequently that I began to carry a bag of stones with me in order to let them finish me off.

A prophetic word that I was given close to ten years ago was in regard to this and condemnation. The Lord said, "Tell Christians to stop condemning and judging. And to start encouraging and supporting each other in going out in your giftings." Sooner or later God's plan will come into place and perception that tries to control the world won't be able to continue.

God did not want us to eat of the tree of Good and Evil. God tried to keep or spare us from the danger in having such knowledge. Our "perceptions" can cause judgement and condemnation of others and ourselves, and that is not what God intends for us!

Of course I know that a Christian can expect a lot of persecution to occur in their lives. It comes with our faith stance. I just did not expect it to come from my own brothers and sisters in Christ. It's a form of the "mark of the beast" because I must decide when faced with persecution if I am going to stand up for my faith or chicken out to avoid a negative confrontation.

People tend either to be drawn to a born again Christian that is Holy Spirit filled or shrink from and detest them. I have been ridiculed and kicked out of churches more than once and once is too much.

I know what you the reader might be thinking. What on earth was I doing to get kicked out of a church? The LORD warned that the bulk of persecution would come from within the body of Christ/church. I must say we can be pretty vicious toward each other if we let negative perception, judgement and condemnation rule our thoughts. Unfortunately Christians can be bad, even known for their judging.

Due to so much persecution, I got pretty tired, fed up and embarrassed for them. God bless-em. The judgement was uncalled for and the attempt to put the guilt on me didn't work. I refused to own their guilt and problem. I refused to make it an issue or take on any guilt when it was not mine in the first place. Nor was I convicted of it by my LORD.

I am saddened by our inability to unconditionally like others. Jesus showed us how to be with each other. Why can't we be more like the brothers and sisters in Christ that God wanted us to be? It is downright disheartening to find it rare instead of common for adults to talk maturely and considerately toward each other.

I desire and long for that always. Kindness and respect is rarer than it should be. To deal with the overabundance of the persecution, I dug my marbles out. Yes, I still have all my marbles! As I said, I started carrying stones. It was most severe when I advised the person(s), to stop! As I said, "Be the one to cast the first stone if you have the right to!"

A perfect example was a night when a past friend came over to tear a strip off of me. Another friend had apparently told her that I had taken advantage of her, even though I hadn't.

She made it her business. She knew my mom was dying at the time and knew I had been traveling back and forth to see her. I had just gotten in from that long drive. Before she started in on me, I intervened declaring I did not want to discuss anything right then. I couldn't handle anything really heavy, and I attempted to close the door on her.

Instead she barged in and barked at me anyway, about something with no facts that was none of her business. I shake my head and cringe at us Christians sometimes. For surely we know not what we do! Famous words last said on the cross by JESUS himself. It helps often to recite these words to myself when I encounter others taking on GOD's job. GOD says frequently that vindication and judgement are HIS alone.

There is one good thing about being persecuted and attacked. If we are acting through our Holy Spirit and making others uncomfortable, then we must be on the right track spiritually. So I consider it all joy when others are convicted by my actions and words.

It boils down to my motive being right with GOD. That must be my main objective. Then for sure I am on the right spiritual track. The key is to keep the main thing the main thing and Do What Jesus Would Do, (WWJD). If there's one thing to learn, it is to ask what HE would do because HE knows the best way to do anything and WILL help you.

Although I was not taking on any guilt or blame for these other Christians, I always check with Jesus anyhow, to see what He thinks I need to look at in myself if anything at all.

It is not easy recovering from these situations. It is very important to find a Christian counsellor as I did. Better yet, a Christian counsellor that operates in the Holy Spirit. Theophostic Ministry is my speciality, although I have further training in other forms of therapy as well. When a heart is ready to heal, the only One to trust and hand them over to is Jesus himself.

That is where the Theophostics and the Holy Spirit come in. If we don't strive to heal as soon as possible, then that ugly enemy spirit rises up and draws one in until they grow in pity, anger and bitterness and more. This in turn pulls us down sometimes to the point of seeing no other helpful and healing options. Then a spirit of suicide can develop.

I know because that was me at first without my kids. When I found out that they really meant what they said, I didn't have a way to solve the problem and I couldn't mend my shattered heart.

I saw heaven as the only way to take the pain of the whole mess away. The Lord didn't seem to answer my pleading prayers for reconciliation. There was no one to turn to.

I then called a Help Line where you can remain anonymous. I like anonymity for a couple of reasons. Particularly so that I am not judged, for one thing. After all the fact that I am a Mother and not with my children may lead to all kinds of unwarranted and unfounded accusations.

Another reason that I like anonymity is it prevents the sin of gossip from taking root. Of course there are times when specifics are needed. So I called this suicide prevention line as a last resort.

Here is what happened to me and I would like to say, NEVER HAPPENS, but it did to me. I was put on hold on the Suicide Help Line! Then the line got disconnected.

When a person is in suicide mode, it is doubtful that they will call back, trust me because I didn't nor did I ever want to again! It would just give me one more shove in that suicidal direction.

I knew about these phone lines ironically after the fact. I used to be someone you called on 100 Huntley St. I was one of those prayer partners you reach with the 1-800 number you see at the bottom of the TV.

While I was still married, I started up another line through "Moms Who Care" for moms praying for their children and their schools. At times I would use another source, Church prayer lines. Pretty much every city has anonymous Good Samaritan Help Lines of all kinds. They might not be referred to by the same name but they are made available to everyone.

Going by my observations and experiences, health care needs to work more on making mental health a protective, safe and definitely a positive experience for those thinking of or who have attempted suicide. I have not seen much for positives in our society's ways of taking care of people in a crisis mode of this nature. I personally am leery about admission to any psychological facility. Society appears to have a double standard on this issue.

I equate it to telling men that it is okay to cry; yet when they do they are questioned, even shunned. The result sometimes ends in others writing them off, so to speak. Even though society suggests that a man has the freedom to cry, I doubt he will truly feel safe to do so in society. It is my opinion that Mental Health care has not reached the potential it must have to reach out to those of us that need support at times.

As a struggling Christian while still married, I often would disclose the problems my family was facing at Bible Studies to get help and guidance. I referred to myself in the third-person so as not to be pinpointed. It seemed if the problems I brought forward persisted, many concluded sin was the issue and that "they need to shape up." How secure would you feel about opening up to someone when that is the feedback you got?

I recall a time I tried calling friends for support because I was fighting off the spirit of suicide tempting me. Out of all the friends I called and left messages with, ONLY one responded. Even though I did not talk to him directly because I could not reach him, he heard my voicemail and called the police.

They showed up and even though I said I was okay and only called a friend to talk with, they insisted I go to the hospital anyway. I had the choice of ambulance or police car. I chose the ambulance because I did not want to be wrongfully viewed and judged by neighbours in my condo complex.

The whole ordeal was a nightmare! Once in emergency, since I came in with that label, I was kept on suicide watch hence not treated with the best of respect or sensitivity. In my opinion, given the circumstances there should be a great deal of SENSITIVITY towards such a person. Yet I was cared for as more of a criminal under guard by the police and paramedics as well as the medical staff.

No one even thought of being very empathetic or even sympathetic. Instead there was only a matter-of-factness about it all in a very sterile guarded manner. An environment in which I was held captive and had to be continually watched.

Even though I had not done or taken anything, charcoal was administered to me regardless. Once it had taken effect, I was dismissed to a dungeon of a hallway and forgotten.

There I was stuffed down some narrow, cluttered, hallway looking up at some dull, water-stained ceiling. Now how you would feel in my shoes? Would you feel a whole lot like living after being pawned off inconsequentially to some hallway after being prodded and poked?

Seriously, is this how the health care system treats a person brought in suspected of attempting suicide? Consequently, I felt at times when I was at my lowest that there was nowhere to turn to get help. It sure was not going to be a hospital.

I phoned the friend, that had said he would be there as a big brother in Christ, to see if he could pick me up from the hospital the next day. He couldn't even bear to do that, GOD bless-em. That only added to the depression. All he could say in response was, that it was too heavy for him to deal with.

Now I know why a suicidal person doesn't want to reach out to anyone. For everyone seems to turn and run at the very hint of suicide! Or they treat you with a judgemental air of sorts.

The other concern I had was it seems to follow you around like a prison record with a stigma attached to it. Therefore, I felt incriminated from then on. Kind of like one has a burr in their saddle and a blemish on their face. That is something I never want to be put through nor be treated like again.

PITY PARTY'S GONE, CARTOON IS ON

When I got hit hard with a number of things coming at me like curve balls I often fell into a "Pity Party." When we are weary, this demonic trap is the most dangerous thing one faces for it's just next door to suicide. It seems to hit a nerve without warning.

It is much harder to get out of the pit than keep a safe distance. Pitying myself had to stop because that was half the battle for recovery, right there. It held me captive. Anything out of the blue could hit me hard without a moment's notice. It could be seeing a family in a restaurant, taking their mother out for dinner and presenting her with gifts and flowers on Mother's Day. I am sure you can guess why that was not my favourite day to eat out.

We can shield ourselves from pity with the use of thanksgiving and praising in order to avoid the crumbling, unsecured edges of the pit. "Fake it 'til you make it", is what I say. I may not feel like thanking and praising but once I start, the act of worshipping will eventually take over and become very real and liberating. Freeing me from the shackles of pity.

The LORD does have a way to help us escape what we can't handle. As I write this, the most gruesome chapter in the whole book, I am watching a cartoon movie and laughing my way through this chapter! How great is that? You may call it a complete fluke, but I definitely see it as a blessing.

It really has only been in the last handful of years that I've not been so affected by my children's absence. I've actually been able to spend all of Christmas Day alone without a tear shed. Yeah, finally! I am getting better at simply taking the moment to feel rightfully sad then distracting myself in order to keep from plummeting into the doldrums accompanied only by my lone self at a pity party.

SUICIDE, THE SPIRIT OF HOPELESSNESS

Hopeless thoughts can so easily invade and flood one's mind like endless storm waves on a seashore. We go adrift without hope in what seems to be a meaningless world without any glimpse of light at the end of any tunnel. For me the only way back then that I could see in my blindness, to relieve the pain in my chest and to stop caring, was to die.

My counsellors have said time and time again how well I am coping now. Some even think it is only a matter of time before it will all be water under the bridge. But I say that the sadness will never be fully gone from my life. Their well-being is always in the back of my mind. I just can't see how a mother can completely get over her children. I have my weak moments but I keep reasonably occupied. However, that sometimes backfires.

In my efforts to go out more often, I was invited to a church dinner. The person taking me never even called to say that she was not coming. Finally with stomach growling I went ahead and made myself dinner.

You see, I would have preferred to stay home. I truly was enjoying being a Hermit as I worked on this book. However, when asked I thought I had better, since I had promised God that I would get out if invited.

When it all fell dead, I had a hard time keeping from getting sad and crying about it. For disappointment was exactly what I was trying to avoid! I would rather have nothing happen for me then to have carrots dangled in front of me and taken away. I say this because that is a frequent occurrence in my life that I pray goes away and never comes back. AMEN!

It seems to be hitting a nerve more than ever this year for some reason. I think it is because I am finishing up with my book.

I think that all invitations and the events in my life are brought about by my LORD, so this was creating a spiritual battle in me. A struggle between trusting the LORD in all things good or bad and not liking HIS plans for me. Which is absolutely not true, for it says right in HIS word that HE cares for me and makes sure the plans for me are for goodness and abundance (Jeremiah 29:11). I just have to wrap my head around the idea that HIS ways are greater than I can perceive or even understand.

We Christians, all have to ask "Why" less and trust more that HE has our best interests at heart. At times I forget that. I really can see the advantage in me trusting, and not disliking or even doubting regardless of my state of affairs. I can't understand myself sometimes. Why can't I simply trust consistently? That is a downfall that I am working on.

SUICIDE IS AN EVIL SPIRIT

My suicidal actions bring me to point out the possibly that one purpose of doing so is to get back at GOD! Heaven forbid I would think that! The very idea strikes me numb. However, I do see eventually how suicide could actually be seen by GOD as a way of getting back at HIM! No way did I premeditatedly think that way!

I must stop here for a minute to say that it is NOT about deliberately getting back at GOD. But thinking of suicide as the only solution, is flat-out ignoring GOD and what HIS solutions would be. It is a total lack of leaning on HIM for help.

At the time that everything was crashing down around me, the idea of wanting to get back at GOD was the farthest thing from my mind. To get back at GOD is a thought that just makes me cringe.

If and when I do realize such a thought developing, I repent as quickly as I can! In humility I am saddened by my very thoughts and actions. I can't believe myself for letting down the most faithful supporter I have on the planet!

Fortunately HE is a forgiving GOD and wants you to be able to share with HIM all your thoughts. Though HE knows them already! HE would rather have you spill your guts out to HIM than skirt around HIM with your thoughts. HE is not going to get mad at your for sharing them either. In fact I suspect HE would be rather pleased with you if you opened up to HIM, angry or otherwise!

What was I thinking, as if HE couldn't help me at all? When I look at it from that angle I can see clearly what a big fat lie it all is! Suicide is a trick of the enemy to take us all out. "He comes to lie, steal and destroy" (John 10:10).

After that unsuccessful attempt at suicide I sensed HIM picking me up and putting me in the big pocket of HIS robe. If you ever saw and recall the TV sitcom, *I Dream of Jeannie*, she lived in a bottle. That is what it was like for me living in HIS pocket. I had everything I needed, and more importantly I was safe. Especially from myself and wanting to opt out of the life on earth.

I did not like the poem, "Footprints" for the very reason I did not think I was being carried. For if my SAVOUR was carrying me like the poem implies, then should I not have some sensation of that? Some knowing kind of comfort, or something of the sort? Well, after backing out of that garage that night, I literally sensed HIM carrying me, from then on!

PURPLE HAIRED HEATHEN

The year 2000 was the beginning of the new Millennium. Whenever there is a birthday or large milestone, I have always tried to do something out of the ordinary to celebrate and make it a memorable occasion.

In 1967 when Canada celebrated its hundredth birthday, I skated my first figure skating solo. For Lethbridge's hundredth birthday I competed by swimming 100 kilometres. So for the year 2000 for New Year's Eve, I had my hair dyed purple with silver streaks through it.

That was all great until a week after it proved to have a terrible outcome. A dear friend in British Columbia called and asked me to come and support him over the time of his mother's funeral.

His aunt and uncle took one look at my purple hair and thought I was a heathen and would not let me stay! Remember what I said about persecution and prejudice? Does this sound similar? Regardless, the Lord showed me to just love them, for they know not what they do, (a phrase I had become very familiar with).

All was not lost though. My friend's younger brother came up to me at the tea afterwards. He asked me what had happened and did the same with his aunt and uncle. Then he brought us together right at the tea.

Though he was the younger brother, I was amazed at his communication skills and tact. I loved how he had us resolve the touchy subject of me being rejected, complete with an apology from both of them. Then he said the most shocking yet incredible thing you would ever think of. He turned and told them to leave right after the tea. I was speechless, yet in awe of his fortitude!

I would have to say that is the most mature experience I have ever had the privilege of seeing. It far outranks the maturity of the average man. I am proud to know him and this awesome family of six close brothers. AND because of one befriending me I now am welcome as family in all six of their lives.

One of his older brothers might remember when he and I would swim across the Thompson River and back. Since that river comes from mountain runoff it's a pretty cold swim! Brrr! One time he got quite cold and was shaking severely when we got back across the river. See, that's where the little bit of fat on women comes in handy. He, however, needed to get warmer and fast!

So I got him out and lying on the hot pavement in the middle of the road, as flat out on his stomach as possible to warm up. I pretty much floored him at first until he felt it working right away! A neighbour of his literally drove over to see what's going on. I wish at times I had videos of many experiences like this.

NOT GOOD

In 2003 I was at an all-time low in my life. So as I mentioned already I decided to approach depression differently by calling everyone I knew and crying out for help! It was a colossal failure and turned out to be a big mistake! Apparently people just can't deal with heavy stuff even if it is a friend in need of support at the time. What a bunch of chickens!

I am not exactly sure what all one should do for someone that approaches them with the thoughts of suicide looming in their life. I do know a few things from over the years and from my counselling experiences.

First, I'd take them seriously. If someone comes to you talking of suicide, I would contract with them to promise they will not carry out suicide before talking to someone they trust. They rarely carry out the suicide attempt after making such a promise. Try to keep from treating them glibly like a number. For that is what often propels them in just that direction.

Another thing that I have already alluded to is that suicide is a spirit. A negative spirit that needs to be shut down and rebuked in the name of Jesus Christ of Nazareth. An example would be, for one born again to say: "I declare in the name of Jesus CHRIST for all negative spirits, plus suicide and death, to go QUIETLY to Jesus to be dealt with by Jesus Christ himself!"

The authority we have will get rid of demonic troublemakers. With that kind of power, always remember you have the right as a child of GOD to call upon HIM to protect yourself and others! Amen!

LIES WE ARE BOUND BY

Here are lies that can run rampant throughout our minds. Do they run through your mind?

Lie	What God says in his Word
I am alone	"You are not alone for I am with you, says the LORD."
I am unworthy of love	"You are chosen by GOD, holy and dearly loved." (Colossians 2:10)
I am unforgiveable	"You are completely forgiven." (Romans 5:1)
I cannot change	"You have the mind of Christ." (1Corinthians 2:16)
I am ashamed of my past	"You are righteous and holy." (Ephesians 4:24)
I am powerless	"You have been given a spirit of power..." (2 Timothy 1:7)

When such lies try to creep in I have to fight them off with the word of GOD as a great weapon in my armour.

A DEPRESSING NOTE

Having been Chairperson of the Substitute Teachers' Committee for both the Catholic school board and the Public school board in Calgary, I would more often than enough get calls from teachers seriously considering suicide. Things were getting worse and worse out there in the education jungle! I'm not missing teaching too much because of that.

At times I'm embarrassed to be part of the education system here for it is considered to be one of the worst in the province. A lot of changes could be made to improve things. At the top of the list it might be time to hold students accountable for a change. So that they leave the education field and go out into that adult field much more capable of handling it.

Another improvement would be to hold students back instead of rifling them through the grades when they can't even read in grade ten. I'm not kidding, I actually know some students that could not read in grade ten! I personally think that the increasingly outrageous behaviour from our teenage students is a real cry for help.

Not to mention the stress it's putting on our teachers today. No wonder they consider suicide at times or have major health problems. Did you know that teachers are fourth from the top on the list of professions for the numbers of suicides?

FAITH, FACT AND FEELING

I remember a diagram from a Bible Study years ago. I was fortunate to get a lot of Kay Arthur's Bible Studies under my belt to flourish correctly in the word. The diagram was of a train with an engine, railcar and caboose. The engine was to be "FAITH" pulling "FACT" followed by the caboose and "FEELINGS."

The point is that feelings should trail behind and not be the leader. My problem was the emotions got the better of me. It is not wise to let "feelings" creep in and take over. They are only there as gauges or signposts, not to monopolise. If one allows feeling free rein, then it is likely that you will de-rail and regret something. HE showed me more and more where HE would take my pain on HIMSELF.

One of those times I remember vividly is the time I came back earlier than expected from being on a Mercy Ship. I was so distraught that all I could do was sleep all day and weep in-between.

JESUS came and sat beside me in that dark basement where I spent all my time in disappointment, crying. It was one of only a few times, HE wasn't just sad with me but that time HE actually sat and cried right along with me. As HE consoled me and assured me HE had something better for me, I sensed that HE had taken much of my pain on HIMSELF to ease my load and the massive pressure of disappointment I was going through at the time.

I thank GOD for these numerous times in my life where I sensed HIM taking my feelings and putting them aside while I went through a major traumatic event. You read how HE carried me through my emergency surgery to remove a massive tumour without taking my ovaries. Further on in this book you will read of the time a biker tried to strangle me to death. That story will move you if nothing else does. It moves me still every time I think of it!

STROKES TAKE MY MOM HOME

Around the same time, over a period of some years, my mom had several strokes. The first stroke was when I was in the Scott Tournament of Hearts, Women's National Curling Championship as the Scott Paper Company's mascot. I was still married then.

The second time, as I was now divorced, I was free to visit her more. I performed for her as a surprise, by reciting my Cowboy Poetry to the whole Remoka Lodge on a weekend visit. She hadn't been too well after suffering another stroke. This time it was scarier, and we said our goodbyes to each other then. I was going on the Mercy Ships and not returning for some time. She even told me not to come back for her funeral.

The third and final time, I remember it was November. She was having a lot of little strokes by then. She had lost her ability to speak. I could see her frustration for she still had things she wanted to tell me. So I did all the talking after that, reminiscing and singing to her.

It was very disturbing to me to see how bruised up her arm was from the IV. So when it had slipped out, fortunately while her doctor was there, I asked her if we had to put it back in or not.

It seemed cruel and I just couldn't see them sticking it in her again. Her doctor looked directly at me and said, "We do not have to if you don't want to. What were her wishes?" Then I remembered she had always said she never wanted her life prolonged. That was when I decided to pull the plug.

I sure didn't think it an issue for my brother and sister. I am pretty sure they would have agreed with my decision and even been relieved to see her go peacefully.

Before that, I was sitting beside her hospital bed asking the LORD if HE wanted to heal her. He respectfully answered with "No, Karen, I want to bring her home." I asked back, "Then why is it taking so long?"

HE said, "You know how tough she is and how strong she can be about hanging in there and not quitting." Often when someone hangs on like that it is because there is an important date or event coming up that keeps them hanging on.

It was on her wedding anniversary she went to heaven. I regret not being with her then. I had to go down to Lethbridge to try to spend the time with my son for his birthday.

I deeply regret not staying with my mom. For as it turns out, I got stood up by my son and never did see him for his birthday. A devastating double dose of sadness since I didn't get to see him, nor be with my mom during her last few moments before she left for Heaven. Looking back, maybe I should have called to cancel with my son and stayed with my Mom. I just didn't want any of my kids madder at me than they already were.

ALL TIME LOW: MY MOTHER'S FUNERAL

I went with a Pastor friend for the day back to Ponoka to deal with funeral plans with my brother and sister. Then I returned later in the week for the funeral. I put this in this suicide chapter because it brought me to an all-time low. I asked the LORD for someone to go with to my Mom's funeral and not just anyone. I truly needed someone that could and would support me there.

The friend that did come with me was not one I would have preferred. He wasn't the kind I could expect to pick up the ball and carry it the way I needed it carried at such a sensitive time. I felt that I needed someone that would anticipate my needs without me having to ask for it. He was a real gentleman, just not one that would know what to do without me having to think of what to ask.

I should have stayed away from the funeral like my mom said. We had already said our goodbyes and I knew she would be okay with that. I was going for everyone else and not for myself. Big mistake! It was a lesson that I learned the hard way. At a time like that, I needed to do what was best for me. That was more important than pleasing everyone but myself.

My ex-husband came and brought the kids. I thought at first that it was a nice thing to do. But it really was not because of what the kids did to me! It was not nice at all!

I had sat in a pew at the front. Along came my kids to sit beside me. What was to happen next nearly killed me right there on the spot. It was so very painful to take that I wanted the floor to swallow me up right then and there!

For when they were beside me, they all stood up together and moved over about three feet AWAY from me! It was the hardest thing for me to stay sitting there and take. In the front of a full chapel. I wanted to run away!

At the tea after the funeral I just could not hold back the tears. No one but my friend came to comfort me! Not even my brother or sister! Why didn't they? It just added insult to injury. The turmoil inside me while all this was going on was unbelievable! I am still saddened over the whole thing.

This is when I really needed a tissue and my poor friend was all thumbs! You know how men get when a women is crying? Well, being all thumbs was not what I needed at that time. I am not upset with my friend. No, I am simply giving you a picture of the whole situation. You can surely see my torment building by then.

Out at the gravesite later, all my holding back of my frustration and hurt came to a head. All three of us were asked to stand up at the grave site. My sister was on one side of me and my brother on the other.

We were given red roses to place on her grave. First my brother was to put his rose down and then me, and then my sister. When it came to me, I did, but faltered after I bent down and almost fainted. Just as I was about to pass out, both my brother and sister reached under my arms to keep me from falling and were going to hold me up for support.

By this time I had reached my limit of torture! I couldn't take anymore! So I wrenched my arms away from both of them saying under my breath, or at least I thought, "Too little too late!"

Oh-oh! I found out later from my cousin that I hadn't said it under my breath as much as I thought. For I asked her if it was noticeable or not and could she hear what I said. Unfortunately what I had intended for their ears only, everyone else had heard too.

I have noticed that about me. I sometimes reach a point where I can't take anymore and then blurt out something without thinking. It is better to take time before making a comment that I will regret afterwards. The rule of thumb for me should be "whenever I have reached my limit I need to REACH for duct tape, and fast!"

Maybe the blessing in all this was I saw most vividly this fact about myself and a good use for duct tape!

I did call both my brother and sister right away when I got home to apologize. In so doing I was able to set things right.

Regarding forgiving others, I find the sooner you do it the better! For the longer you wait the more acid seeps into your soul and eats away at you. Affecting of course YOU and only YOU and not the other person or person(s)! I pray we all gain the ability to forgive and let go of past hurts before they cause diseases.

My biggest apology had to be to my GOD whom I did offend. I doubted my God over the lack of support I had prayed for. I no longer question HIM on the timing of things nor how they go down. For HIS plans are far better than what I may see as the best way to go. This is KEY even if I still don't always see HIS plans as the BEST way YET. So I keep working on my perspective it until it becomes a habit. I hope.

For example, in the very recent past I've needed a new hip. As far as I am concerned, HE should heal it before my surgery as a testimony of HIS power. I apologize for being as presumptuous as to conclude HE should heal me and nothing else.

I now realize it is up to HIM to determine the best way for me to go: healed by surgery or by HIM, my Master Physician. It is not for me to decide like I was doing. Forgive me LORD, for all that and the past times when I did the same. I am learning to see the good in all that happens, regardless of how bad it might seem at the time.

Before I close on the subject of my mother's funeral, I need to reveal a miracle in its midst. I felt a loneliness like never before when I got home. And this was after I made my apology phone calls.

Not even when going through my divorce and the issue around my kids, was I struck with such deep and dangerous loneliness. I found it so scary that I prayed immediately to GOD to take it away. I knew right away its danger and that I had to rid myself of it as soon as possible!

As I prayed, out of nowhere came my friend the Coyote. Yes, you read it right, a coyote! I had become friends with a couple of coyotes where I lived backing on to Edworthy Park. This coyote would frequently visit me.

The very first time I met him he came out of nowhere and sat beside me as I painted my desk out on my patio. He just sat there, amused, and watched. I found him friendly so I kept on painting but chatted with him for the longest time before he sauntered off down the hill.

Well, after my mom's funeral he came and sat just outside on the patio. He seemed to have been summoned and instinctively knew I needed company. He looked intently at me with a comforting look in his yellow eyes. He seemed to be saying, I understand and I am going to stay with you as long as you need for the loneliness to go away. AND he did stay for the longest time, until he heard a noise coming from a balcony above and got startled.

Here is the neatest thing: he goes to bolt but stops abruptly to look back at me as if to say, are you going to be okay? I give a nod and he takes off. My deep scary loneliness had gone! It just disappeared while my coyote friend was with me and it has never returned. The whole experience boosts my spirits even today. Animals have been such a helpful part of my life.

CHAPTER 19:

CARRIED

Newly single, I didn't know what to do so I prayed and got the answers. I asked HIM for three things. One I needed a roof over my head. HE gave me a 20,000 square foot home with a 3000 square foot indoor pool with fountain and slide, all glassed in and overlooking the mountains to the west. It was a massive acreage home I house sat.

Two, I need rest and recreation, so the acreage and pool did a good job of providing that for me.

Thirdly, I needed to know what to do. Since I could not get a job in all the places I tried, HE gave me acting. My prayers were answered, but take note, not in the way I would ever expect.

TEACHER TO STUNT WOMAN

To my shock of all shocks I could not pick up a subbing job anywhere to save my soul. I happened to run into a past acquaintance and friend of my brother from elementary school days. He is a famous chuckwagon racer and Hollywood stuntman. At first I kiddingly said to him, "Got any stunting jobs for me?" Then I re-thought that and said, "No, actually, since I can't get a job teaching, I am serious. Have you got a stunting jobs?"

The next thing I knew I was acting. He gave me his agent's phone number. I called right away and arranged to have coffee with the agent first thing the next morning. I was in wardrobe that afternoon. Hence my newfound career as an actress in movies.

I am still in my agent's file as an Aquatic Stuntwoman. One group I enjoyed being part of was a group of extras called "Backgrounds." I even went in the Bowness parade with them and the Gunpowder Club, during Stampede Week.

ANOTHER SURGERY

I was growing more physically exhausted by the hour. In my lifeguarding, I could handle emergencies but they lasted only for a certain time. This was lasting forever! My divorce took seventeen years, from 1994 through to 2011. Way too long for my body to handle an emergency. I had three surgeries in 1994 so my body at the time was saying to me, "You can keep on going but I quit."

I was going to five or six interviews a day at times. I collapsed while on the phone at my niece's making more appointments for job interviews.

After the collapse the doctor would not even operate until I went back to my niece's where I had been staying after I tore my stomach wall from moving my furniture myself. He said that I was too exhausted and physically not able to handle the surgery I needed. I had to stay there and relax until I was strong enough for the surgery. My niece even had to assure the doctor that she would not let me lift a finger to make any more calls for interviews or even glance at my resume. That meant I could no longer stay in my mansion with the 3000 square foot pool.

I got my surgery and it took a long time to recover. Not like my birthings where I could jump off the delivery table.

The counsellor I had been seeing managed to get me a room in the Sheriff King Women's Shelter. There I could rest and recover from the surgery, not having to worry about a roof over my head or three square meals a day. Counsellors were also there and I could access them any time of day or night.

As soon as I was able to travel I left my niece's home in order to move into the shelter and receive the blanketed care that I would be getting. GOD bless her and her family for opening up their small home to me in a time of need. I can't thank them enough for the great deal of help she gave me when I was in a bind.

Sheriff King was a helpful resource on so many levels. Besides the basic necessities, I could have twenty four hour in-house counselling. This I very much appreciated because I was very deep into the throes of the divorce at that point.

I was very appreciative of the shelter and glad that I could stay a bit longer over the Christmas holidays. That was such a crucial time for my well-being, That Christmas that would be my very first one all alone without the children or without my family.

Just as a side note, I met a male counsellor at the shelter that was an answer to another prayer of mine. I had asked the Lord to let me meet healthier men. Men that were more confident in themselves, sure of themselves, healthy and wealthy in all areas of their life. This counsellor was just such a man. We became good friends and talked often into the night.

He confided that he had more of an interest in me then just professional, but of course could not pursue such a relationship that would compromise his professionalism and my rights.

He also told me that before I had arrived he had accepted a job in another province and would be leaving at the end of the month. So at the end of December, he went one way and I another. Wherever he is, I pray extra blessings and thank him for blessing me with answered prayer.

INTER-VARSITY INTERNATIONAL CHRISTMAS

I was supposedly going to be an embarrassment if I went to my brother's for Christmas that first year. What would I do instead for my very first Christmas EVER ALONE? Then I remembered that I used to support an "International Campus Christmas," in my married years.

It is interesting how events can overlap at times. As the saying goes, "What goes around comes around!" First I became one of those that are sponsored at Christmas dinners instead of being the donator. Then I will tell you later how I ended up working there at the camp.

I spent a fantastic time at Pioneer Ranch Camps for my very first Christmas alone. How interesting to come a few hundred miles to turn around and meet some interesting people from around the world.

One Russian fellow became more of a friend. I also met others from Lethbridge. In all this I marvel at God's great abundance! I had a growing sense of Philippians 4:12: "Be content in all my circumstances and He will provide abundantly!" Therefore I continued to experience "Footprints" to the fullest.

I did not spend any money that Christmas. Not just because I didn't have any money to spend, but also it helped me avoid stores and the malls at Christmas time. That being my very first Christmas and the hardest away from the kids, I would break down at the first sight of a Christmas tree or a single Christmas decoration.

I didn't even have to buy a box of chocolates. I wanted to take chocolates to this international function to give everyone. So I was wondering and asking the Lord if I should buy a large box of chocolates or not. He said, "No wait." So I said, "Okay I will but please can You keep in mind that I have to have something by the end of the week?"

Every night at the shelter we always had an encounter group meeting. I learned a lot at these meetings about abuse such as how to recognize controlling people. Or, how to be empowered as a woman and all of it through the fun exercises that we did together every night.

There was always a door prize at this meeting in order to coax us all to attend. Guess what?! I won a door prize that night and guess what it was? It was the largest box of Turtles I had ever seen, and boy do I love Turtles! When I took that box of Turtles to share at the International Christmas I had hoped there'd be a couple left for me. To my delight I had three left over to enjoy over the weekend stay: One for GOD, one for JESUS, and one for the HOLY SPIRIT.

After Christmas my main objective was to find an apartment for January, since my stay at Sheriff King would be over. I was thinking of getting a small cheap dresser from IKEA and one of those couches or love seats that fold out as a bed.

One of my last nights at the Shelter I happened to be sitting in the office with one of the counsellors when the phone rang and it was someone donating furniture. The counsellor said, "You need furniture don't you Karen?"

"Yes, you bet I do!" I explained in anticipation! The person was giving away a bed and dresser and two love seats, a table and four chairs, which is exactly what I was hoping to get from IKEA. Right down to the white dresser and foldout love seats for my bed.

Over and over again I was getting the full picture of how my Lord can be as a provider. HE proved to me that I could be really content in all my circumstances, for HE was already working on it.

CHAPTER 20:

MERCY ME (1994-2000)

Since 1978, Mercy Ships have impacted over 2.35 million people with life changing surgeries and ongoing community development. All of the Mercy Ships were converted into mobile hospitals, housing three state-of-the-art operating rooms, a 40-bed hospital ward, a dental clinic, a laboratory, an X-ray unit, and three cargo holds.

*An estimated 25,000 volunteer crew members served onboard over the years from 1994-2006, in Central America and the Caribbean basin, docking in more than 18 countries. (*www.mercyships.org*)*

I got to be one of them in 1996.

Up until Mercy Ships I had been staying with friends and keeping myself busy with acting, modelling, volunteering and getting involved in church groups.

I heard about Mercy Ships through the Turner Valley Discipleship Training (DTS). I knew for sure that I was to go, but I needed sponsorship money around the amount of $4,000. Impossible, I thought, as I hung up the phone. I simply lifted a quick prayer to GOD.

It went something like this: "LORD, you know very well I can't come up with that kind of sponsorship money." I had only just moved to Calgary, had no home church and only a few dollars in my pocket.

After the singles group meeting had ended and I had shared this new desire, one of the guys came up to me and said he had just gotten a large inheritance. He said he was going to donate it to the church but felt led to give it to me to go on Mercy Ships training.

Now if that is not a God thing, prompting me to go, I don't know what is! The amount he gave me was the exact amount I needed to go! I had found my passion and what I wanted to do for the rest of my life. My plan was to work on one ship and then go from it to another. Or so I thought! That did not happen, however, I did get to experience some of it.

Here is what really happened, and what GOD really sent me there to do. It was not to work as long as I had hoped on the ship. Even the Medical staff were encouraging me to stick around no matter what and to go to the University of Hawaii to complete my DTS.

I was on the ship to teach the children of the doctors and nurses on board. It was a medical floating triage ship that primarily did hair-lips, cataracts and tumour removals. Until I was needed to teach, I helped a lady with computer data inputting, to keep their inventory records up to date.

Take it from me you do not want to be putting data into the computer while floating on the water. Trust me, it makes your head float for weeks after going on shore. If any of you have ever been on a cruise ship, you will know how it feels to walk on land after being on the water. You walk a little tipsy, don't you? Now take that tipsy and put it in your head. Close your eyes and picture what that might feel like.

I prepared to be onboard the ship a long time. So, I went up to the top of the Calgary Tower to say a heartfelt goodbye to Calgary.

I went first to Houston where I stayed with a Geologist friend. Then a day or two before I was to leave I stayed with a missionary and his wife just outside Houston. He now works for the US. Space program. He happens to be one of about 3 people that can cancel a space shuttle trip. His job is to make sure that everything that is hauled is accounted for. All weight, going and coming had to be completely in balance with the entire cargo or it was a no go.

I love learning things about space, so he took me on a tour of the Houston space headquarters. It was pretty impressive to say the least. What a very memorable way to leave land for the ship the next day.

I boarded the ship just before lunch. I sat with two couples that were leaving after lunch. Their job had been to put air conditioning in. I told them they were MOST appreciated. I had being praying there would be air conditioning on board and it was there because of them! YEAH!

I had a shoebox of a room that happened to be just over the propellers at the back of the ship beside the engine room. I could hear and feel rumbling noises and the vibrations were enough to give me the shakes for days!

Even the cockroaches for bunk partners were better companions than that engine room. It gave me a good excuse to sleep out on the Aft Deck. It was stupendous, under God's vast blanket of stars as the ship itself rocked me to sleep at night in the warm slow breeze.

Shortly after lunch that first day, we set sail for New Orleans to pick up supplies. Not too long after, a message came down to me from the bridge inviting me to come see the bridge. I was thrilled, naturally, and went right away. After 10 or 15 minutes of being given the tour and watching them run everything I shared my abundant thanks and said I better leave them to carry on.

That was when the Captain interjected and asked if I would like to give it a go. Wow! "Can I really? Sure I'd love to!" I sailed way into the evening. I had so much fun gauging the swells with the radar that I lost track of time. Realizing I had taken up much of their time, I thanked the Captain and said, "I should probably give you back your ship."

To my delighted surprise, the Captain said that I was doing a great job and could continue if I liked. So I did! I ended up sailing the ship all the way through the Gulf of Mexico. I found out that it is not a straight and direct course as I thought it would be. No it is not as simple as that. Besides having to gauge for the swells each time, I had to watch for other ships and giant oil derricks. Meaning, I had to stay a minimum of a 1/4 of a nautical mile away from all traffic and derricks.

I had no idea how many oil derricks are in the Gulf! Needless to say, I was dodging and ducking all the way. Really, it was no easy task. So much for wide open seas. The Off-Shore Oil Rigs we passed along the way, were like enormous, gorgeous chandeliers!

As night fell on us it was beautiful! The Ship's Mate said that I caught on quickly. It was no easy task, he said, because one had to steer opposite to the way the needle showed and that is what made it so difficult to catch on to. He was the one that taught me as I took the wheel.

By the time we got to the mouth of the Mississippi it was about midnight. We had to wait for a Pilot to come on board to tender us up the river. Apparently the river is dredged out every year to avoid build up and dangerous sandbars. This Pilot knew the lay of the bottom of the river and where the ship could maneuver up the Mississippi River to New Orleans.

Where we prayed, we would have favour and get docking privileges. I met many on board and went with some of them on shore to see Bourbon Street. I did not get to the aquarium which is supposed to be quite famous. I would have loved that, but there was no the time.

Bourbon Street sure was not boring, I will tell you that! In fact a rather embarrassing thing happened to me there.

We were walking along trying to find a coffee shop. I saw a beautiful full-wall fish aquarium in the foyer of a club.

I stepped in, asking two bouncers if it was okay to take a look. So I peeked into it and then I realized that I was looking right at a bare butt on the other side of the aquarium!

Apparently there was a strip joint just through and on the other side. What I saw was the stage and a dancer half naked. Red from embarrassment, I gasped and started to back right up and out on to the street. I suppose it was sort of funny because the bouncers sure laughed their heads off!

On my trip I was supposed to say "Hi" to a few people. One was a brother of a friend of mine back in Calgary. I was able to have time to go for coffee with him over the few days stay in Houston. Interestingly enough it turns out that he and my geophysicist friend had careers in common!

The other one was the mother of the CEO of Schlumberger back in Calgary. While in New Orleans I was only able to give her a phone call. I like that there can be a link to people pretty much anywhere in the world.

It takes a day and a half to sail from Galveston to New Orleans. Once we docked, I was served a greater blow when given a copy of a fax. It had apparently been sent to me some time ago. A fax I never did receive in Calgary.

It was a personal note from the Coordinator that she had prayed and felt that I was not to come on the ship, but rather to go home and connect with a church for stronger support.

Oh my LORD! I had everyone praying back home and sure enough our prayers were answered for the Coordinator was unable to get a hold of headquarters in Lindale, Texas. So I was to continue on with them on the ship for as long as need be.

After all, the Coordinator herself said she had never heard of anybody getting all their required sponsorship money in less than 48 hours like I had! So that had something to say for itself all right. Once she did connect with the base it was decided I was to return to base.

Once I returned to the base, I found it surprisingly quiet. With classes out over the summer, the kitchen was closed. I was far from starving though! My LORD provided all kinds of surprise things for me to eat. Even "Red River Oatmeal" from Manitoba, Eh!

There was what everyone referred to as the "Surprise Freebie Kitchen Cupboard." This cupboard was the one in which anyone leaving for home left all their groceries behind. Anyone arriving on base could help themselves.

The food selection in that cupboard was quite the International Food Buffet! I could get plenty from that cupboard alone. I may not have known what the heck I was eating, but I didn't go hungry or get bored with the selection!

In addition to the cupboard, there was a great big huge Quonset in which the Food Bank was housed. I could go in there and select any number of grocery items that I needed so I sure wasn't starving by any means, even though I had come unprepared.

I had gotten to know and was well favoured by the medical staff on base. So one time after coming back from the food bank I noticed at breakfast a number of little bugs in my cornflakes. Obviously things at the Food Bank had been in the Quonset for some time.

Anyway, I just asked my medical staff friends if the bugs were safe to eat once I at least froze them first or cooked them well. They all laughed as I mentioned this and were surprised and very impressed that I, a "Green-horn", rookie Missionary, would not be phased by the bugs and would be okay about eating them if it was safe. They confided in me that I had skipped a few steps to becoming a full-fledged, true, veteran missionary. This is when they shared their standard missionary joke with me.

The joke is: you can tell a Rookie missionary because he or she throws everything out when they see the bugs! YUCK! How do you tell the Short Termer? He or she will sift through the food and pick out the bugs to throw out, before eating. A Long Term missionary will just eat them along with everything else. How can you tell an over the hill missionary? He picks out the bugs to eat and throws away the food! (I hope you had not just finished eating when you read this juicy tidbit?)

FUNNY FEELING

While back at the base and only a few days into my stay the new Coordinator was introduced at church that evening. Before he was even introduced I got that FUNNY FEELING where the hair on the back of my neck stood on end. Well it was an accurate ALERT. It was a form of warning to beware and if led by GOD to tell others as well.

You can imagine my surprise to find out the man I had the prickly sensation over was their very own NEW base Coordinator. I did not feel I was to divulge my prickly experience to anyone at that time.

Then all heck broke loose between me and that man, even though I had NEVER met him personally! On the base over the next few days he personally started pressuring me to leave and immediately! He wanted me kcked off the base, and he was not going to be easy on me a bit!

The Lord often spoke to me at night. That night HE said, "KAREN!"

I woke right out of a sound sleep as if alerted! I looked over at my roommate. She was still asleep. You would think the volume to the voice calling me awake would awaken her too but it didn't.

I replied with a "Yes?" realizing it was the LORD calling out my name loud and clear and definitely URGENTLY!

"Is that you LORD?"

"Yes" the LORD said, "STAY HERE KAREN! For now stay here!"

Then I went back to sleep just as if I was never awakened! Oh how sweet HE is! For I was thankful for HIS guidance and confirmation I very much needed it because I had been asking what to do about all the threats this guy was making that were so obviously non-Christian in behaviour.

One obvious cause of my prickly feeling was when I did sit down with the Coordinator and he demanded that I leave. I asked for us to pray first to see if that is what the LORD was showing us. For I was personally getting that I had to stay there for the time being.

Yet when I suggested that we pray, he would not allow it! In fact it angered him! So I knew right then and there his actions and words were NOT of the Lord. It also affirmed that I was to stay steadfast and NOT leave. Which was what I thought was given in my direct message from my Lord.

And stay I did, dodging the Coordinator by hiding with the help of the medical staff for a few days before he discovered where I was keeping.

When he found me he barged right in with not so much as "Hi" to anyone. He reached down and snapped the plug right out of the wall for the computer that I had been working on! The whole medical staff just froze in shock and stared in silence!

The medical staff advised me to go see the Head of the Board on the base before I left for home. So I did and they were pretty shocked. They seemed glad to get information from me about this fellow's behaviour.

DANGER VERSUS THE LORD

I felt covered by the LORD's protection in more ways than one, the whole time I was there at the base. Not just protected from this man but I learned to identify poisonous Copperheads, Water Moccasins, Rattlesnakes, Black Widow Spiders, Brown Recluse Spiders, Tarantulas and those Teeny-Weeny, but NASTY little Fire Ants!

They are no bigger than the head of a tiny pin but they sure can pack a wallop! OUCH! I got just one tiny bite on my little toe and it didn't go away for months. In fact I still have the scar.

After that, I prayed that the ants couldn't come near me. Hence I never got another bite. Even when accidentally, I stood right in an ant-hill in my sandals! Now if that isn't the LORD, I sure do not know what is! For greater is HE that is in me than he that can bite!

Another time I stuck my hand right into a swarm of them. I had been working on the computer and kept a granola bar still wrapped up in its package in my briefcase. I had just finished a long day of letters and went to reach in my briefcase to get the granola bar. Big, big, huge mistake! Can you just imagine what I saw? My briefcase was loaded and completely covered with a swarm of Fire Ants crawling all over in and out of my briefcase. It was amazing that I wasn't bitten by any of them.

Thus my life carried on side by side with these critters. Cockroaches and all!

The LORD is so good! HE made sure I was given favour in spite of the harsh reception that I was given by the Coordinator. He was hard to deal with, but I had lots of support from others.

I even had a person I met on the bus buy me lunch and then offer to donate money towards my Mercy Ship sponsorship!

I have had a few others like that too. A guy gave me a spare pair of earphones that he had for my own had broken. It really wouldn't surprise me if I truly did arrive with just the clothes on my back; I would honestly be fine.

Believe it or not, I actually get excited now when I'm challenged and have to lean on the LORD for provisions and to see how HE will provide the next thing I need! Only this man's personal vendetta and threatening was my Christening moment so I was not quite as delighted as I get now about my daily calling.

Not to be discouraged. The LORD showed me there were a couple of serious things that I might be required to report to the CEO of Mercy Ships.

That was probably one of the coldest Christian welcomes I had ever received. Yet I was well-liked on board and by the medical staff. Everything wasn't all bad.

I was given a ship uniform which we were to wear when we were departing from the dock or arriving at a dock in which case we all joined in waiting and saluting when coming into port. I thought that it was pretty cool. I looked really important in that tight navy blue pencil skirt, white officer's shirt and Navy Hat. I guess it's called a Purser's Uniform.

RETREAT TO DOLDRUMS

When I arrived back home from the base after loss of my dream job I stayed down in my friend's basement. I slept on a cot in the dark almost around the clock. I didn't want to do anything, not even eat but sleep and cry and cry and sleep. I had finally found a purpose to head for, only to have it nipped in the bud. It just seemed totally unfair.

I had lost my purpose as a Wife. I had lost my purpose as a Mother. I couldn't even fall back on another purpose I also loved, as a teacher. I loved being all those! I thought and I was told I was pretty good at them as well. I loved and knew I was good at teaching and parenting too because of the great efforts taken to get me on staff to teach educators and parents. Now the very thing that I felt was getting me back on my feet, that gave me both a passion and purpose, was prematurely cut off from me.

I honestly thought that the opportunity had come from GOD Himself, especially since I got the sponsorship money so unbelievably quickly. It seemed perfect but came to an end over the silly technicality of not having a "home church" that Jesus Himself shook HIS head over. I just cried and cried because I felt so empty and without a clue what to do and of course suicide was not attainable anymore.

I would read scripture and cry out to the LORD for "H-E-L-P! Where are You LORD? Why did YOU let that happen to me? Why, why, why? After all it was You that got me the money and took me all the way to New Orleans and back. I get that You wanted me there for other reasons, but did it have come to an end too?"

It was the first time ever when Jesus sat down on that cot beside me in that blackened basement and literally cried with me. HE had been with me thousands of times when I cried but this time HE actually cried with me.

As HE held me and cried with me, HE said something that has stuck with me. HE said I was not to worry. That HE had something better for me. I was so forlorn I didn't even catch what HE actually said, so I snapped back with, "What could be better?"

I saw being on Mercy Ships as the ultimate way to work with Christ and use my gifts! Getting to restore people's lives when due to some abnormality they were shunned by their own people for superstitious reasons. I really thought that there was nothing better.

But what HE said was closer to the truth than I realized. A couple of things were to happen that would cause my life to head in a completely different direction. As if I had not taken enough 180s, up came another one!

Since that fateful day I no longer ask why or put limitations on GOD. Now I just wait on HIM to orchestra HIS plans for me that are beyond my imagination. And like HE said, I didn't have to worry about how or what to do.

I was reintroduced to my Holy Spirit on a whole new level! The Holy Spirit would be teaching me what to do and say (Luke 12:12).

DULLING THE PAIN

After a better than ever Christmas and New Years with "Agape" (Christian Skiing/Hiking Club), that year I was into MY own place.

I had volunteered 11 years at the Martha Cohan Theatre so I could enjoy live theatre. I could go skating in the plaza after with a dear friend or go for a nice wine with another.

From 1995 to 1997, I had some pretty jam-packed times of laughter and life for a change since I was still dealing with a very nasty divorce. Belonging to a couple of Christian Singles Groups helped considerably when the usual holiday dinners came along. There were other functions such as Bible studies and retreats.

It was at a retreat I met a guy that said confided in me much later that I saved his life! He was planning on killing himself when he got home. Instead he has been such a helpful friend over the years.

He did something else that I was in awe of and had not seen much of before. I would just have to admire something in a store window and he would buy it for me. I had to quit admiring things so he would not buy them for me because I knew that he really could not afford to do so.

That is the kind of giving I treasure in someone: a cheerful giver. If I marry again, I want "my man" to have the same giving nature and be a good steward about money. Money is one of the main troublemakers in marriages.

It was Square Dancing and riding where I met and got to know a fellow that pursued me and won. I became engaged too before I discovered Mercy Ships. We both agreed to take our time with it since it was not something I really wanted to do just yet. When my dream job came along I was graciously set free to sail away, literally!

Another 180 in regards to my identity! I was blown away at the number of guys that wanted to marry me over these few years from 1995 to now. And the reason I bring this up is not vanity. I never really thought of myself as beautiful or gorgeous. Now more than one guy would tell me that I was beautiful and fun to be with. Sure the odd one only said it to try to charm me for their ulterior reasons. However, I could tell the majority meant it by the way they said it.

Some that said it didn't even have a vested interest in me. So I began to realize something totally different about myself and own it for myself. And this is why I bring it up: to point out a valuable character builder.

Until then I did not see myself in that way at all! The families my ex and I grew up in did not verbally uplift and encourage one another. As a teacher and mother I saw the significance of it, and asked my ex to regularly praise and point out to our daughter how pretty she is. I also told him, contrary to popular belief, the fathers are the ones that establish the gender in our children.

With this new feedback I now believed and took on the attitude that I was beautiful! I owned it and walked with it. The outcome was one of newfound victory in myself. I was no longer plain nor undesirable.

So much so that a couple of years back for my birthday month of June, I decided to try something that I read one guy did for a whole year. He tried to go out on a date 365 days in a row. Wow! I sure as heck would not want to do that, but I was willing to try it for the whole month of June to see how things would go.

I actually went on a date every day for the whole month and then some. There were even days I ended up going on three dates in one day! CRAZY! I will not do that again. It was just way too stressful trying to end one date before I had to go meet the next one. Whew!

It was a bit tricky at times because I would get their names wrong. I divulged this to a friend and she came up with the idea to make up a spreadsheet with them all on it. I recorded notes on my phone to help remember a few of the guys.

Just so you know, I wasn't trying to find a lasting relationship or a husband. I felt bad that some of the guys were wanting that I was just not into. You see, I only wanted a date and some of them wanted more.

All in all though, the experiment was a success, since I did go out every day of the month of June and some of July as well. However, I wouldn't want to do it again!

I FOUND WHAT WAS BETTER THAN MERCY SHIPS

Remember when JESUS cried with me and said that HE had something better for me? That was in October of 1996. By November of '96, it began to take shape for me. I was actually made aware of it way back when I was still married. The real beginning occurred at a conference, only I did not pay any attention to it because of the source it came from.

The lady that had a word for me was into auras and New Age things. Consequently I did the usual. I asked the Lord to fill me in and clarify it for me. Until then I shelved it. A good thing I had gotten in the habit of doing every time I heard something was to ask HIM to show me what part of that message was "wheat" and what part of it was "chaff."

That November it materialized for me. I knew it had something to do with "healing." For the lady from Pittsburgh with her eyes bugging out of her head points like an arrow at me and exclaimed, "You have the biggest healing aura around you that I have ever seen!"

I didn't think there was anything better than cataract or hair-lip surgery on the Mercy Ships. But there sure was and JESUS knew that!

I got the same message two more times. By then I was willing to throw my hands up in the air and admit to HIM; "Okay Lord I'll do it but you have to tell me exactly what to do 'cuz it sounds pretty heavy duty to me."

Only a few short weeks after HE told me HE had something better I was doing it. HE just set it up so I wouldn't see it coming and maybe bolt.

HE set it up for me at church one Sunday evening. After service people were asked to come up to the front if they needed prayer. I did what I usually did, I gave words of encouragement and information, like I had since I was little.

I was in the habit of asking the LORD if there was anyone HE wanted me to give a word to. HE had me focus on a certain woman and prompted me to go and stand in front of her. Only the shocking thing was, this time I had no words for her.

Puzzled and nervous, I went up slowly in hopes that HE would give me something to say to her. Still nothing. All I did was go up and stand in front of her with my head bowed. I probably looked calm on the outside but I was praying like the dickens for a word and fast!

I remember taking her hands in mine, still waiting on the LORD to tell me what to say. "Any time now LORD. I could use a hint as to what to say to her, any time!" No way, I couldn't believe it, still no word!

Instead HE asked me to lay hands on her stomach area and pray for healing. Whoa! That was different, I must say! So I motioned as I asked her if she minded me doing so. She was okay with it. WOW! When I did so, she immediately felt a change of some kind in her stomach. I learned later from her that she had a medical problem in her abdomen.

Once I had done what the LORD said to do, then HE then gave me a word for her! HE said HE also wanted to heal her head only she had to give up something. Again she immediately responded with a slight whimper, "I know." And in between whimpers more: "I know. I know!"

I was flabbergasted, it worked! It really worked, to pray healing for someone! I was always one of those Christians in doubt. One that would pray healing for others by lumping it all under one sentence: "If it be your will LORD, heal them." Or "Your will be done, LORD."

So I must say slightly embarrassed but delightedly blessed to find out GOD's healing is real and alive TODAY! That very first HEALING prayer for that women in November of 1996 set me on a path that has never ended. Oh and my apologies to my LORD: YOU'RE right. YOUR way is WAY BETTER!

CHAPTER 21:

UNBELIEVABLE EXPERIENCES

After I got back from being on Mercy Ships, I started to look for work. I never thought in a million years I would not be able to fall back on my teaching degree. Nor did I ever think I was OVER qualified for a job!

In this time of my life when I desperately needed a job, it called for desperate measures. I found myself contriving ways to get past the receptionist in order to be heard. Whenever I was in an office I would observe closely where the Superintendent's or CEO's office was located.

Once I figured that out, I would watch closely for a time when the receptionist was away from her desk and then would bee-line to their offices to pass them my resume, then thank them for their busy and valuable time. Every time it got me in the door for a quick interview.

I knew I was needed for my ideas because of my experience in Lethbridge when I was asked to be on several boards, such as the YWCA and Symphony Boards, to name a couple.

I knew that I had the ability to be ingenious about coming up with big ideas for some of the businesses in downtown Calgary. It was a bit tricky finding the right balance in how much to tell the company to get them interested but not to give away my whole idea.

So here I was again, sneaking past the receptionist to give the CEO my ideas. I knew for example, Telus needed something fresh for they were getting ready expand into British Columbia. So I came up with a fresh NEW ad campaign for their launch.

It turns out that I was right about the need and the CEO did like my idea! He actually felt a bit disappointed in not meeting me sooner, because they had just signed on with a company to create one. Interviews like that became a standard procedure. Following are examples of a few of the more unusual ones.

INTERVIEWS

I have experienced numerous interviews over the years. When I had applied previously for jobs as a lifeguard, the "interviews" normally consisted of exchanges sent through the mail. They weren't necessarily face to face interviews.

On the other hand, interviews for teaching jobs were much different. I have to commend the University of Lethbridge for a job well done in this department. Superintendents from all around, even parts of the United States, gathered during Reading Week. We just had to sign up for as many interviews as we wanted to all week long.

I got seven offers from that week of interviews alone. Some were very appealing. Had I not been married at the time, I would have accepted a few of them. Stettler, Grande Prairie and Fort Vermillion, appealed to me the most. The northernmost ones were the most appealing since I would get isolation pay on top of my salary. In addition to that, Fort Vermillion was appealing because it offered 6 fly ins and outs every year, the school was brand new and so was the "Teacherage."

I had another interview for a teaching job with a whole board. There were something like 12 people across the table, all facing me. Not only that, but I was up against an Olympic basketball athlete and the job was to work with them as a Phys. Ed. Teacher. To our surprise neither one of us got the job.

In some cases there wasn't even a formal interview for a job. One time I was offered a job while lifeguarding at the Strathcona Swimming Pool, in Edmonton where I guarded while attending university. The job offer was for a cruise director job. A friend of my boss owned a cruise line and was there swimming.

Another time I was offered a job at the Michener Centre in Red Deer, Alberta. Again in Red Deer I was offered the job of the city's Recreation Director. You usually need a degree before you can apply for such a position, but I had an extensive sports background. For that job I had to take and pass a test to become a hockey referee. That's the reason that I became what I understand was the first female hockey referee in Alberta.

As I mentioned, I was offered another job similar to the one at the Michener Centre in Red Deer. What was similar was that I would have to teach nine severely handicapped young adults. I know my capabilities and my inabilities. I knew right off the bat I couldn't take on a job where I knew I wouldn't be able to help them make any progress whatsoever.

I was offered another postgraduate teaching position and I did accept. I enjoyed creating new courses such as "Parenting for the Gifted" and a Series for kids with their parents.

My own children were proof of the success of these courses and the discipline used on my strong-willed boys for sure, is tried and true.

I have left the worst teaching interview of all time (in my life, anyways) to the last. The interview was with a company that hires a number of Teachers for other countries such as China and Japan to teach English as a second language, (ESL).

For this interview I had the privilege of meeting some of the greatest people in the province. I would have preferred to walk away from there with all their contact emails. There was quite a variety of people, from Judges to Musicians, and I was rather impressed. Even my travel expenses to Edmonton were covered which sure was nice.

It's important to arrive early for interviews so I was the first to get there. I was given my number (#1) on arrival and asked to go into the main meeting room and instructed to enjoy a beverage as I looked around at my leisure at the various information they had on display about their company.

Well, guess what? That was a TRAP! We weren't told but what we observed in that waiting room was a test! AND the #1 meant I had to go first! YIKES, talk about pressure! That was the hardest interview ever! We were even given a sealed and timed, English test! Sheesh!

Remember when I got my first apartment in Calgary because of my honest smile? Well, something similar happened to me in 1994. I was at my brothers visiting and heard of a possible job available so I went to see the owner and ask about the job. I explained to him that I had not expected to do any interviews or seek any jobs therefore I had no resumes with me.

To my delighted surprise the owner returns with: "You're hired, if you want the job. For your smile is enough for me to hire you!" He added that my smile was a commodity to him! He went on to say "Because you will be working behind the counter and greeting the public, a smile like that is important for the job."

I now have that sentence in my resume: "My smile is a commodity!"

AMBASSADORSHIP

I could not find a teaching job and grew increasingly desperate for an income. I was seeking anything and everything. I left no stone uncovered.

An old school mate of mine was down east in Ottawa working for the government. Given all the positions my friend in Ottawa was surrounded with, and my previous experiences in ambassadorship and public relations, I thought, "Why not, it is worth a try! What have I got to lose?"

So I sent her my resume to pass around. Nothing came of it, but it affirms how diligent I was in seeking employment and why I ended up in some of the positions that I did.

I looked at my predicament as a blessing in disguise most of the time. I saw the tremendous abundance of the Lord in it. Regardless of the hardships and lots of crying time, there was also further healing time. Who knows, maybe I'd become an international ambassador for the Lord. Although I didn't think it at the time, little did I know that I was actually going to do so later on.

1996 – CAMP - SPICE

I joined Christian church groups to keep active and ward off depression, the plight divorce and Mercy Ships had on me. I went on retreats with them and volunteered a lot to keep busy until I could find work. I volunteered at Pioneer camps so my children could attend free. I was still trying to see my kids and thought if I offered them a chance to go to a riding camp they would go for it. My camp name was "SPICE."

When I ride, I like to know the horses. It just isn't my style to pile on any horse without knowing something about'em. Some cowboys see that as chicken; I see it as plain stupid if you don't know something about your horse's personality.

Trust me horses have one! In fact, when you watch the top bronco riders and bull riders in the Calgary Stampede, every one of them has sized up their ride in order to know what to expect and have the edge when they finally pile on.

I don't think I'm supposed to be brainless and only have guts in order to rate or prove how tough I am! I know that not all cowboys are like that of course. However, a number that I have seen and met over the years seem to be.

Even the Christian ones, to my surprise, revealed a suspicious level of pride I am cautious around. I am just saying. I may be a sucker for a guy in western wear, but you can see why I don't get involved with one if I can help it. You never know though, maybe I will meet a cowboy that isn't like that.

ACTING

Since it was too expensive to be in the Actors Guild I wouldn't get the big jobs but that was okay. I still relished the opportunity to have such an experience. I occasionally met the odd lead actor. On one movie set I met Sydney Portier's brother while watching off set. On that movie set I was discovered by the movie director doing the movie.

I had bit parts in some Disney productions and a couple of commercials. I also remember being in a sitcom series called *Honey I Shrunk the Kids*.

A couple of amazing things did happen in my few short years modelling and acting. One, I was introduced to an agent that took a video of me marvelling the whole time as to how dead on I was at duplicating a couple of actresses. So if ever, Joni Mitchell, Leona Boyd or Meredith Baxter Bernie come back to town to do a movie, I get to be their stand-in. Doubles get paid a lot more than extras without lines. So I still hope I get that chance to be a double for at least one of them. That would put a nice finishing touch to my short acting career.

The second thing that happened to me while acting was what I did on set one day. It was a movie with Sydney Portier, called *Children of the Dust*. We were on site at the rail station in Heritage Park. My job was to be a passenger on the train that blocked the way from the leading actress seeing her brother.

I did my stint, pausing on the threshold gazing in to the crowd to locate the make-believe person I was to meet at the train station. Then I stepped off the train and headed out past the cameras.

Once I did that, the director, a Mr. Greene, followed right after me. It was an experience I will never forget. The crowd of extras just parted like the Red Sea for the Director to come after me. He walked right up to me as I seated myself on the platform. He asked me very directly if I had ever acted before.

I really did not want him to think I was only there for the money. So I hummed and hawed, then blurted out that I had done some acting in school. His response back at me was, "Well, you are very good!" I really was caught off guard.

A guy that I went out with sometimes said to me after that I should have given the Director a business card. I never had a business card, except the time I was going to Japan with the team. It is something I do have now that I made to give out when networking, which can happen at any given moment. That's a book in itself!

Anyhow, after the Director walked back to the set, everyone swooped in on me to ask, "What did he say? What did he say?" You the reader may not know the complete significance of that. You see, Directors and Actors did not speak to us and we the Extras were not to fraternize with them either.

So for this Director to come straight over to me and speak to me was a significant and rare occasion. That is why they all swarmed in to me to see what he had said to me.

Upon reflection I hope that I did not miss an opportunity. However, when I turn my sights on the LORD, I realize that I did not miss any opportunity. For after all these years I am really trying to cement in the very fact that when something is meant to be for me, then GOD himself will make sure it happens.

I know that more than ever now, but not so much back then. Back in 1995 I was so busy being stressed out, yet still having to jump through lots of hoops to get anywhere and back on my feet again.

SUBSTITUTE TEACHING

Ta-dah! I finally got on the Sub-Teaching Roster for the Calgary Public Education system. I got on the list but it was not by the conventional way I assure you. A good friend of mine from as far back as grade two is a CBE teacher. Even when we lost touch off and on over the years, fate kept us together.

The unconventional way it all happened was through her. She knew the Superintendent and figured that she would listen to what I had to say. Sure enough she agreed to listen to me. As a result she put me in contact with another person high up in Human Resources. He agreed to meet with me but emphasized that meeting me did not mean that I was getting on the Roster.

The interview was a "behavioural" type one. I actually prefer this type of interview, where the person is asked what they would do in certain situations. All the way through the interview he kept on saying, "You realize this will not get you on the roster." I replied, "That's okay, I just want to be heard."

As the interview progressed, he asked me what the most embarrassing teaching moment was. So I began to tell him about using an Ant Farm to depict "Community" to my kindergarten classes. It backfired during the lesson when one student observed and asked why there was only one live ant wandering around looking rather wounded.

OOPS! That was not supposed to be what happened! Apparently my mistake was in collecting two different colonies of ants that will kill each other off. So here I was trying to illustrate community! When the exact opposite had occurred right before the children's impressionable eyes. So to make the lesson work, I switched it to what it is like when we don't get along and there's no community existence! It can turn out to be all-out war.

By then I had him in stitches! Still laughing, he excused himself to go get something. He came back in with a handful of papers of all different colours. Then he proceeded to fill me in on how to complete the forms in order to be placed on the Substitute Teacher's Roster. I couldn't believe it! I had to ask him a couple of times to clarify. By the way, he became one of my references!

YEAH! The salary was going to be far better than my acting one. The hours too were going to be far better. With acting we often got on a bus at about five in the morning and would work until sometimes eight at night before loading up on some bus, exhausted, to head home.

I loved subbing, and really appreciated the teachers. One thing I did was to leave each teacher that I Subbed for an encouragement note with a "Thank U!" and... "YOU'RE WORTH A MINT!" with a real mint taped beside it.

To network, I would make up little paper crayons, cut them out and leave them in Teacher's mailboxes. I wrote on the paper crayons this: "STRESS FREE Absence... (4X Teacher of the Year Nominee), Miss K= Karen McKenzieSmith. So colour your day away with me as your SUB by calling: 403 _ _ _-_ _ _ _!'"

I have great memories of subbing. My very first assignment was the best experience ever. I still have the notes and presents given to me on that day as well as the hundreds since then.

I was okay with not teaching fulltime. I preferred to pick and choose my holiday times. The LORD wanted me to Substitute Teach and said that HE would cover me! I also think because I had lost my three children, the Lord gave me thousands!

One grade two class I subbed a lot for nominated me for the PanCanadian's Student Choice Awards, for Teacher of the Year. I was nominated every year after that, four in a row, until it came to a close with the sale of PanCanadian to Encana.

1997: HUGE BUT I DID IT

I was terrified, but a realtor assured me it was the best time to buy. Mortgage rates were the lowest they had been since 1961 or '67 I think he said. So I was buying my first property all by myself! It was a beautiful condo backing on to Edworthy Park (the largest, natural inner city park), overlooking downtown.

Years later when I bought the third condo (that I am still living in) I thanked GOD, for that amount of money I fought for and received from my ex's pension. It paid off my mortgage! Believe it or not, unintentionally, I paid off all of it on my ex-husband's birthday! It dawned on me later that there was something about that date. I thought, after the fact, it was rather prophetic!

It nearly killed me to fight through a divorce settlement and three lawsuit attempts but I obtained my rightful portion of his pension. "However, one gives or takes will be given or taken to/from them." So call it Karma or I prefer to call it "You reap what you sow" (John 4:8).

My ex is a perfect example of that. When a spouse is nasty in a divorce, it will come back to haunt them. It is not my intention to point fingers at him or anyone in particular. My intention is only for this book to reveal reality.

CHOICES

During this time I was learning many things that were very new to me personally. Things others may not think anything of. I didn't even know I had such a common thing as choices! Take a restaurant menu. For years I did not know that I could get more than a cheeseburger and fries.

It was not a bad thing that happened to me when I was growing up. I can see why my parents did not give me a whole lot of choices. For several reasons, mainly to make life simpler to deal with for them and for me. After all, a child can get over-stimulated by a bombardment of choices. Frankly as a parent I too would limit the choices my children could have until they were older.

The unfortunate thing was that I did not see beyond that in many aspects later on in life. Not with regards to a menu of course, but in regards to options I might have had.

That is where my problem arose. I didn't see it until I would be frustrated and a bit angry toward those that would say such things like: "You had the choice." Or, "It was your choice." I just couldn't comprehend that! I still struggle with the concept that even though circumstances were thrust in front of me it still boiled down to me having a choice! I don't entirely believe that I could always make a choice.

I still don't believe that I'm free to always choose. Is it not true, there are some things that simply do not give one the option to choose? The good news is, GOD can take the bad choices that we have made and turn them around for our good for those whom believe in HIM (Romans 8:28). We might not see such results right away, but it is so, thank GOD!

You know, Christianity is so simple that many don't get it. Hence they turn away. We humans somehow or other feel we need to make things more complicated than they need to be. We seem to need rules and a ladder to climb. So we find GOD's simplicity confounding. GOD does not acquire us as Christians to climb any ladder. In fact HE has achieved it, for us!

Even our visions and dreams from HIM are more reliable than life as we know it and see it. For GOD is really stripping us of the worldly way of thinking. The lies in our upbringing, strongholds and so forth are what isn't real! They only become real if we ourselves believe and manifest them. I am seeing that fear is something that man has come to believe as a reality. I see it as a lie from the enemy, spreading like the plague.

My dreams and visions and prophecies align with GOD's Word. I have realized there is no need to fear. I am not saying that I do not have fears, but I know now more than ever to give them to HIM directly in prayer and supplication.

I have been able to see what it really is like surviving without strongholds overruling my choices and without being co-dependent on them. The only co-dependency that is healthy is a dependency on JESUS CHRIST. Living co-dependent on HIM is a sure thing. It's the only way to go! HE is the one we can count on for protection and to aid us in discerning the best route to go. Amen!

There are times GOD knows very well that I will grow tired of trying to do life all on my own; trying to make it work and weary of its battles scars. Never fear though, for HE can turn scars into stars! That's how good HE is!

It is actually reassuring and good that I cannot do life on my own. HE is ready every time I am too weak to step in and take over. If I let HIM. HE in turn picks me up and guides me in HIS paths.

WRAPPED AND FROM THE LORD

The LORD knew how important it was to me to get wrapped gifts at Christmas time. I tried surprising myself with a wrapped present at Christmas but it just fizzled to say the least. So every year since my divorce, which is a total of 19 going on 20 years now, HE makes sure I get a wrapped gift or more each and every Christmas. I have never found out where some of them came from.

The first Christmas was UNBELIEVABLE! The Sheriff King staff asked guests to submit a Christmas list. I didn't think I was supposed to take part because I was without kids. They insisted I submit something anyway and include my kids regardless.

So I put a couple of things down for myself and another couple of choices for each of my three kids. I asked for pajamas since I had none as well as a Christian cassette tape. I had absolutely no Christian music and cell phones or IPods were non-existent then.

All the other mothers had received their Christmas hampers, which consisted of a box about the size of an apple box heaping full. Mine had not come so I just figured I was not getting one for the same reason I was not going to submit a list in the first place.

It was a couple of days before Christmas Eve. I was still in bed. A knock came to the door announcing that I was to come get my Christmas hamper. I moaned back for them to just move it out of the way and I would get it later. The messenger at my door replied back "No you have to come now! It is in the way!"

A bit annoyed, I hoisted myself out of bed abruptly and stomped to the door, mumbling, "Alright then, okay!" When I got to the front entrance and the office, they told me to come around the corner to get my hamper.

So I stomped around the corner still annoyed, only to come face to face with an entire trolley stacked full of gifts and goodies just for me! I whispered, "Oh my GOD!" as I broke into tears of surprise, mixed with awe and gratefulness.

The trolley was stacked about 3ft. high and the trolley itself was 3 feet by 5 feet long. Oh my LORD I was overwhelmed! I just stood there in tears. I got my pajamas and my Christian tape, plus plenty more! When I sent a "Thank You Note" to the family that adopted me, I couldn't stop saying thank you over and over throughout the whole letter.

One year it was a pink fuzzy bathrobe, another year the best kind of journal with a coil binding and hardcovers to make it easier to write in. Another time it was chocolates, a further time candles. Once I received a red purse with a matching change purse. Another time it was a gold sparkly necklace wrapped up in a bag with some goodies. There were more things wrapped up, a pink sparkly pen and notepad. An additional Dutch blue writing paper and a pen set to match. Oh and yum, short bread cookies wrapped up in a nice tin.

Another year I received crossword puzzles and a book to read. One of my favourite was a big huge stocking full of all kinds of tiny little wrapped gifts. I thoroughly enjoyed unwrapping each little gift.

I have attended the CUPS clinic and the Alex clinic (low income health clinics) ever since I came to Calgary. My doctor is a doctor that I have known since I spoke to a number of graduating doctors while at Sheriff King. She of course knows my plight, along with the other staff at the Alex, who have learned of my situation with regards to my absence of children over the years.

My doctor has always been conscious of making sure I'm taken care of at Christmas. Each year they seem to come up with one or two wrapped gifts for me. One memorable time the receptionist asked me to follow her to one of the back rooms. She came out carrying two huge gift bags for me! Both were full to overflowing with wrapped gifts!

"This is all for me!" I exclaimed as my eyes welled up with tears. Wow unbelievable! My, was that a delightful Christmas that year! I made sure I that I spread it out over several days opening one or two gifts per day.

The same occurred this past Christmas and the year before. I received about 17 gifts one Christmas and I think it was 22 wrapped gifts the other Christmas and 9 another time. I took as long as possible to slowly unwrap each one, savouring the moment again with my traditional Carols playing in the background with all the Christmas lights on and a cup of cinnamon hot chocolate by my side, (which was another gift)!

It couldn't be more perfect. Thank You GOD, and the saints that honour You by playing Santa!

A COMPLETE ASIDE: THE THINGS I LEARNED FROM A LEAF

In Matthew 11:28, the Bible refers to coming to Jesus Christ when we "are weary and heavy laden and He will give you rest." Therefore we do not need pain to have gain.

This brings me to a story about a leaf. Here are 3 Bible verses to help explain how well a leaf taught me an important lesson. They go something like this: 1) "Lean not on your own understanding" (Proverbs 3:5) and... 2) "I will give you no more than you can handle" (1st Corinthians 10:13) and ... 3) "I have a way out always for you" (also 1st Corinthians 10:13).

One time I was tubing down the river, struggling through and out of periodic rapids. At first I leaned on my own understanding and used my oar to maneuver unsuccessfully through the rapids, falling back in complete exhaustion. Finding my own way through them resulted in all work and no play. I was losing the battle.

I noticed a leaf floating by at leisure. I watched it for as long as I could before it blended in with all the other leaves that disappeared around the bend in the river. The thing I noticed the most, was how effortlessly it glided and maneuvered its way through the rapids. I felt silly as I slumped back in my tire tube exhausted from the struggle.

I decided to stay that way for the next set of rapids. Sure enough, I slid around and in and out of the rapids; taking what appeared to be the best way around and through them. Wow, what a big difference! There was no struggle at all! My experiment worked!

The leaf showed me, that if I simply rested and let nature "literally" take its course it will guide me just fine! Since nature is controlled by God, the simple solution I learned from this lesson, was this: rest in God by letting Him literally direct my path. This will give me the best way through life's problems with the least amount of effort. So it is with life, whereby I follow Holy Spirit's lead.

GOD AND NATURE WORK HAND IN HAND

I know that some people think nature does its own thing, without God. That may be, but I don't think so. I have experienced enough proof that God can and does intervene at times with nature.

For example on a trip I took to Mexico it was pouring rain all around us as we were heading to the stadium for our crusade. We had been praying for rain, for it was very dry and in desperate need of moisture. There had just been a volcanic eruption before we arrived in that district. The air smelled of sulfur and was filled with dust and smoke.

Though there was need for rain, we prayed that the rain would not fall on our crusade. Sure enough, within a short distance before the stadium we drove through a wall of rain!

The whole area within the stadium was completely dry! Yet we were surrounded with pouring rain. You could see lightning and hear thunder all around as the rain poured, nourishing the land! I will never forget seeing that wall of rain that we drove through with our vans as we neared the stadium where the crusade was set up to go.

I was in awe of the intense support through the power of prayer when we entered the stadium. There were people every 10 to 15 feet apart around the whole stadium perimeter, around the stage, and walking through the rows praying for the crusade!

The interesting thing about this was they had been doing this for as long as three months before our arrival. WOW, impressive!

Another example when God intervened was when I was in Tulsa, Oklahoma. The State is riddled with tornadoes throughout their summers. While I was visiting there, the radio alerted us that a tornado was coming right for us.

There were underground shelters spaced about every two or three blocks and people in the neighbourhood were in charge of opening them up and debugging them and having them ready in case we had to evacuate to the shelter for safety's sake.

I remember us gathering together at a neighbour's house right next to the shelter and praying that the tornado would jump right over the city.

I bet I don't even have to tell you what happened after that. The tornado, according to the news report, actually did jump directly over top of us and missed the entire city completely!

I recall another time in BC way up the mountain, in a treehouse that my friend and I camped in overnight. I had prayed that there would be no dew when we woke up to in the morning and that our fire would not die in the night. Sure enough to my delight our sleeping bags were completely dry, the fire was still going and there wasn't any dew!

I've also prayed as a teacher that field trips would be on a sunny day without the weather hindering our trip at all. Amen!

I remember too, flying over Mount Everest on my way to Kathmandu, to minister in Nepal. I asked the Steward to let me know when we were getting near Mt. Everest, so I could view it from the plane. The Steward did just that however he mentioned that it would be very unlikely that I would see anything of Mt. Everest for it was always in the cloud cover above the clouds and not visible. So I just prayed that the Lord would give me the chance to view Mt. Everest anyway.

Sure enough, just as the wing of the plane was moving past the spot, the cloud cover lifted and the sun beamed right over top of Mt. Everest, looming above the clouds where I actually had to look up a bit to see it. I asked the Lord "Why did You make Mt. Everest?

He said, "So that my people will talk to me." And he continued to clarify saying, "People will either praise him me for the view when they get up there or they will be up there calling out to me for help." Either way they would be talking to HIM! Ummm!

Most recently God intervened with the flood of 2013 in Calgary where I live. How so you might ask? I prayed that the church that I attend, the Jesus Loves You Society, located right down near the Elbow River, would remain dry.

Sure enough it was safe from the water level. But it taught me to be more specific with such a prayer. For I didn't think to be that specific and forgot about the problem of electricity being shut down due to water levels. That meant the food freezers were compromised. OOPS!

MYSTICS AND SAINTS

Besides finally getting to Substitute Teach for the Calgary Board of Education other things started to happen for me. A lot of my Christian friends would suggest that I read books where they felt I was a lot like the person in the book.

My Catholic friends would give me books on Mystics and Saints because they felt I was a lot like them. Meaning, that I have similar experiences. Like the Mystics, I also actually see Jesus, Holy Spirit and God my Father, (my Daddy). They talk to me and show me things.

I know that many Christians are going to say that I can't see GOD or I will die! However that is not literally what it means. It truly means that I will die to self when I see GOD. In which case I have. I know for sure that is the case since Jesus took me to the Throne Room one time to meet GOD my Daddy.

The very instant I was face to face with HIM, all I could do was drop prostrate on the floor, face down. So I know I was no longer myself in a fleshly, sinful state, hence dead to myself. I had become filled with Holy Spirit and therefore dead to myself. Dead to my sinful fleshly self.

If you are not a Christian and do not know what I mean here, please ask GOD to explain it to you. HE does not keep HIMSELF from us. HE wants us to visit HIM and get to know HIM personally. When we do, HE teaches us so much beyond our own understanding.

HE spoke to me when I got back very disappointed with my stay on the Mercy Ship. HE said HE had something better for me and HE did. In two and a half months I was Prayer Healing and going on Crusades. That could amount to a whole book in itself. However in the chapters to come I will provide a very much abridged version for you.

POTENTIAL TALK SHOW HOST

In October of 2001 I had an opportunity come my way that I thought was worth pursuing. A Christian radio talk show in Lethbridge was looking to hire a "Co-Host." So I got to go down and do a job shadow cold turkey, co-hosting a radio talk show program!

It was fun but the timing was off. I liked the chance to try it out though and maybe sometime in the future that will be a possibility. I also got, while down there, a chance to go see one of my second son's high school football games at the College field. He was a Wide Receiver and wow, could he run like the wind! I was impressed!

This was going to be interesting because I had never done anything with the kids and their dad together! I asked their dad if he was going to the game and he said yes so I said I would join them.

I really didn't get to join him. My ex was just there, moving down in the stands a bit to sit instead of beside me. Our daughter came too to watch the game and she brought a friend with her.

Now here is where it gets weird but interesting. I am not sure what to call it. When we all got sitting my daughter up and went over to sit with her dad. However, I was not left alone, for the girl that came with her decided to stay with me. In fact she openly stated that I was fun and that my daughter had a "cool Mother!"

She was a GOD-send for me! It showed in living colour that I was someone kids would feel safe around and enjoy being with. That was something very important for my daughter to see. AND on that note, in relationship to my teaching, I discovered I had a rapport that made the kids feel safe and free around me. I lost three but gained thousands by Substitute Teaching!

ANT HILLS TO SNOWBALLS IN THE CLASSROOM

GOD specifically said to me to, "Substitute teach and I will cover you." HE was so right about that. I must tell you of some of incredible teaching moments.

My very first subbing job was with a lady I met through church. She said if she ever needed a Sub she would call me. Sure enough I got called to teach her grade five class. It was the most incredible and edifying introduction to my eleven years subbing in the city of

Calgary. The children kept saying how much they liked me and they didn't want me to go!

At the end I was given individual notes from students. I was also presented with a card signed by all of them and a couple of little gifts as well. It was the beginning of many subbing jobs where students would crowd around me and love on me and open up to me. I was finding that when I went into classrooms to teach, the students would run up to me and hug me and give me thank you notes when I was leaving. I have kept all my notes in a big valentine cake box.

The Administration could also see how quickly I gained rapport with the students. It didn't seem to matter what age they were, all seemed to warm up to me instantly. I believe it was GOD giving them HIS love and me receiving love from HIM that way!

I missed out on love from my own three but instead got loved by several thousand! See what I mean by HIM being amazing! HE was giving me more than just a job.

I had so much fun teaching over the years! I always introduced myself by asking "Do you want to know how to have fun learning today?"

I would teach Physical Education with ketchup in first aid class. I would have a snowball fight in math class. We would all enjoy a treasure hunt at the end of the day to clean the floor and tidy up. Students doing well got little papers to write their name on and put in a draw that was made at the end of each teaching day.

One time my principal in my second job came into my room looking for me when I was in the TV. He had to duck his way over to the middle of the room to ask the kids where I was. They all pointed to the TV Set.

I had one of those old model TV sets that was a large wooden furniture piece. I gutted it, making it completely hollow. So I really was inside the TV set giving the news and weather for the beginning of the class day. My poor principal had to bend way down to find me in the TV. Set. Ha-Ha. He seemed a bit surprised yet impressed.

I loved to help my students! For example, one of my Kindergarten students had a hard time concentrating and printing well. So I gave him a "MAGIC PENCIL." It was bigger than usual and all fancy with a tassel on top of a clown.

When I gave it to him I told him it was magic and could help him print easier and longer. I also showed him how it would help him stay on a line to read so as not lose his place. I had assessed that was his main problem, keeping him distracted and therefore interfering with his comprehension.

I also had a party for the best class of the year! I let principals, superintendents, and other administrative staff in on it by making the draw in May. That way a party could be held by me at the end of the school year and sponsored by a popular restaurant franchise. I kept this up until new privacy legislation came along and ruined the idea.

THE LORD HAS CHEMISTRY

It was a Chemistry class. I came into the classroom a few minutes early to prepare notes on the blackboard before class started, only to find a student asleep in his desk. I made some comment like, "Good morning! Did you have to work late last night?" We chatted back and forth a bit before other students started trickling in.

Then just as class was about to start, a guy came to the door to motion for that same fellow to come to the door. I pretty much figured out what was going down. Sure enough, the student retrieved his books and skipped class.

However, not before I claimed them for Christ, Amen. By claiming them, I mean lifting them in prayer, to HIM. This is not the end of the story on this guy. NO, it certainly isn't so I will fill you in later. I am just going to skip over it for now to let you know what went on in the rest of that Chemistry class.

I felt led to allow another student that seemed eager to teach. So I let him take over. First though I suggested to the class that sometimes when a student teaches, other students pick it up from a different angle and even learn quicker.

The result was a phenomenal success! I think the reason it did work so well, was the fact that the method was unique. It drew the students in right away, first out of a desire to see this student flub-up or not. Once in, they discovered it to be quite interesting!

All the credit goes to my Holy Spirit for my successes. HE is the main reason I am sure, that I was nominated four years in a row for "Student Choice Teacher of the Year Awards."

Now the best for last! I can tell you what final discovery I made about that one lone student that was asleep and then skipped out of class. Here is where the exceptional comes in.

Remember, I prayed and claimed them for the LORD? That is a common tendency of mine with just about everybody. So you can imagine my delight when given some good news only a month and a half later.

I was at Tahieliah Monday, a "super soaking" worship service for teens and young adults, when I met him again. I was saying "Hi" to a friend of mine and he was with him. My friend introduced him to me as a "New Christian!"

I turned to him, (not recognizing him at first), to say that I would be praying for him. I know that when someone comes to the LORD and as a New Christian, it can be hard, and that spiritual growth is tough. So I wanted him to know I would be in prayer for him to cover that.

Saying "Thanks," he added that he thought he knew me from somewhere else. That I looked familiar. I couldn't think where.

I added "Unless, either church or school."

That is when he blurted out, "Now I remember where it was! Did you teach at E.P. Scarlet, a chemistry class, about…?"

I interrupted him and said to him, "Oh, you're going to like what I am about to tell you! You won't believe that this Substitute Teacher was praying for you, way back then!"

I shared what I had done when I figured he would skip out of class that day. Touché and look at him, already a new Christian! And in record time I thought! YEAH!

He couldn't believe that a teacher was praying and looking out for him. I was delighted that my prayer was answered. YEAH. A month later he had graduated from grade twelve and we became good friends.

I met another guy in a similar way. He was a student too, only a bit older and in college. It was at Taheliah another time, a pastor friend of mine had come with a bunch of young adult friends, and we went out for coffee after.

As we sat down, one of his friends came directly up to me, like he was on a mission and tapped me on the shoulder. He looked straight at me and asked to if he could sit down beside me. I said, "Sure, you bet!"

At the same time he blurted out a declaration to me. He said,"Cuz I want what you have!"

"Okay then, sit right down and we'll talk." To this day we are great friends, although he eventually moved away too.

FRIENDS LIKE NO OTHER

My friend always seemed to know what I was going to do next. For example I pulled over on the side of the road one time when we were coming back from BC. I had no sooner gotten out of the car to run over to the snow in the ditch when he jumped out right along with me, as if knowing what I was going to do. Sure enough we both made snow angels and had a small snow-ball fight.

Another time I was coming back with him on his motorbike from Clearwater where he worked for a White Water Rafting Co. We both had spotted an old abandoned house and he leaned back to say, "Are you thinking what I am thinking?"

Now keep in mind that neither of us knew the other had looked at the abandoned house. I simply said "Yes" and the next thing you know, we were checking it out. It was so neat seeing old calendars dating the house, and finding other knick-knacks that gave a hint to the old owners' lives.

Though he was much younger than I, we seemed to really click! It was not a sexual relationship at all as you might think. No, in fact we both appreciated the fact that we helped each other ward off any unwanted attraction from others.

It was refreshing to have a male friend without all the sexual dynamics added. Plus, we liked a lot of the same adventures. He even had me white water rafting the most dangerous rank of river.

I have so many good memories of the times we had. For my birthday one year, he blew up a bunch of balloons and had me pop one at a time to follow the instructions on notes inside each balloon. The memories are bountiful. Thanks to you and your brothers and their families!

KETCHUP AND CUTTING

I was teaching first aide to a junior high gym class. I decided to get real to bring home a point. I let the other necessary staff know what I was up to. I got some ketchup packs from the cafeteria.

Just as the students finally all got into the classroom, I proceeded to set up the projector and suddenly pretended to get a severe cut on the palm of my hand. Then as I looked at it I fainted right there in front of the class. This was all to see what they would do to handle the emergency. Most froze, a couple gasped, one girl screamed and got all flustered.

Finally one lone person ran to get the other gym teacher. When he finally came, that is when I miraculously recovered.

Of course the gym teacher knew what was up and didn't blow my cover. I thanked him as he left the classroom and began to explain my strategy to the students. I emphasized that one out of three of them would face an emergency first aid situation at least once in their lifetime. They needed to be able to respond immediately, but could they? I gave them a close-up and personal reality check.

The lesson was to show as vividly as possible what they could or would do in an emergency. At first the girl that screamed was so mad at me for pulling that stunt. I in one way apologized, yet said that I needed to get the class to take emergency readiness seriously.

Then I asked her "Have I made my point? And would I have if I hadn't made it as real as possible for you? She assured me that was the case. Therefore I succeeded in getting my point across. I concluded with, "Isn't it better to find out this way than in a real emergency?"

Here is another story, about a grade three student on a sadder note but successful in its outcome. I caught him cutting himself with a paperclip. I knew about cutters to some degree but had never seen one so young. I found it disheartening and it saddened me to see someone so young cutting. My instinctive impulse was to deliver him out of that self-damaging obsession promptly.

I called it out of him in the name of Jesus Christ. He stopped immediately, dropping the paper clip he had been using to cut his arm up. At the same time, his whole demeanour mellowed, indicating he had been delivered from the demonic presence that had captivated him for some time.

Thank Heavens he was now free from the dangers of cutting himself up. Teacher or no teacher, I couldn't help but help. When I saw a student in dire need like that I acted immediately for their sake!

It definitely was not something that I did all the time. But when required, the faster the better.

There were and are many students besides him that I pray especially for. Whether they were good or bad all my students (and others of course), are in my prayers often. Eventually there got to be so many of them that I finally exclaimed to the LORD that we had to figure out a faster way to pray for them all. So we did. And I have been using it ever since.

God has an unimaginable, unique and incomprehensible ability. He came up with me simply having to sway my hands by my side as I walked around the classrooms or hallways and staff-rooms. Since then I have expanded it to anywhere I feel compelled to do so. Sometimes I can actually see the effects of this shortcut. In addition, I requested the Lord to allow me to pray as I sleep. My thinking was "Why not use me every minute I can to pray?" This included my sleep time. Keep an eye out for the proof of this when I share about my trip to Nepal.

Substitute teaching was going so well, I restricted the zones I would work in. I narrowed down radius within which I would drive to work. I was getting booked frequently to the same classes over and over again. So much so that I got to know the students and teachers very well.

2006 MY TEACHING DAYS ARE NUMBERED

One afternoon I was coming out of a Chiropractor's office on Seventeenth Avenue, SW right by two funeral homes, kitty-corner from each other. I was crossing at a green light and had the right-of-way when it happened: I got hit by a car!

A car second from the light in the lane that travels straight ahead, suddenly pulled out and around the first stopped car to make a right hand turn instead of waiting for the light to turn green. In so doing, he did not account for me coming across the street into the intersection.

Though I managed to jump out of the way so as not to get hit directly by the car, I fell into a parked car and jilted my hip, pelvis, and groin. I also pinched my sciatica nerve that went down the back of my leg.

I continued to teach for another year but found it extremely painful to continue. So I quit in June of 2007.

I did not quit entirely for that one reason alone. I was assaulted in school. I walked out of a high school and my career in teaching in Calgary and never looked back.

I was subbing in a physical education class. Someone(s) on the sidelines threw rock hard dirt lumps and stones at me when my back was turned. How I wished they had missed. For it became necessary for me to file an assault charge with the Resources Officer in the school.

Can you believe it, she wanted to know "Why press charges?" REALLY? As another female couldn't she at least empathize? So much for sticking up for women. I was floored to find no support whatsoever.

I told my Curriculum Head. He was sad to hear such a thing and apologized to me on behalf of the Phys. Ed. Department. The Vice Principal came and also apologized to me on behalf of the school and allowed me to leave for the day. I didn't argue and was relieved to get the heck out of there! So that my readers, that was the day I walked away from teaching!

I was always the kind of person that picked a job I liked to do. I no longer liked to teach. The passion was gone when the students were no longer held accountable for very much of anything. When that happens I don't want to be a part of it. So I figured that last assault was the straw that broke my back, (pun intended).

I loved teaching and realized early on that it came easy to me. I've been told that I was gifted at it. For as much as I enjoyed the students, they enjoyed and wanted me to teach them, even though I was a Substitute Teacher. I actually had a number of classes I taught over the years as a Sub go straight to the Principal's office to demand that I become their regular teacher! I am not kidding! How unbelievably sweet! I can't get a better compliment than that.

Near the end of those teaching years, I could see a shift occurring in the student's attitudes, and not for the better. I wanted to phone a student's parents one time when I was on a contract job and the Administration wouldn't let me. The principal turned on me, accusing me of not being capable of handling the class.

Now let me see; having taught for 11 years as a Sub Teacher and only needing to call parents once over all those years, getting nominated for Student Choice Awards, four years in a row and being asked personally by the Sub Office to take the classes from HELL that no one else would teach. Does that indicate I couldn't handle it?

No, it indicates that the kids are not like they used to be. They are sadly more belligerent, they are held unaccountable and they are never failed. What do you think that produces? It is not good, I'll tell you that. It makes for more policing, and less teaching. Disciplining them became more consuming. It's not fun anymore so I do not miss it, and I am sad for students, parents and society.

Sure the end for me may have been a bit of a downer, but there were many more amazing years that compensated for it. I had a whole class come to the LORD one afternoon. It happened when I prayed for a student's ankle and the pain disappeared right away. So she went out for recess and prayed for everyone. The whole class was so excited they wanted to know more and that led up to them praying the Sinner's Prayer!

ASSAULTED

About a year before the assault I just described, I was also physically assaulted. It was again during Phys. Ed. class. That time I had a very risky situation to deal with. It all could have been prevented though, had the teacher documented his case.

Teachers tend to give their students an inch but this one took a mile! He had slashed his teacher across the knee-caps the day before I filled in. The students also said that they would not play with him anymore because he was so dangerous. So the teacher banished him from class.. Then I come in to Sub for this teacher, unaware, the very next day. By the way, this was occurring a lot with my job, making for very dangerous predicaments to deal with.

According to the students, this guy could no longer attend that class, but he showed up! The class filled me on the whole incident from the day before, stating that they refused to play with him. I called the office to inform them. Without the teacher's report of the assault and expulsion from class I was required to include him.

I sure didn't want to and sensed it would have a bad outcome. The students were mad and I was not too happy either. I turned to the guy and read him the riot act then turned to promise the rest of the class that if he did not cooperate, he'd be benched right away! Everybody was fine with it but me! I was leery the whole time of my precarious position.

Here is what occurred next. The problem guy got benched. While I placed him off by himself to shoot pucks, I went to the aid of a guy that had sprained his ankle.

POW. I got a slap-shot right in my chest just above my heart! I would have fallen over had it not been for the wall I was leaning up against when I was helping the injured student.

I went to deal with the source of the assault but he ran out and disappeared. Immediately after class I reported him and went to the Resource Officer to charge him with assault.

Again, not only did this cop brush me off but the Principal did too! I was absolutely mortified at the poor treatment I received. I was kept there after school, like I was the one at fault. I diplomatically stated so and expressed my concern for this student. I felt that he was crying out for help and that they should do something about it.

Needless to say, I did not go back to that school to work and dusted my feet as I left. I never did get any satisfactory results from school or the police for either assault! Well, God bless them for they will reap what they sow as I know that GOD will vindicate. "For vengeance is mine says the Lord" (Romans 12:19). It will be unfortunate for them.

A wonderful thing did come out of getting hit by that slap-shot. I immediately started praying for healing and got healed almost right away. That was so helpful on so many levels. Mainly because it took the severe pain away.

With that went the terrible mark it had left on my chest. This greatly relieved me, since I was going to a Christmas Dinner that evening and would be wearing an evening dress that would have shown that terrible bruise!

On the other hand, my evidence was gone! By the way, I prayed for the student that had been injured and his ankle got healed.

I would pray healing for hundreds of students over my eleven years of subbing and HE would in HIS love, mercy and grace, heal all of them! As well HE was true to HIS word when HE said HE would cover me as I taught. It is not hard to fully see the scope of that protection now.

What was incredible was that when I offered prayer for healing to anyone, they would be so grateful! They actually could not believe that I would do such a nice thing for them. I was thrilled too, for it was not the uphill grind I expected to experience.

God wanted me to cover as many students as I could and Subbing surely did that. I'll share a few of these amazing healings here. The rest could be another entire book.

CANCER GONE

It was the end of another teaching year. I was teaching in the biggest high school in all of Calgary. The year before I had met a grade eleven student dying of cancer. Now she was in grade twelve.

I saw her walk by earlier in the day and noticed that she was bald. I was heading into the office at the time. The LORD was beckoning me to pray healing for her. I frequently prayed with students, teachers and even secretaries as well. So, as usual, I would wait on HIM to set the whole opportunity up in order to follow through. HE worked it out so I didn't go against school policy either.

I did not preach in school at all. When HE set things up, students themselves came up to me and started the conversation in some way.

As I said, I was in the office. Just outside was the big foyer to the high school. The students hung out there ALL THE TIME.

Still prompted to pray for her, I said, "Okay GOD, if I bump into her as I leave the office I will obey." Not much later as I left the office, she was coming around the corner and literally…. You guessed it, I bumped into her! She remembered me, so we both exchanged greetings. I shared with her what the LORD told me to do and that I had learned it was for the best to follow through, if she was okay with me doing so.

To my enchanted surprise she jumped at the offer! In fact, she insisted that I take her phone number, and she shoved it into my hand. She was adamant that I call later the following week to find out her test results. I obliged, and to her most incredible delight she was healed and going to live a long fruitful life! Amen!

Another student I had known since Junior High School was in High School when I met up with her again. Glad to see me, she ran towards me in front of another school office. She was holding her burned hand, in great pain from having picked up a spotlight in the drama class that was still hot.

I offered to pray for the pain to go. As I spoke, she was already exclaiming to me that her hand felt free from pain and a cooling effect was coming over her whole hand. Another Amen! I could share more but I think you get the picture.

SPIRITUAL SHIFT

Things began to shift for the worse around 2005 or so. Students even began to refuse prayer! Such things were no longer readily acceptable anymore. I was starting to get kicked out of schools for praying. I could see a drastic spiritual shift developing.

I was teaching Social Studies at another high school in Calgary, again in June. The next thing I knew I was called into the Vice Principal's office at the end of the day and asked to not return. There would also be a letter sent to the Board. Just guess who the student was that reported me for so-called "preaching?"

She herself was a Christian! I figured as much because she had questioned in class if I was preaching. I had not, I assured her. I was simply answering questions that the class had tabled. Then as the period ended I wished them well on exams and said that I would be praying for them.

Apparently this is why I was called into the office. Again I dusted my feet, as the Lord reminded me to do, when I left that school. When one dusts their feet so to speak, they are removing their blessings as GOD refers to it in scripture. The following fall, all hell broke loose in that school, all in the first month. Interesting!

By the way, I don't mind being asked to leave. I would rather find out they don't want me than stick around where I am not welcome. I'd rather sift the wheat from the chaff. The sooner I can get those two sorted the better! That was one of the more obvious times I could see a distinct difference when I removed my blessings by dusting my feet.

The very result shows the watchful eye of our Creator and HIS promise of vindication. Be watchful for a "two-edged" vindication in times to come. I believe that it is time to REAP what is SOWN.

I don't care whether one calls it karma, religion or a faith or whatever. It's going to happen!

About the time this Christian girl turned on me, I was given a prophetic word of warning from GOD for all Christians. HE said for us to, "Be careful and aware of dissension from within the ranks!"

Meaning, He said, that fellow Christians will judge and condemn each other in these times. HE also said that fellow Christian friends, relatives, siblings, mentors and others should watch that they hear each other correctly and not misunderstand each other.

I see that happening a lot! Kind of like physics, for every action there is an equal and opposite reaction. Therefore, where evil rises, so does Christ's power and victory. Just as evil is making a spiritual shift, so is GOD!

This has been and is going to be on the increase more and more, in the coming years. Even though I find myself para-phrasing back to make sure I am understood, I am still not heard correctly and still misunderstood. It is evident through this issue that the enemy is twisting and manipulating conversations to create confusion and dissention. Hence we face opposition regardless.

Here's another example: A Christian friend started tearing a strip off me, condemning me. I knew very well what was going on. Therefore under my breath I rebuked the enemy and his dissension tactics immediately, sending them to the pit. I demanded the enemy leave quietly too, to be dealt with by Jesus Christ himself.

While she rambled I actually asked the LORD to shut it down in MID sentence if it was not of God. Sure enough, she shut up in mid-sentence, shook her head and said, "Sorry Karen, I don't know what happened!" I answered back, "That's okay, apology accepted."

EVIL LURKS

Evil is even in the schools. There is a reason I ask Gothic dressed students why they dress the way they do. Some do it to be different. Others do it to follow the occult at varying levels. I asked three grade 9 girls one time if they dressed like they did for a fashion statement only, or not? All three whipped out their satanic bibles. Whoa!

Another time I walked into a high school classroom while the students were all reading quietly. All except for one guy. As I walked to the desk at the front, he glared with searing eyes at me the whole time over his book. If looks could kill, I would have instantly been dead. Then he did something unusual.

As he glared at me he slouched down further in his desk and raised his book up higher in the air, as if to make sure that I noticed it. It was a satanic bible and I do not think he was into it as a fascination like the grade nine girls were. I think he was in it deeper and took it more seriously than the girls. For his spirit was actually challenging me and attempting to put me in place.

However, little did he know what satan knows, but he doesn't let anyone that follows him know. Which is that he and his troublemakers really do not have a leg to stand with Jesus and His followers. The only way out of a trap of satan's is through the help of Jesus Christ. So as much as this student threatened me, it was only to fall null and void as I spoke in tongues under my breath.

There is evil out there around us - more than what meets the eye. I actually had a boyfriend who came from an ancestry of voodoo, and tried to put a Love Spell on me. Needless to say, I didn't go out with him any more even though he would still like that to happen.

I could go on about voodoo and such but that topic is more suited to another book. I just wanted to give you the idea that some things can be kind of crazy at times to the naked eye. It may make me appear crazy.

There is a lot in this book you may find unbelievable, but I assure you, is completely true. At first glance you may assume my motives in some cases were not okay. I assure you that was not the case.

I feel it is time for people to know that evil lurks out there. Maybe now when I touch upon this aspect of my life it will at least give you a glimpse of why weird and crazy things happen to people like me.

The LORD is asking me to now share more openly the things we must become aware of out there in that jungle of a world captivated by satan.

PEARLS

I learned a valuable lesson while at university living in the student residences: To not cast my PEARLS amongst swine.

Whenever I got back from a fantastic, over the top, ski trip, I was just dying to tell all! However, I quickly noticed with the very first person I came across, that they didn't share the same enthusiasm for the sport as I did and therefore they were not the least bit interested. Hence I "cast a pearl amongst swine." (Please, do not read into this that I am saying you are all swine.)

So the visions and visits to heaven are best left untold until He deems otherwise. Like my story of going to heaven when I was taken by JESUS to the Throne Room.

By the way, I don't feel I have a corner on this over other Christians. I just think He shows me lots because I am open to it and do not limit Him I suppose. Plus I've always been one that thinks outside the box.

It has only been in the last handful of years that HE has me sharing these pearls that I have kept close to my heart. HE has been compelling me to be more revealing and open about my faith and experiences with GOD, the TRINITY. Which is good because I can now feel free to share these well-kept secrets. I know some of this will be a jaw dropper, and I hope that it is inspiring or even convicting too. And that is perfectly okay in HIS eyes for HE knows what you the reader, need to get out of this book and HE will make sure you do, guaranteed! Quite the good deal, Eh?

The second or third time I was in the throne room I saw off in a grand office the LORD seated at an elegant oak office desk. HE was handing out assignments to the angels as they walked in one door and out another with their individual assignments in hand. The angels did not look hurried but moved smoothly with great precision and order. The chaos of the world does not phase them whatsoever. They just keep on moving steadily on demand through the Office of the LORD's.

I have seen this numerous times since and it appears that the line gets longer and longer and moves faster and faster. The angels seem to be given more and more assignments at a time. No longer are they handling just one problem. This tells me that it is all in line and a sign of the times. I mean by this n line with where we are in Revelation, where things have begun to speed up. That is why I can now share such secrets openly with others. It is time!

HELLO, I AM A VAMPIRE

It is time now to share about my relationship with a vampire. Yes a real live HUMAN vampire. I met and prayed with a real vampire that turned his life over to the Lord.

I was as usual attending Taheliah Monday. Just before worship started, a friend showed up with another person that he introduced to me. Within minutes he received a call that required him to leave suddenly. So he asked me to stay there with his friend

The friend and I chatted a bit before going into the sanctuary. I noticed rather quickly after meeting him something about him that I was suspicious about. His spirit didn't seem to be quite on the level. Also while we chatted, I was the only one that was calmly sitting down and listening while he paced back and forth. He appeared extremely restless and uncomfortable. At the same time he kept on saying over and over again: "You won't understand. You don't understand!" and so on.

I assured him that I felt okay about anything that he had to share. I didn't want him to think I would not understand whatever he was going through. On that note, it wasn't long after that he blurted out, as if I would be shocked to hear his confession: "I am a vampire!"

I said I thought something of that nature, due to my earlier suspicions. I assured him that I wasn't really surprised given his extreme uneasiness about being in a church. He agreed and was a bit taken aback by my relaxed tone. This helped him to relax a bit and begin to share more. He pointed outside at the full moon and said, "You see, I should be busy finding blood right now because of that."

I knew what he meant and agreed calmly with him. In a roundabout way we eventually got on to the topic of God and Christ. At some point he felt a real urgency to make a do or die choice for him. Little did he know that I had been praying intensely for the demonic presence in him to be rendered still and unable to interfere. Which is one reason why he calmed down somewhat.

This of course gave him a breather, and time to reflect on his chance to make a choice that would be a game changer in his life. In that free time undaunted by the demonic presence of his vampire nature controlling him, he was clear to follow through on the new urge he had to take a 180 in his life. Right then and there. In a church of all things!

Boy, did the Lord have him prepared to receive HIM into his life! It was like he couldn't wait another second to ask the Lord into his life as his personal Lord and Saviour. That made it easy to walk him through deliverance of the ever possessive demonic spirits that had taken control of him. Such spirits that gave him that vampire state of being whereby he needed to consume human blood and be highly ill-at-ease in a church of any kind.

I loved how his demeanour switched to a much calmer state. He himself even exclaimed in awe of the change that had come over him. He was so excited and knew instantly that he was unaffected and unoccupied any longer with his previously demanding vampire characteristics.

He even felt comfortable to enter the sanctuary with me to worship. Wow, that was a big and confirming step to take for him! Since our friend never did return he felt so relieved and at ease with me that we went for coffee afterwards. He was so relaxed and secure in himself for once, that we got into a lengthy spiritual conversation, mostly about Jesus.

So here I was, having coffee with a vampire, I mean EX-vampire until after three in the morning, which by the way tends to be the hexing hour of the night. The whole time he was oblivious to the menacing full moon outside hovering over us. Again wow!

BAD TURNS GOOD

I did have a bad story that turned out good. I was dismissed from another school near where I lived at the time in Marda Loop. I was dismissed right after 9/11. I had just gotten back from being locked out of the country, (another story, for later).

While I was teaching a grade seven Religion class, a student asked me if she could make up a word for her assignment. I said, "Sure you can! In fact I just made one up not too long ago. I made up the word, 'Revelationizing Here We Come!' when 9/11 hit the US."

I went on to explain that I felt because of 9/11, and other signs that we were definitely into the time the Bible refers to as "The Book of Revelation."

Well, my Aide apparently did not like that and reported me to the principal. He in turn called me into his office at lunchtime and informed me that he was going to drop me from his school. He went on to say that Catholics did not believe in Revelation and that they only saw it as an allegory.

I am so glad he did not insist I renege on what I had said because that would be going against my faith. As a Born Again Christian, I do take the Book of Revelation to be the most prophetic book in the Bible. John was given its valuable information word for word to relay on to us to guide us in the last days of this age.

Apparently the Aide thought that I was scaring the kids into believing the world was going to end! Whoa! I assured the principal that the kids, as far as I could tell, were not in the least concerned about that.

In fact I went so far as to invite him to come in on the last class of the day when I had the same group of kids for home room. Then I would come right out and ask them as subtlety as possible if I did anything in any way scare them. Sure enough, I was correct! When I questioned the students, none were alarmed or even took what I had said that way at all. However, I was still dismissed.

By the way, for every letter written against me that was filed with either the Public School Board or the Catholic School Board I attached my own letter of rebuttal so as to clarify any of the Administrative Staff's accusations and condemnations.

My conscience was clear of all fault or guilt. When a student in a class asked me a question regarding GOD/LORD, I proceeded to answer them. I replied right back with total confidence that I would not be a good educator if I did not provide students with the basic information. Then they could go ahead and research and seek out all they needed to in order to make an educated decision on their own regarding ALL Faiths. This is preferable obviously to sending them to go blindly stabbing in the dark and making only uneducated guesses.

Many parents these days use the strategy of throwing their lambs to the wolves and letting them decide about God for themselves! How could we do that to them as educators? I would not be a good teacher nor a reliable parent in my opinion, if I took that approach.

OOPS, I got side-tracked there a bit. I meant to tell you what happened after I was dismissed from that school when I spoke of

9/11 as a part of Revelation. A couple of years later, I got a call from the Sub-Desk offering me a substitute teaching job at that very school. So I figured, if they were going to invite, I was going to go back! Only this time I was going to stay in my room and not go near the office at all.

You would not believe what happened to me that day. Shortly after the first morning class began, a knock came at my door. Before I could go answer, the principal marched in. OMG-in-Heaven! I thought he was about to tear a strip off of me right in front of the whole class.

I was not going to allow it, and I marched across the room to insist that he speak to me privately out in the hall.

It is unprofessional and abusive for any Employer to tear a strip off of any Employee in front of others. I have learned the hard way to carry out just such discussions of confrontation, privately or with a trusted witness. In the case with my kids, I started to bring a trusted witness to help when the other party tends to play their word against yours. Or maybe I have taped the confrontation on my phone as a last resort.

At any rate, I was relieved to know that the principal did not tear a strip off of me. Not one shred! In fact he did just the opposite. He actually started complimenting me to the whole class on my expertise as a teacher!

He actually said, "Good morning class! I would like you, to give a very warm welcome to Ms. McKenzieSmith here. She is probably the best Substitute Teacher in the entire city!"

He proceeded to say more and more and I blushed redder and redder. My teeth nearly fell out then, as I stood there almost with my mouth falling open.

That's good news that is nice to know! People will be vindicated, restored, renewed and upheld. That is part of the "Karma" I was referring to. I believe there is still more to come! Keep in mind not to expect it though. Let it be a nice surprise! Just let it come in HIS timing.

FURTHER ADVENTURES IN TEACHING

Most substitute teachers stick to their specialty area and more than likely just the school they used to teach full-time at. When I first started in November of 1996, I said on my profile that I would go anywhere, anytime. Once I established a network of teachers close to where I lived, I narrowed down the work field.

By Christmas that same year I was starting to pick and choose the jobs I wanted to take. I also like to take a variety of jobs for my own interest's sake. So below is an actual work week sample for you to see: Physics 30, French 30, Spanish 30, and Cosmetology and on Friday, Kindergarten.

Most teachers would not touch some of these subjects if it was not their specialty area. I may not have known much about cosmetology but I did tell the students "I know something about being a customer!" So I taught from that perspective.

When I was teaching a class of grade tens that only worked with mannequin heads, all I said as I walked around the classroom evaluating, was, "If that were a real person, would you get a $ TIP? Ummmmm? That made them think. ! If I was teaching grade twelves for example, I would let them do my hair if they needed a willing subject and didn't have one. They were totally blown away to think that I would do that for them!

My math students were also open-mouthed when I let them have a snowball fight in the classroom at the end of class! Say they had a test coming up. I would have each student write an exam question on a page of paper, crumple it up into a "snowball" and voila! At my signal they could have a snowball fight. When I flicked the lights they were to stop and pick up one snowball to take home and solve.

It was fun to see their faces of shock when I first said that we would have a snowball fight. Then their facial expression would change to one of delight when I gave the signal to fight! I love to bring fun into learning as much as I can.

TENSE NO MORE

A most unusual thing happened to me when I was starting the day teaching a grade seven class. It happened to be during exam week. The atmosphere of the class was gloomy. The despair was so thick you could cut it with a knife! While writing notes on the blackboard I was sensing all this. I felt in my Spirit that I must do something to alleviate the situation.

Sure I was a Substitute Teacher, but I'm primarily Christian and the first thing I thought of doing was praying over the situation. I bet you can't imagine what happened next? As I was writing on the board I began to chuckle in my Spirit. I couldn't stop when I tried to, so that affirmed for me that GOD was up to something.

It was a relatively quiet laugh that no one really noticed but me. Something miraculous happened to the atmosphere of the classroom when I continued to laugh and chuckle. Believe it or not everyone's Spirits were lifted. The whole class enjoyed a very positive upbeat period. It was math and the students were laughing and joyfully enjoying it all. YEAH!

CHAPTER 22:

MY CRUSADES AND TRAVELS

How blessed I was and am with all whom I met and will meet on the wonderful journey through my crusades! I truly see how foe or friend have touched me so. Whenever I think of any of you, I lift a prayer on your behalf even if you are foe.

MEXICO FIRST

You may recall friends giving me books on various people they felt I resembled? One of those was on Len Lindstrom's story. He was also coming to speak in Calgary. So I went and found that I had a passion for HIS ministry. So much so, that I went up after the tent meeting, to see what I had to do to be part of Len's team.

I was given a spiel by one of his helpers and told to put my name on a mailing list. I did so, but felt that was going to be the last I'd hear from them. I figured it was just a tactic to brush me off. Just as I figured, I got only a newsletter and nothing more.

Then a few short months later in the New Year, I got a letter directly from Len of "World Harvest Ministries" asking me to pray about it because he was inviting me to join him as a team member on a crusade to Mexico that coming Easter. Through prayer and GOD providing the flight tickets, it became clear the answer was yes.

That first trip was addictively amazing. From the minute the pilot announced our descent into Mexico City, I was instantly overcome by my HOLY SPIRIT. I actually started laughing endlessly pretty much until we got to our luggage.

A few things come to mind as I recall that first trip of many with Len's team. I was sitting on the edge of the stage off to the side the first night while Len was speaking. Near the end when it was time for us to pray for the people, I began to pray for help from the LORD.

I was feeling a bit overwhelmed; scared silly to say the least. After all, I was going from praying for one women at the front of a church to a stadium jammed with high expectations for us to usher in the LORD's amazing healing power.

There was little me off to the side on the stage. I distinctly remember crying out to the LORD to not send anyone hard, like in a wheelchair. Still praying frantically for help, I whispered "I can't do anything!"

HE answered "Exactly! That is exactly what I want you to do, NOTHING!"

Then I saw a vision of me being a large golden filigreed vase with a hole in the bottom of it. HE was pouring in, HIS anointed healing and it flowed right through me and out on to the people. I totally got what HE meant by that!

Just then, with my eyes still shut, something hard and horizontal like cold metal bumped up against my ankles as they were hanging over the edge of the stage. It caused me to jolt my eyes open in a reflex move. Oh, no, no! Guess what it was? You're right! A wheelchair! I just stared startled at the man that was pushing the wheelchair. Then my eyes were diverted, down at the man sitting in the chair.

What should I do? The pause seemed to last an eternity. Then the circle of immediate silence was broken with a BIG voice that said, "Get up and walk!" Whoa, that was different! HE spoke right through me! So this man walked! He was truly healed right there before my eyes. Everything is possible in Christ!

The man in the wheelchair looked at me as he struggled. Then he got to his feet and stood for a moment. Then he gradually appeared to have stability in his legs. So much so that he started to make little hops around, that became bigger. Everybody cheered!

Boy did I wish I had a video of it to capture that million dollar look on his face. The rest of the evening until 1:00 PM at night was a blur of healing by the LORD through me and the 18 others on the team that trip.

When a person like me starts to fully commit to doing what the LORD wants them to, it is never the same and it certainly never ever grows stale. I use to think that sitting in a front row seat watching the LORD perform was awesome enough. It does not hold a candle to being allowed to join in and be part of the action!

Sure the LORD can do all this Himself but it sure is a pleasure beyond measure to be welcomed to walk alongside in the HOLY SPIRIT. Which is exactly what happened when I went on these crusades.

Later, I began to travel on my own when Len Lindstrom quit traveling. I also carry out the same types of prayer and healing in between crusades right here at home.

It's an absolute relief to be assured HE steps in just when needed. Christians know HE died a perfect man and is the one and only man to do so. Therefore when HE gives HIS word it is golden.

The next night, I felt charged as I stood on stage off again to the side until Len had finished speaking. Then it was our turn to go out into the audience in the stadium to pray for individuals. I was just about to do so when one of the team members came staunchly over to me to scold me for attempting to upstage Len. I was appalled and shaken by his ghastly, fleshly comment. (Just an FYI: A person when "reacting in the flesh," is sinning and not operating in the HOLY SPIRIT.)

When he was finished tearing a strip off of me, I ran behind the stage all crumpled, deflated and hurt. I felt dumbfounded by what had happened, so much so that I felt I should just stay behind the stage and pray for the others in intercession. Though I did have enough sense to pray and say to my LORD that if HE wanted me out there HE would have to come and get me.

So I started to intercede in prayer for all involved. That didn't last long. Out of the blue while my eyes were shut, someone wrenched by my arm. As I popped my eyes open, the mother of one of the families that I had prayed for the night before was yanking on my arm. With a determined stride she pulled me right out from behind the stage!

According to my interpreter, she had specifically sought me out. Nothing was going to stop her from pulling me along behind her out directly into the crowd.

My gosh she was purpose driven! Not long after she plucked me from behind the stage, we were standing directly in front of her Padre. Her grandfather was wheelchair-bound. Obviously she had retrieved me to pray for him because of how she positioned me directly in front of him and motioned for me to do something.

I moved into action, kneeling down by him with my hand resting on his hand on the arm of his wheelchair. Even before we had arrived at her destination for me, I was intently praying. I continued as I kneeled there beside him. Not much time passed before I was led to get up and step back away from in front of him. Then I motioned for him to get up. I was really glad to have an interpreter come to my aid.

By now the Padre was standing in front of his wheelchair. As I saw him reach for the cane I reached out too to snatch it away before he could get a hold of it. Then I stepped even further back and beckoned for him to walk toward me. At the same time I asked the interpreter to gather the rest of the family and any around that were attentive to what was going on in our little circle near the back of the massive crowd.

I motioned to all of them to begin to pray to JESUS as I pointed to the sky and placed my hands together in a prayer formation. All to get their power of prayer to help with the healing of their grandfather. Simultaneously my interpreter kicked in beside me to share the same information complete with the copying of my sign language. That is the sign of a good interpreter, (pun intended).

This all happened in a matter of five minutes or so. All eyes were fixed on the Padre. He was attempting a shaky step forward. Everyone was looking on anxiously to see what would happen.

We were all elated to see him take another step and another, causing me to step further back. I kept beckoning him and motioning to the sky for prayer. I said in Spanish, "Mucho gracious Jesus Christo!"

Miraculously the crowd opened up behind me like the Red Sea, as I continued for some time to back up, until I bumped into a ledge. I had bumped into the stage!

There happened to be another one of our team near us and he cried out in delight to the Padre saying "Padre! Do you see how far you have come?" He motioned with his arms down the long "Red Sea" path all the way back to that lonely old vacated wheelchair!

"Your wheelchair is way back there!" Everyone erupted into cheers and clapped for joy. Once again I pointed to the sky and spoke in my Spanish, "Mucho gracious, Jesus Christo!" Then I tossed the cane up onto the stage.

After that I was swept away into the crowd to continue my job, praying for more of the same. This went on way into the night until after midnight. I finally had a second to look out over the little crowd that had formed around me. I tried to spot any others on our team.

That is when I discovered something rather startling! They were all gone! Here I was in a strange land with no familiar face around. I did not even know where my hotel was, nor its name! I really felt stupid at that moment in time but I learned a valuable lesson!

As soon as I wrote "stupid" here I regretted it, but I left it in to bring home a spur-of-the-moment point. Please don't ever tell yourself that you are stupid or think that of yourself. There truly is no good that comes of the negativity that we as individuals plague ourselves with.

Because I was with a team, it didn't seem necessary to even need the address of the hotel, so I wasn't actually being "stupid." There were three vans. Everyone assumed that I was in the other van but I was stranded back at the stadium all alone.

I ventured toward the exit where the vans had been parked. Just as I was about to round the corner I spotted a truckload of policemen. I recoiled right back around the corner so as not to be seen by them. In many countries the police are not the safest to be with. That only left me the option of returning to the stage to see if I could find help.

As I rounded the next corner, I literally bumped right into my interpreter. She said, "Karen, you're still here!"

She knew of my hotel and would be able to get me back to it and my team. YEAH! Thank Heavens GOD kept track of me and kept me safe! That sure was not the last time HE saved me from potential harm nor the first.

FURTHER CRUSADES

It is interesting, how HE was already preparing me long before November of 1996 and into 1997 and on for a life such as this. I seemed to handle the heat well in tropical countries. I had no problem adapting to the culture and to the kind of food I would be eating. And as a side note, the nice thing about eating strange entrees, is that it makes a hamburger back here look like a steak!

I went on a number of other crusades. I travelled to Mexico a second time. In between I went to Nicaragua and Guatemala. The last crusade I went on with Len to Nepal was in 1999, at Easter break.

By that time in my spiritual walk I was getting visions a great deal of the time. We were having trouble finding an appropriate stadium. Due to an election looming, the authorities were putting pressure on us. In fact we wanted to go and stand beside the Christians that were being beaten by clubs with barbs on them.

Our Pastor liaison insisted that we stay put in our hotel room; so we did. We stayed and prayed. It was memorable in the sense that for the first time ever, I "SWEATED" when I prayed. It wasn't blood, but not unlike JESUS.

Though our Christian friends remained passive, the police still tried to exacerbate things in hopes of inciting a riot. Although 79 of them got hurt and taken to a hospital, the Christians still remained passive and at peace.

My vision showed me where I thought the crusade was going to be held. I saw high solid walls with huge angels at each entrance guarding and brushing off any evil attached to those coming in. There were people climbing up trees, and standing on buildings, and sitting on windows to take in the crusade. Sure enough where we held it looked just like that!

In just a few short years from 1997 to '99 I had grown so much in the LORD. Before I even left my marriage, the LORD had been prodding me to be BOLDER for HIM. It seemed like once I left my marriage HE moved me into macho speed with the gifts HE instilled in me.

TO DIE FOR

Out of all the crusades that I went on with Len Lindstrom's teams, I think I enjoyed the Nepal trip the most. It was the most spiritual of them all. There were only three of us on his team this time besides himself, and two camera men. I am still friends good with my teammates. One of the team has been a dear friend that has taken me into her home on numerous occasions.

A couple of things occurred even before we arrived in Nepal. One of those things happened just to me. The other happened to all three of us but at first we didn't know that. I had asked the LORD some time before going to Nepal to allow me to pray as I slept. Years ago I was often awakened in the middle of the night, to pray through the night. Sometimes it lasted an hour or so. Other times I may have been kept up all night in intercession.

At some point this stopped and I was no longer required to get up in the middle of the night to pray. So I got thinking, "Why not use me in my sleep to pray, LORD?" Of course, how would I ever really know if I was or not?

This is where Nepal answers that question. The other women on the team was my roommate. While in Nepal, the LORD woke her up in the middle of the night to pray. When she woke up she told me that before she went up on the roof to pray, she had stopped by my cot for a short time to ensure that I would be okay.

It turns out that I had my hands in the air. Yet I was sound asleep. I was so glad that she shared with me what she saw. It was then that I knew the LORD was using me in that way.

The other occurrence happened to all of us unbeknownst to each other. We all were asked by GOD if we would die for HIM. This was divulged in the hotel room while praying in intercession for the Nepalese who were being accosted by the police.

The lone male member of our threesome team mentioned in our prayer time together that the LORD had asked him if he would die for HIM. OMG! The very second that he said that my roommate and I, one after the other, spoke up and said that the same thing had happened to us!

We were all asked by God if we would die for HIM before we even left for Nepal! I began to wonder if that was what was going to happen to us while there. Would we be dying for HIM? That pretty much was the silent thought in that room after all of us shared what HE asked us and what our replies were.

I prefer only to share what my answer was to the question that GOD posed to each of us. I told them that I answered with "maybe." That I honestly didn't know for sure if I could die for

HIM. To me that seems to be something that I would have to think about for a longer period of time, than just being asked out of the blue like that. Mind you it remained on my conscience long after getting home from Nepal.

Could I actually die for HIM? Over the years since 1999 after Nepal, I came to the realization that I could die for HIM. Of course in my little chicken way, I request that I die fast and preferably from the back! Otherwise, could I die in my sleep or better yet be raptured, Lord? I have always set about making a difference in my corner of the world, so dying for HIM would make a difference.

Hence, I travelled to Israel in 2005 with the intention of dying for HIM. I wanted to be an organ Donor too, to donate all the parts that were needed. So that got me thinking that if I was walking this tight rope of spirituality anyway, what would be the best possible way to leave while doing the most for HIM? Since I have no family, why not make my spiritual walk the ultimate in being worthwhile by allowing myself to die for HIM?

That is how I came to my conclusion about life and death. Going on the Mercy Ship helped me make this decision regarding my death. When going on the ship I had to sign a form stating I was willing to be buried at sea. Once I had done that it only seemed practical to make the organ donor decision next.

It makes sense to share the body God has given me with others after my earthly death, as I sure won't need this body anymore. I will get a new one!

EVIL PLOY

In Nepal, I didn't care to go shopping. However, my roommate wanted to get something for her husband. We were supposed to go out in pairs or as a group so I went with her. That made sense, if for no other reason than to find our way back. There was rarely a straight street to direct us back.

In one particular shop, the owner relentlessly hounded me to buy a drum I picked up to look at while waiting for my roommate. He was so adamant that I bought it for a buck just to get him to leave me alone. I am serious about the pressure he put on me, because when I bought it I had already left the shop and was half a block away with him trailing along behind me still badgering me to buy it.

I may know the reason why such pressure. There are times when black magic gets in the way to try to undermine our walk with the LORD. This drum might have had something to do with it. Christians are confronted with Black Magic in more ways than one.

I got all the way back home to Canada with my Drum. I had a good friend, now in Heaven, who was very proficient at discerning evil spirits. She clued me into more about that drum that I did not want to hear. She sensed a strong evil presence, a Spirit of Death coming from the drum, especially when I played it!

The question I will never know the answer to is: did that store-clerk know this, and is that is why he hounded me to no end to take that drum? Or was he a typical peddler?

SPEAKING OF EVIL

The drum wasn't the only thing. The same spirit was on a few Estate Sale items that I picked up at a garage sale some time ago. My friend and I gathered up all the things we felt were culprits and went and burned them at a campsite so as not to let such spirits go anywhere else to potentially cause trouble elsewhere.

There were a couple of items in that Estate Sale that were too big or too important to burn. One was a hide-a-bed. The other was actually an old special print Bible I had been looking for. Now I absolutely refused to burn a Bible. Plus, in my opinion that is a ruse. Who more than Satan would love a Christian to burn a Bible. Umm? Well I was certainly not about to help him out!

There are ways around this problem regarding evil. In the case of the Bible, we prayed off that spirit and cleansed it with further prayer.

Evil can appear in many forms. Very subtle forms, hard to detect, and more obvious forms that one can spot even with the naked eye. Like in Mali, where sorcery signs were visibly placed around the small church we met at.

Once we came across a section of the market place in Bamako, Mali where items for Black Magic were sold. Medicine Men, Shamans and others would purchase items to use in their medicine, potions and concoctions. Items like bats' wings, snakes and snake skins, teeth, internal organs, skulls, powders of sorts and so on were displayed.

I asked to take a picture and the guy manning the specific booth selling these wares seemed to not mind. Once the picture was taken, however, he jumped down from his seat and came right for me and my camera! He had a hold of my arm and tried to grab the camera out of my hand by twisting my arm and forcing me to let go of it.

I held firm and stood my ground as I prayed for the violence to cease in the name of JESUS CHRIST!

The Engineer that was with me reached into the middle of things at the time I was praying off this eruption. Now the guy had turned his focus on him. My camera and I were released.

I continued to pray but felt the LORD wanted me to start praying peace and blessings over this mean-looking brute of a man. He was kind of man that lifts weights, and could be a Bouncer in a bar.

At once my prayers were answered, for his look of rage turned soft and a slight smile came over his face. That is when he let go and left us alone to walk away safe.

A crowd had developed, which is no surprise. Anything draws a crowd when it looks as if something is up. Once we started walking away, we were accosted by the crowd wanting to know how we got away so easily like that. They seemed in awe and rather excited to find out how.

All I could say was, whether the Engineer translated that into Bambra for me or not, that GOD did it. I think I pointed to the sky as well.

FUNNY, HOW WE PERCEIVE THINGS

The Pastor I lived with in Mali when I was going on mission trips on my own referred to us "White Women" as lazy. Please don't take offense. The only reason he said that is that he did not have sufficient knowledge to know better.

That right there is most likely the number one reason differences occur between people in the first place. What a shame that is!

Once I explained the reason we appear lazy, he no longer saw us that way. My answer to that was obvious.

Take for example, when I would scrub the laundry with his wife she would wash circles around me. This was all due to my inability to move as fast as them in such tropical heat. Mali is just a few miles from the Equator and on the edge of the Sahara Desert.

Another thing he made comments on was how we used so many creams and ointments in Canada. Again I conclude it was due to the climate in America/Canada. In tropical countries I found I could get by without using all that gobble-de-gook we need to use in the colder and extremely dry climate in Alberta.

I am bring this up to reveal a major revelation I got from just such comments. This is called the "Spirit of Judgement," a universal viewpoint that blankets all cultures regardless of race, skin colour, or geographical location. It could very well be the root of prejudice and war.

To judge before knowing anything about someone or something is to put an automatic wedge between us. That can grow into estrangement and conflict between individuals or whole countries, for that matter.

The LORD showed me a vision at one point where I looked down from Heaven and saw all kinds of people all over the world conversing with each other in an angry way and when they did so there was a big wedge stuck between them. HE then gave me the assignment to pray for removal of these hindering wedges.

It worked too, because I knew some of the people I was asked to pray for personally. Some were couples, or siblings in the throes of divorce or becoming estranged toward each other. I found myself plucking out the wedges. So when I went to pray in tongues over these situations in peoples' lives I was seeing behaviour changes, whereby these very same people were coming together and breaking down their walls.

I was also given a follow-up vision that affirmed my real life findings. The second vision showed the same people. Only this time I could see the wedges being plucked out as a result of all of the prayers. Amen!

VANITY EVERYWHERE

I discovered that judgements and vain habits are universal. It does not matter where you live or what culture you are in. You will have some form of pride and vanity prevail. We all, whether it be woman-kind or man-kind as a whole, seek the same thing but go about it in a different way.

This is maybe ingrained in each of us to some degree or another. The point is that people want to look good, no matter where they live on the planet. It is just sought out differently in different parts of the world.

In North America we have been convinced in some way or another that in order to look good, beautiful or gorgeous women must have that "Barbie Doll" look. We must stay skinny. Anorexia is on the increase in teenage girls.

On the other hand, vanity is established in an entirely different way elsewhere. In Africa, the way a women looks good is if she has a large butt, or "Booty" as it has been labeled. They will go to great lengths to enlarge their butt for the same purpose. They will even use injections to create a larger than life buttocks.

Vanity seems to be universal. So you see both are striving for the same thing. Only different tactics are used to seek it, with entirely different ideas as to what is beautiful. It is sought out almost at any cost, whether rich or poor, you could even be obsessed by it. Plastic surgery used to be just a Hollywood thing, but not anymore!

HITCHHIKING

The first time I hitchhiked I wanted to catch a ride out to the local ski hill in Camrose. In those days, it really did not seem to be a big deal as far as scariness went, and hitchhiking was totally acceptable.

There was an ongoing policy that anyone standing on the edge of the road to the ski hill with a pair of skis would be given a ride. So my mom would drop my sister and me at the road. I do not remember hitchhiking much, most of the time I caught rides with friends.

I hitchhiked was when I was attending the University of Alberta. Again it seemed normal due to the fact there was a bus strike on, and everyone was encouraged to pick anyone up they saw hitchhiking by the side of the road heading to work.

Since I worked at the Strathcona Pool while attending school I had to hitch to get to work. I actually found that I got to work faster than when I took the buses. So I didn't mind how long the Bus Strike lasted!

I hitchhiked another time at university because I needed to get back home quickly. It was winter time. I remember that because I had my ski toque on and my hair all up underneath the toque. My hair at the time was down to my waist.

So I was standing hitchhiking, just outside and down a bit from the Army and Navy store on White Avenue in Edmonton. No one seemed to even notice me, let alone stop and give me a ride, even though it was wintertime. I guess no one expected someone to be standing outside a store hitchhiking.

Anyway, I thought to myself, "Enough of this nonsense!" So I just took my toque off and shook my hair loose to cascade over my shoulders, sliding down over my ski jacket to my waist.

I heard a Screech! Well, actually more like a slide to a stop by tires on wet pavement scattering the pea-gravel. A guy in a pickup truck slid to a stop just beside me.

As it turns out he was heading out of town too and could give me a ride to the overpass at the Ponoka turnoff on the highway. However, when we got to the overpass he turned off the highway and headed right into the town. What a gentleman! He dropped me right off at my parent's store.

Do you know what a Leroy Slush Turn is? When he pulled over outside of the Army and Navy Store to give me that ride home, we ended up stuck in traffic. So he said, "Excuse me. I hope you don't mind if a do a Leroy Slush Turn here?" Before I could even ask what that was, he was doing it!

He simply said, "Watch this." As he drove up onto the city sidewalk some 70 to 100 feet or so, where he reached the alleyway to turn into and off we went. Until we got on to 104th St. to head out of town. So now you and I both know what a Leroy Slush Turn is!

I remember another time I hitchhiked, but much later after my divorce. I was down in Lethbridge when Alfred that owns Alfred Chev-Olds ran into me. He asked if and whenever I want to sell my Suburban to let him know.

I was short of money and still without money from my divorce settlement, so I said "Sure." So it was a deal, but how was I to get back to Calgary? So I was hitchhiking again!

When the guy that gave me a ride let me off I wanted to give him what money I had. Other than the certified cheque for my Suburban, I only had a handful of change. So I dug all of it out and gave it to him with a verse from the Bible that says, "... you have just entertained an angel unawares" (Hebrews 13:2) and I prayed a blessing over him.

Whenever I do that, if prompted to by the Lord, I will state what a blessing really is. It doesn't just mean a glib comment like, "How's the weather for you?" It is way more than that! A "blessing" is actually a prayer lifted on one's behalf by another to ask the LORD for a specific blessing to come their way as soon as possible in order to know that the prayer was heard and delivered.

Then we are all blessed and the LORD is glorified! The difficult thing is that I do not often get to witness their blessing because I have prayed it for someone and then left. Therefore I do not see the glorious outcome!

A friend and I hitchhiked in Israel too. We had stayed way up the road off the highway at a Hostel. On our way down we couldn't decide whether to go back or keep on going on the highway. My friend went on ahead down the road to the highway in hopes of catching the bus for us.

I didn't want to us to miss the only bus back. So I turned around and stuck my thumb out at the first car to come along. As it turns out the guy was going all the way to Tel Aviv. As I hopped in I asked if we could pick up my friend just up ahead around the corner. It was no problem so all we off went to Tel Aviv.

I have hitchhiked as recently as last year. I have had no car for a while so I was taking the bus. Unfortunately the bus outside our complex is horribly unpredictable. As a result, I got so that I would stand in the entrance to our complex and hitchhike with anyone coming out of the courtyard.

The advantage I had was that there were three nearby C-Train stops. That usually meant that I could very easily catch a ride to any one of those stations without it being of any inconvenience to anyone. Every time I prayed I'd catch a ride I would.

PICKING UP HITCHHIKERS

Just so you know, I do not pick up hitchhikers unless GOD tells me to. Consequently, every time I have given someone a ride, it has been GOD given. I know almost right away that it was meant to be.

I recall one that was hilarious! I was coming back from Kamloops with two good friends when the Spirit of Laughter ensued as I was driving. Up ahead was a young guy that I felt the LORD wanted me to pick up and give a ride to. When he got in the car behind me, I was still laughing and could barely stop enough to say "Hi." I could only get a little wave out to him. My friends chuckled. They explained to him, as he stared at me and my laughing, that I actually am a safer driver when in the Spirit.

We explained also what the Spirit was for the hiker's curious mind. When we came up to the entrance to his driveway to let him out, he looked at me and thanked me. He said that I had shown him Christ was real and that it had restored his faith.

He said that he was back-slider until then and he wanted a real Christ and that I gave that to him. It was awesome to see that my laugher had such a purpose. After all, I had been asking GOD why I was still laughing once the guy got into the car. Now I knew. The hitchhiker needed to see Christ in action and alive in someone in order have his faith won back. GOD has HIS ways, beyond our understanding.

Here is another time. This story was astounding! A male hitchhiker shared was heading back to Toronto and wondered if I could drop him off at a big truck stop. We chatted all the way into Calgary. When I pulled into the truck stop, he shared that he always wanted to ride in one of those, as he pointed toward a MacCosham Van-lines truck, because they were big semi-trucks and they were orange.

Before he got out I stopped him to pray that he would get a ride from the second person he asked. And that it would be with a guy driving one of those big orange trucks. And that the driver would be able to take him all the way to Toronto where he was heading.

You are bound to believe by now what happened next! The way this book has been unfolding, you can pretty much guess he did get that ride I prayed for him to get! Yes sirree!

I excused myself to the washroom where I stayed and prayed for a while. When I came out the young hitchhiker rushed up to me all bug-eyed and as excited as a Mexican Jumping Bean. He got the ride! He kept saying to me. "You're an angel! You're an angel!"

I kept replying back that "It wasn't me. It was the Big Guy in the sky, not me," as I pointed upward with a glance in that direction to accompany it. I sure hope wherever that guy is today that he has not forgotten about what the LORD did for him.

A STAB WOUND

I picked up another guy in the pouring rain one time on my way to Lethbridge in a brand-new rental car. I was coming up to the overpass at the 22X on the south end of the city and there he was under the overpass. The LORD told me to pick him up. I retaliated with "But LORD did you see what he looks like and that stab wound he has on his hand. I know it is a stab wound LORD. I am pretty sure it is a stab wound. I will pick him up if you say so but he looks like one of those terrorists I have seen on TV!"

So I pulled up to give him a ride. He was more shocked than I was at who was picking him up. In shock he said, "Aren't you afraid I will stab you and take your car and everything?" Now this has to be GOD talking because I am pretty sure I couldn't come up with it myself. I retorted right back at him as I stared straight into his eyes and said, "If you do, I will go to Heaven where I want to be and you will have to RECKON with GOD!"

As soon as I said GOD, he totally changed and melted into this inquisitive kid eager to climb into the seat beside me and hear all I had to say about GOD.

For as soon as he settled in, he said, "Tell me everything you know about HIM. I enrolled in Philosophy at university to find out about GOD, but quit in disappointment because I learned nothing about GOD."

So I answered all his questions on GOD all the way to Lethbridge where I dropped him at a place that I knew would take good care of him. I gave him my Bible and we prayed and talked over the Sinner's Prayer before I dropped him off at a safe place, Victory Church's Street Stop that I told him would take good care of him.

HERMITAGE

I like to do a hermitage every once in a while. I prefer to retreat to either Kings Fold just west of the city in the Foothills or to someone's cabin or boat. I was on my way out to Port Moody on the west coast where I would stay on a 75 foot sail boat for a week, away from many of civilization's distractions.

I stayed over with friends along the way into Port Moody then Vancouver and finally Comox on the island where a friend from the Mexico trip lived. One friend was a Christian singer, another was the secretary with the office of Prayer Canada.

I loved being in that sail boat all by myself, especially since it rained most of the time. I got a lot of praying and reading accomplished. It was the time alone with GOD that I looked forward to. One of the books I focused in on besides the Bible, was one of Watchman Nee's books, *The Normal Christian Life*.

I surprisingly learned a great deal from the Blue Heron outside my porthole on those rainy days. He illustrated patience and endurance. These are two traits I wanted to ingrain in myself on that hermitage. So thanks Blue Heron!

I ended up in what I called a "Crack House" of all things in Vancouver. I was supposed to stay with a sports agent friend of mine. I was really looking forward to it too. No such luck though. It turned out he had something else in mind for me when I was to stay there.

So at the very last minute and in the late evening I was looking for somewhere else to stay. Other friends were not home so I headed to the hostel. They were booked completely up. However, I guess I had the same name as someone else that had booked, and I got their bed.

The only clue to this came in the middle of the night when others came in and one peered at me in the bunk bed. I vaguely heard her say, "Someone is in my bed!" Therefore that was the only night I could stay there.

Another girl and I were in the same predicament, so we joined together to find a place. Our only choices were a "wino" hotel and a Crack House. I called it the Wino Hotel because it was full of old men scattered randomly on the staircase in the entrance with the brown paper bag syndrome, if you get the picture?

We went for the Crack House. The reason I nicknamed it is that there was no lobby. You had to ring a buzzer and a wooden window would open up soon after to a little peep hole with a voice on the other side. The price was right so we took it.

You will not believe the time I had. It was on the bad end of town, I guess, because even the firemen I visited told me to get the heck out of there! Now does that fill you in enough as to the environment enveloping me? Let's just call it an unusual adventure that is off the beaten track.

There was good in it. I got to brush up on my Japanese with the two guys next door that we shared our kitchen with. In fact they were the ones that got me interested in drinking green tea.

At night the neon sign outside flashed on and off as prostitutes lined the narrow sidewalk below. Mornings were filled with derelicts lining up along the sidewalk waiting for the soup kitchen down below on the street to open.

One morning when I was heading out, I got an eye full. Just outside my door was a prostitute rooting through another older woman's shopping cart full of various clothes with blouses hung around the outside of the cart. Something caught the prostitute's eye in the cart, so she stripped right there in broad daylight, to try it on! I walked by her without as much as a bat of an eye. Very colourful neighbourhood!

While I waited for my friends to get back in town, I spent the next couple of days checking out Gastown. Not a dull moment was had. I met a prostitute that I took out for lunch. After a prayer and best wishes, the prostitute and I said goodbye

That is when the owner of the restaurant came out and walked with me along the shops. After a while he treated me to supper. He really was pretty nice and wanted to know more about the Lord. He actually wanted to establish a closer relationship with the Lord.

On our date, he took me to an Iranian night club for dinner and dancing. It was very different and very interesting! The food was great!

The dancing was the most unusual type of dancing I have ever experienced. I stood in the center of a circle of young handsome guys and they took turns doing the dancing around me to impress me. It reminded me of animals prancing around the female to win her over. I must admit they made me feel like a Queen!

He wanted me to stay and meet his parents. Then he proposed to me of all things! When he started in on pressing me with the "M" word, I was glad to be leaving town the next day.

INVITED TO AUSTRALIA

In 1999, I had gotten involved in a two to three week long stint volunteering for the Police and Fire Games. They are an even bigger event than the Olympics. They even have Canine Events. I took the time off from teaching to get involved, and am I glad that I did. It was one of the most enjoyable experiences of my life.

I had the good fortune to host 31 VIP Policemen from Australia. I spent almost every waking minute with them. Since they were a public relations show band, they had gigs every night to put on. So I attended all their performances with them.

They would often play late into the night, and then I would have to get up fairly early to go over their schedule for the next day and help make contacts for them to put on more shows. Sometimes they would have three shows in a day! It was very time consuming but totally worth it! They even stayed after the games and performed at pancake breakfasts for the Calgary Stampede.

Heehaw! They even wrote a song about me. They called it, "The Lady in Red," because when they first met me at the airport I wore my red riding jacket and white Stetson cowboy hat. I remember passing out Canadian pins and maple sugar candies. Later that year they invited me to Australia for the Christmas Holidays. So I went again to stay with them in their home land.

WOW, good on-yah mate! I sure would have stayed in Australia if I had met a handsome rich man. I loved petting a Wombat, Koala Bears, Kangaroos and some little Fairy Penguins. They were so adorable! The first three were all in a nature preserve where we could walk through and pet some of them.

Someday I might go back and visit them again as well as friends I have in Perth. I would still like to see the Great Barrier Reef. Of course I made sure that I swam in the Pacific Ocean.

After the Police and Fire games that summer I prepared for the trip the LORD set up for me. The one where HE said not to take anything with me nor plan a specific route or make reservations.

I did follow HIS orders, only I could not help but take some clothes. I found that I really didn't need them much, even though I fudged a bit and did.

That road trip was phenomenal! The miracles that occurred were liberating and after that I really think I could have gone anywhere in the world and not taken a thing. I met so many wonderful people and stayed at some out of the ordinary, remarkable places. I made no reservations and traveled by stopping where I felt the LORD was telling me to stop and stay. Hence my "Wing it Holiday!"

A "WING IT" HOLIDAY

You may not believe it, but I found non-Christians (unless some of them were actually ANGELS?) on the trip to be the more hospitable than the Christians that I was visited along the way. It had a lot to do with the way the Lord wanted me to travel. He did not want me to plan or book ahead. I was to WING IT and not even take clothes.

I was to stay however long the LORD said to stay. The more ill-at-ease I felt, the shorter the stay. In general my friends welcomed me with open arms. It just surprised me that some "Christians" could be so unwelcoming. That was behaviour I naively thought Christians would be exempt from.

I went full circle through BC via the Crowsnest pass, stopping over in Kimberley, Cranbrook, Kelowna, Agassi, Chilliwack and Abbotsford before hitting Vancouver. Then I headed across the border to Bellingham, and Portland, crossing back into Canada at Caraway, Alberta, to make sure I stopped in Lethbridge.

While in Cranbrook, I loaded up on some books to bring back and pass out. They were by GOD written by the hand of George Warnock. He actually is GOD's stenographer and will get whole books in his head that the LORD has given him to write. Then someone helps him publish them so that he can give them away rather than sell them. I feel privileged to get any of his books and have passed them out just as freely. I am sure you can look him up online and get his books free.

While I was in Kelowna, I stayed with an artist friend and he is led in the same way. He paints massive pictures that the LORD tells him to paint. I had a chance also to visit Len Lindstrom from "World Harvest Ministries" and I spent a few days there helping preview and catalogue lots of their camera footage.

At the same time I was able to get a tape of my own of the trips I had taken with Len. Then I travelled on to Bellingham, Washington, Seattle and Portland where I would be able to visit some more firemen that I had met at the Police and Fire Games. I also wanted to reconnect with friends I had met at a Singles Retreat in Hungry Horse, Montana that I had not seen since 1995.

My friend in Kellogg was blind and had a Seeing Eye Dog. When I stayed overnight, the dog snuck into my room during the night to stay by my bed. As a Seeing Eye Dog he really is not supposed to do such a treasonous thing. OOPS! I noticed he did scamper back early in the morning to where he truly was to be stationed, so as not to be missed. I miss him!

FLAT TIRE ANSWERS PRAYER

Back on the road again, I chose to cut across country to Polson, Montana in order to make it to Kalispell before dark where I hoped to stay with a couple that were both colleagues and Christian counsellors. They lived on the lakefront and I really was looking forward to a couple of days of swimming and simply laying in the sun.

I was told the road was not a well-travelled road. It was paved but very narrow, with no shoulders nor any real main stops along the way. On top of that, I was having trouble along the way with my credit card not being accepted in some ATM machines. I was caught off guard without cash.

On my way across country it poured rain. I did not mind so much as I was on the road anyway and my whole trip had been blessed with sunshine!

I did have an answer to prayer by having a flat tire! Yes a flat tire answered my prayers! I had prayed long before this trip was even a thought, that I would never have a flat for fear of my car going out of control. "No blowout, Lord" I asked, and if I were to have one that I would be able to maintain control of the car on the road.

And HE did do just that! I was driving along around a bend in the road when I saw a piece of timber that most likely had fallen off of a logging truck. In order to miss it I had to straddle it. A piece must have caught underneath and impaled my rear passenger tire.

Here is where my prayer got answered. I didn't even notice the flat at all. It was so smooth that I wasn't even sure that I had one. I only felt a slight vibrating at the wheel which prompted me to pull over to see.

A grave situation occurred while I was trying to change my tire! I could not budge one bolt on the wheel. Now what was I going to do, Lord? Just as I was pondering in prayer what to do next, a man appeared, standing beside me asking if he could help.

You bet! So he proceeded to change the tire while I held an umbrella over him.

After he finished he revealed to me that while there was a town not far ahead, it had no gas station nor much of anything to fix my tire. There was another town further on but nothing there would be open by the time I got there. As he told me I gave him a dry shirt before he disappeared almost as quickly as he appeared.

Slowly proceeding on my way, I thanked the Lord more than ever for that man's help. I was pretty sure that he was an angel sent to take care of me. Having lost a fair bit of time, I decided I would stay at the next town he mentioned rather than drive on a spare in the rain.

IN PARADISE

The man was right. There were no services or store or hotel or church or anything of that nature in the town, only a saloon. I went in to inquire about a service station, and a man at the bar piped up and said that he knew the owner and mechanic of the service station in the town further on.

He said that he would phone ahead to see if the service station would stay open if I went on ahead to get them to repair my regular tire.

"Okay LORD," I prayed, "You decide if I go on or not." No such luck, the shop mechanic must have gone home early. As I thanked the man at the bar and turned around to thank the bartender for the quarter for the phone, they invited me to stay and party since it was too wet to plough! Again I thanked them and went back to my car. I pulled out and drove around the block out of sight and pulled over to pray in the rain.

Since I couldn't find a church, I felt prompted to drive around the one block once again and I prayed to find a little old lady's place. I came up to two different houses a couple of doors apart.

How did I know they were little old lady's places? I didn't actually. I just looked at each house closely to determine to what degree they were rundown. Yet kept. Looking like just a few little things needed fixing.

Once I picked the house, I knocked. No one came to the door. I didn't understand because the door was ajar. The lights were all on.

Just as I was about to walk away, I heard a meek "Hello." So I turned back to reply with the same. She wasn't really old, maybe in her early 70's, and she was in a wheelchair.

I explained my situation, and asked by any chance if I could stay the night and I would pay her whatever lodging at a hotel might be. She welcomed me in whole- heartedly.

She was so welcoming that I cried as she offered me something to eat. She said "You must be tired and starving. So help yourself to something from the fridge. I have some Cordon Bleu, Caesar Salad, baked potatoes with chives and sour cream!" OMG! Better than a restaurant!

That is why I started crying because I told her "I am so overwhelmed I just can't raid your fridge like that!" I hadn't eaten as well before as I did that night. I hadn't even had Cordon Bleu before! I must say it was delicious.

But wait! It didn't stop there. She insisted that I take a bath in her jet tub.

Ohhhh, now that was nice! I felt like I was in a Spa Resort. Only it was a Little Ole Lady's house in a little hamlet. Now get this, this is priceless, the place was called "Paradise!" I had a flat tire and ended up in Paradise because of it. Pretty good deal I thought. Thanks LORD!

After my soak and massage time we got into a really good discussion that went well into the night. To no surprise, we got on the subject of the LORD. Believe it or not within a short period of time, like about thirty or forty minutes, I knew that I was supposed to be there.

She mentioned something about the Toronto Airport Church. Since I knew a bit about it, she wanted to know all about them. Apparently her daughter, I think it was, went there.

She actually thought her daughter was in some sort of cult. I assured her that it was nothing like that at all. It was a Born Again Spirit-Filled Church that just happened to have an anointing for healing. People flocked there from miles around and lined up to get in to be seen.

I actually went there myself on my way to Mali to live and minister. I had a layover there near the Toronto airport so I made an effort to go and get a blessing from them before flying out to Africa. Guess who I was paired up with for that prayer? Two people from Africa, and one that had ministered there! I thought that was providence.

As we talked into the night, her fears were dismissed. She was so thankful to have had me stay there and tell her all about that church.

I really felt that I wanted to paint a little angel somewhere in her house for her. When I was married I liked to paint little angels in every room in our home. I had an angel that was reading and soaking her feet in the kitchen. Another was having tea in the living room, another was asleep in one of the bedrooms.

Well lo and behold, I got to! The next morning when I was finishing breakfast, she asked me if I wouldn't mind painting something for her on one of her walls. Little did she know that I wanted to do that, but of course had never mentioned it!

So I went to work on painting a little angel over the light switch in her library. The angel was seated, curled up in a wing-backed chair reading a book. As I was going to leave, I wanted to get her address to send her some money or a cheque for my stay. She would not hear of it. In fact she wanted to give me some money.

As much as I protested she countered, so it was a matter of me giving into her desire to give me some money or I might still be there dickering with her! Once I got to the next town to fix my tire, I found out that the money she had given me was the exact amount I needed to pay for the tire. Wow!

To summarize, it turned out to be a bomb with my friends in Kalispell. They actually were annoyed that I was not making reservations ahead along the way. I felt uncomfortable staying there and only visited for a short time before I moved on.

I should have turned around and stayed longer with that sweet, sweet lady in Paradise! It is at time like that I realize that "what is meant to be will be."

Up until my divorce I really did need to rely much on others. Since then, I am still learning to ask for help. I am just not clear at times on who to ask. I have learned to accept good things when they come my way because they are meant to be. Like the money I didn't want to take, that ended up being the exact amount I needed to fix my tire.

ELECTRIFIED

I was driving to Medicine Hat to minister and visit my good friend. Remember the roommate I got to know on Len Lindstrom's Crusade to Nepal?

All of a sudden I was spinning 530 degrees in the middle of the Trans-Canada highway! On the last spin I straightened out, only now I was going backwards down the highway.

I knew I couldn't keep going that way at a 112 km. an hour, with traffic coming right at me. My rear wheel was just about to hit the edge of the ditch. I figured that my best bet would be to turn into the ditch and get facing the right way. I hoped that I could just keep on going right back up on to the highway and on course again.

The plan would have worked except for one teeny-weeny thing in the way. The one and only railroad track on the entire Trans-Canada highway between Medicine Hat and Calgary was right there in front of me and I was about to crash right into it.

So I made a quick switch to "Plan Z": I turned sharply in towards the field. Thank Heavens there was no fence line, so I thought that it should work.

Unfortunately I had another problem to contend with. There was just enough of a skiff of snow in the ditch to create slippery slimy conditions. As much as I tried to aim for the field, there was one obstacle right in the way.

A main line power pole just would not get out of the way! My car headed straight toward it. Boom! Smack in the middle of the car I hit the pole straight on! OUCH!

Now here is the miraculous part. As I was careening straight for the power pole I prayed quickly to the LORD to keep me from getting hurt. Everything had gone into slow-motion. I hit that pole dead on. I took it right out.

Here is the incredible part! It seemed like I was in a big marshmallow cloud and I felt no impact whatsoever. Keep in mind my car was too old to have any airbags. Yet I still hit the steering wheel as if it was a cushion!

The other major miracle was the power pole and what it did! I saw it break off, lift up and move over to fall down beside the car. Not on the car. I even asked the policeman while sitting in his car waiting for the electrician to come and shut down the power. I asked him what direction a power pole falls when one drives right smack into one straight on? He said that they fall straight over and on top of the car that hit them. Making them an instant pancake. So I told him what I saw.

The electrician came to the car all bug-eyed and stared right at me. He told me that I was a lucky lady for I should be dead! Fried by the electricity on the ground.

I really was on a Spiritual HIGH. I realized so very much that the LORD was looking out for me, big time! Again! The more the evening wore on the more I fell into deep, drunken laughter as the joy of the LORD came over me.

First when I stepped out of my car on to the wet ground and didn't get electrocuted I was protected. Six people with cell phones came running to me in the ditch as I sat on the seat of my car with my feet outside on the ground. Again, not electrified and without a cell phone!

I had two hours with the policeman in his car while we waited for the electrician and the tow truck. In that two hours we talked about GOD and how he cares for us and loves us so very much! He seemed to have a lot of questions. It was a great time well spent as we waited.

Once all had been sorted out with my car, the policeman drove me into Bassano and he bought me a bus ticket back to Calgary. Then he called a friend, a pastor he knew, to come to the cafe and pick me up to take me home to his place for supper to wait for the Greyhound bus to arrive. I was on such a high with the LORD that I was going around in the cafe telling everyone there that I should be dead but HE saved me! (Pointing to the sky.)

At the Pastor's home I also shared how HE took care of me during the accident. Boy was the LORD being glorified that evening! Amen!

Finally the Greyhound came. I prayed blessings over all of them before I left and then boarded the bus back to Calgary. When getting on the bus I just had to tell the driver that, "I should be dead."

I sat up at the front and began to laugh all over again. I did not know what to say to the bus driver so I just kept telling him, "I am so happy that I am not dead, "and "I am not drunk. Just real, real, happy to be alive and totally fine!"

I couldn't very well tell him I was drunk in the Spirit of the LORD. Even a lot of Christians don't entirely understand what that means. So I am sure the poor bus driver wouldn't be able to swallow that either. He seemed to be okay with what I gave him for an explanation so I left it at that.

The policeman had let me make a few long distance calls for free, to a couple of friends that I could count on to come and pick me up. I was able to reach one of them, and she said that she could pick me up and to call when I got to Calgary.

Once at the bus depot, I headed towards a pay phone to call her. Realizing that I had no change on me, I prayed there would be enough money in the phone for me to call. Sure enough, there was and my friend was pulling up in no time.

As I approached her car to get in, she said, "OMG! You're glowing all over, Karen!" I could not see it myself but it sure did not surprise me given the spiritual state I was resting in. It made me think of Moses.

Later when looking at other cars, I came across a red Del Sol.

My good friend in Medicine Hat said she had a vision of me driving a little red sports car. She did not know that was the car the Lord told me I could have. I was going to be practical and buy the Taurus because I did not think HE wanted me to get the sportier car. Not so though.

CONVERTIBLE HAT

This is a story that I used to share with high school students about following your dreams and passions. You see, I saw a perfect, "convertible hat" so I bought it as my first step toward getting a convertible.

The LORD reminded me of something that I commented on some time before I even saw this Del Sol for sale. Before I even needed to buy a car. I recall way back one time, in one of my glorious states of worship, when I was raising my hands up to praise HIM and kept hitting the roof of the car.

I laughingly said to HIM that I needed a convertible so I could raise my hands in worship without hitting the roof of the car all the time. So HE laughingly reminded me of having said that to HIM.

HE said "I want you to get that convertible instead, to raise the roof in praise for ME!"

Hence, the next time I went to Medicine Hat, I surprised my friend by pulling up in that little red sports car she saw in her dream!

TULSA OR BUST

It was a very long and extensive trip into the US. I covered Montana, Wyoming, North and South Dakota, Kansas, Missouri,

Arkansas, Oklahoma, Colorado and Texas. So many states that I hope I listed them all! My main destination was Tulsa. I was going to attend a couple of conferences with a friend down there.

I put ALL my money into the collection plate at the Maybe Centre on the Oral Roberts University campus. It was the first time I had ever done so.

I'm not particularly pleased when I hear sermons that go on about giving and getting a "hundred fold back." I prefer to simply give as a "cheerful giver" where I am not expecting anything in return, just wanting to freely give without ulterior motives.

In this case, I didn't get the hundred fold nor did I do it to get a hundred fold back. I did however, get enough money to get me all the way back to Calgary, Alberta, Canada.

I stayed with friends along the way. In Montana I stayed with a dear friend at her cabin on Flathead Lake. It was beautiful being able to swim all the way out to Horse Island and back again. I love being able to do that first thing in the morning on calm waters when it is safest.

My next stop was South Dakota. Around half a million bikers converge on the little town of Sturgis, South Dakota every August. I spent time with a ministry team there. I had been invited by another good friend that does roadside ministry for "HIS Labouring Few."

The two ministers that held tent meetings use to be part of the "one-percenters" themselves. Meaning, they had been members of the bike gangs like the Hell's Angels. When they came to be Christians they both were given motorhomes with garages in the back of them to carry their bikes in.

That is what GOD can do for a person when they have a gift to give others. He provides all that is needed to carry it out. We just have be willing to do it. HE provides the money for me to travel and minister. I've been invited back to Mali and Ghana. HE knows when and where I will go next.

A certain small percentage of bikers would just as soon kill you as look at you. Well that almost happened to me! A biker woman came up to me starving for the word of GOD so we talked for some time.

I advised her to not share becoming a Christian with just anyone, especially her biker family. Rather, I told her to find someone trustworthy to talk and confide in, before praying for her and giving her a hug goodbye. I then turned to head on my way down the main street in Sturgis.

That is when this biker yanked me around by the shoulder. I would have fallen backward had it not been for the crowd that I fell into. As he wrenched me around to face him he hollered at me, "Whatcha talkin' to my woman for?"

He dove for my neck to strangle me. That is when the most holy of holy things happened to me; that set me on a course of freedom from fear, from then on in to my ministry.

Attempts have come in a number of ways, in a number of countries. But of course the enemy cannot prevail against us. So no harm came of it. Actually not even a touch! The biker's hands were frozen in one spot just inches away from my neck yet not able to touch me.

AND wait, that is not the most awesome part. The best part about it was the PEACE and the SAFE feeling that came over me. He ended up getting so frustrated that he threw up his hands and walked away.

It was totally God! It had a profound and lasting impact on my spirituality. So much so that from then on I knew that I was fully protected by my GOD. It made it considerably reassuring when I was out there ministering in areas where Voodoo, Sorcery or any Black Magic or weaponry resides. It freed me up not to fear attack. You just don't forget something like that.

Since you are still alive and reading this, there is no time like the present to ask HIM into your life! If you don't know the LORD yet, you can. Simply ask HIM to forgive you your sins and then invite HIM into your life.

It is that easy. Believe me HE is reaching out to you. HE really wants to be your best friend because HE loves you so very, much! HE just won't invite himself in for HE leaves that up to you to choose all on your own with your own free will.

LOCKED OUT OF MY OWN COUNTRY

On my way home something else happened on that trip that blew me away (pun intended) and I was going to be affected by it. In fact it caused a delay that resulted in me getting back to Canada late for the start of another year of teaching that Sept. of 2011.

Do you know what the LORD prompted me to read that summer of 2011? I never liked Revelation, yet it was time, HE said, to read it. So while in Tulsa, I was able to read it from a Van Empy's Bible which specializes in writing on the book of Revelation.

I am bring this up to show you how timely GOD can be. For guess what happened just weeks later that kept me from getting back into my own country? Yes, it was 9-11. So you can see that it was pertinent that I be up to speed with the final and most prophetic book in the Bible.

To me, 9-11 meant Revelationizing, here we come! If people could not see Revelation times in these present times then here was blatant evidence of catastrophic proportions.

I was heading home when I got as far as friends in Bozeman, Montana. I was going to leave that very morning when I was called out to the living room to see what was being shown on the TV. It was around 9 AM that Sept. 11th.

At first I thought it was hype for some movie when everyone else said, "No! It's for real!" We all stood there watching the Trade Centre Towers implode from two airplanes flying straight into them. Oh My LORD GOD! On top of all that they announced that all borders were closed. That meant I could not leave that day and head home.

I finally crossed back into Canada about 4 days later. If you recall I was coming back with a trunk load of clothes and literature. As I pulled up I could see two cars ahead that a dog was searching through the vehicles.

I was relieved to see that it was a quick and easy procedure. However, as the next car in front of me began to pull up for its turn, the dog was whisked off to somewhere around the corner.

That meant only one thing. Now it was going to be a manual search and would take forever!

I just started praying, please, please, that the dog would show up when it was my turn. I sure didn't want to have them tear my whole trunk apart. I would be held up further.

Now it was my turn as the officer waved me forward for my security check. OMG! Just as I am coming to a stop, the man with the dog in tow, shows back up again. Yeah!

I was done in a few minutes. The dog did it all! He walked through the car and trunk, then circled me, as I was made to stand outside my car. That was it! Whew! Sweet, I was now in Alberta and heading home... But to what?

FLOODED OUT

I was now only a couple of hours away from home and looking forward to sleeping in my own bed; which was not going to happen! Just when I thought that I had enough excitement for the whole year, I got back to a flooded condo. OMG! It turned out to be one giant nightmare that went on and on into the next year.

To make a long, ridiculously tedious story short, in the end, I sold my condo, "as is," after living away from it since 9/11. I then lived in hotels until Christmas of 2001. I stayed with friends after the insurance money ran out.

I had so loved my condo overlooking downtown and having Edworthy Park as my backyard! No worries though, for after a few transitional places, the place I house sat in Marda Loop had for my pleasure a swimming pool! So I really just moved from one Sanctuary to another.

IT IS NOT OVER FOR ME

Len Lindstrom was no longer taking big trips overseas but I was still anxious and certainly willing to travel some more for the LORD. So whenever I had invitations come my way, I would leave it up to the LORD to set it up for me.

If it was a go, then I knew it was meant to be. I myself didn't even put the money towards the trip. That way when it showed up on its own, it made it very obvious that I am to go on that trip.

In 2003 I went to live in Mali, West Africa. Besides going for ministerial reasons, I was also wanting to observe whether I enjoyed living there or not. For if I did, I decided ahead of time that I would move there permanently to live. However, that did not happen. As much as I really like living there, I did not like the bureaucracy one had to contend with.

I got along fine with the way of living, even the type of food, etc. However, I sure would have a hard time with the laid-back never-ending way to get things done. For example, the entire mouth of the Niger River could feed all of Africa. Yet for that to happen the people would have to get their act together, and therein lies the problem.

I loved the pastor and his family that I lived with. His wife was the most prayerful women I've had the privilege to know. She believed GOD, for every meal and item they needed. I still wonder at times what she thought of me. I was always doing some unusual thing that may or may not have made sense to them.

For example, the road next to my hut/bedroom, was really a creek bed when the rains came. Since it was a creek bed and we lived near the bottom of this creek, the rains would wash lots of items down to just outside my hut. I was always rooting through it when I saw something I thought maybe of use.

Once I went after something shiny with such fervour! I was delighted to find it was exactly what I thought it was when I dug it out. It was one of those electrical spools that you find wire wrapped around. Not the big ones but just the perfect size as I smiled over at the Pastor exclaiming "Toilet seat! Toilet seat, yeah!"

You laugh but I was so delighted to finally have one. For in Africa, many of the family type toilets are simply holes in the ground that go down to pits or cisterns.

There were a few other things I'm sure didn't make sense. When taking buses I would want to go on a certain one because it had shocks! I also remember sitting on a wooden bench in one bus and when more people got on we were required to shift along the bench to make room.

One particular time I didn't want to slide down the bench. I am pretty sure it looked like I was being arrogant. I pray not, but I was determined to stay where I was. I just didn't want sit on the split wooden bench where it would pinch my butt every time we went over a bump. That would be all the time because their roads weren't real roads, but more like pasture paths along a fence line in a field. Only worse because they were filled with ruts and pot holes.

Just before I arrived in Mali I met someone that demonstrates how the LORD looks out for HIS children. I was able to sit by a lady I met from Edmonton. She was the wife of the head of the UN there in Mali. Where Timbuctoo, (Tim-buck-too) is by the way. So she gave me her contact information.

This proved to be most helpful just after landing in Mali. One thing I had brought were 300 Nikon filtered water bottles. The customs man saw me and pulled me out of the line into his office. I was held there because he expected a bribe in order to let me go. The LORD said, "Don't give him any money," not that I had any. So I insisted on calling the UN phone number that I had just been given on landing.

Pretty neat EH? Between my demands and Pastor M. insisting to speak to his Supervisor, I was immediately released.

We kept up a friendship after that although my Edmonton friend passed away unexpectedly, about a year and a half later! I did not find out until I came back to Mali at Christmas in 2004 when I went to stop in at the UN to drop some more items off. Her husband was on the way then to attend to her funeral arrangements in another country to the west of Mali: Niger.

She had been so considerate and empathetic to MY needs when she heard where I was going to live she insisted I stay with them. Of course I insisted as well that I felt it important I stay with the Pastor and his family.

So we compromised: I promised to stay with my new UN friend the last few weeks before flying out. I did and I must say that it was wonderful! I had my own bedroom with a toilet, sink and shower, not to mention electricity. The meals weren't cooked in a lean-to with dirt floors for a kitchen either. I had Canadian-type food as well which was a treat.

I did however ask the LORD to help me like everything I ate when I travelled to other countries. I ate Kangaroo in Australia, and I've eaten Teriyaki grasshoppers and chocolate ants. I used to kid around and still do about not wanting to know what I am eating until long after I have digested it. !

When I finally arrived at the Pastor's home, I was pretty hungry. One of his boys ran out to the market to get a can of sardines for me to eat as we sat under the shade of a big tree in the empty lot next to their home.

Now I may have told you earlier that when I was pregnant, I ate sardines in my 1st Trimester but I just hate sardines! Yet, remember what I prayed for? To like everything I was given to eat. So when I was handed that open can of sardines, I ate it like it was a steak! By that I mean that I actually liked it and ate all of it up! UMM!

A remarkable thing happened while there in Africa. First and foremost, the Chief got healed! Then there were others. A huge plus came when I found favour with the Mayor. In fact, he offered me his car and chauffeur whenever I needed.

Oh boy, is there a good story behind that for another time. With this favour, I was resourceful in securing land for the Pastor for his church, school, orphanage, garden, clinic, house and store.

Now the Pastor has all that established with electricity as well. He even put walls around the church too. I suggested not to, for I felt it was prophetic in a way to have it remain open on that hill that overlooked the city. That way it could be a spiritual pinnacle for the community and a place to pray out over the city.

However, I do get that walls may have helped in other ways. We faced "sorcery" every time we went to the church.

Even the Muslim alarms that sounded to alert people to pray would bug the Pastor. He was especially annoyed by the ones that went off during his church service on Sundays or their Bible Studies. I said, "Let's make their chanting music a time of intercessory pray in the form of tongues. Therefore, the annoying music will become an asset for warfare! TOUCHE!"

Another oddity that I will never forget was the "guard dog" that guarded my place every night. I never did see that dog. At times I would hear it growl and would jump out of my bed and run outside to see if I could see it but I never did! Are you starting to get the picture of how our LORD can take care of us?

I knew the dog was there to guard me. When the other dogs that ran in packs at night would come around they were not able to persuade him to join them. In fact he would fend them off and send them away whining. He stayed on guard just outside my door growling at anything suspicious.

The Women of Africa Conference was going to be held in Mali that year. The Mayor asked if I would like to go. I said that I would love to attend. So he had his driver come and pick both Pastor and I up.

At noon many went out under the trees to eat their lunches. The men outside played the drums while the women danced. I could not resist dancing to the beat. One of the men saw me and came and took me by the hand to join in!

MARRIAGE PROPHECY

Some years before I even went to Mali, a prophecy was spoken over me. The prophecy was that I would meet my husband either in a place called Mali or Bali. I was also told that I would marry an African Tribal Chief as well by a completely different Christian!

I really put very little thought into it other than recalling it because I was going to Mali. Needless to say, I was a bit gun shy around any of the men I would get introduced to, especially if they were a Tribal Chief!

I also prepared myself for guys wanting to marry me just to get into Canada. I decided with the LORD and ONLY the LORD before I even got to Africa, that any African man that showed any interest in me was to be drawn to me not by what they saw but without having seen me!

Lo and behold that is exactly what happened with my fiancé to be. He was a linguistics teacher and lived nearby. I was on my way to church one Sunday, talking to the children as I went. I was like a Pied-Piper, for they were all following along with me to church.

It was not until a few days later when he was on his way home that Pastor M. called him over to meet me. I had no idea that he was the same guy that wanted me to meet me because of my voice he had heard that Sunday past.

We ended up visiting a lot in the next few weeks before I was to fly out. He invited me to meet his family. His mother and I hit it off right away. I frequently had supper with his family and liked that they all spoke English.

He took me up to a lookout above the city one evening, on his motorbike. It was there he sat me on his bike and kneeled down to propose to me.

I accepted, but also said that I had one condition: I would help as much as I could with letters and meetings at the consulate, etc. but I would not sponsor him to get into Canada. He had to do this on his own and I would be waiting. So we kept in close touch through emailing.

There always seem to be a loop holes that couldn't be resolved. It grew more and more unlikely that he was going to get to Canada. Another year passed. He emailed me to tell me he had met a nice German lady at his school and was seeing her.

We still kept in touch but a few months later he shared with me that he was going to ask her to marry him. A couple of months later they were married.

I was happy for him and had no regrets. Our romance seemed more like something out of a Harlequin Romance novel, and I enjoyed it. I'll treasure it long into my years ahead.

I was actually glad not to marry him when I found out that he was quite a bit younger than I thought. He was only four months older than my oldest son! I suspect that we may only have lived in a happy marriage for a handful of years before he would have found himself drawn to younger attractions here in Canada.

What I don't get is that the bulk of men attracted to me are much younger. I suppose it is because I am so spontaneous and young at heart. I am very careful to make sure it is not an Oedipus complex by the way they interact with me. I sure was not going to be a mother figure. I made that clear right from the start.

I must say, I enjoyed dating at this older age because I was able to call the shots more than when I was a teen and young adult. I was wiser and I didn't need to have a boyfriend like I felt when I was a teen in high school. I knew more of what I was looking for and was much more mature at establishing my terms right from the start.

When I was online dating I declared right away what I was looking for and stuck to it. Usually when men come on strong with "I love you" messages that are all syrup, they are "scammers." I look out for that, and have also been asked to advise other women on how to avoid these scammers. I have been glad to tell other women what to watch for and avoid.

A GIFT OF MUD (2005-06)

Just after Christmas a friend of mine and I headed to Israel for a month. We went thinking we may very well not come home alive. We were focusing on a message that came from Revelations 10: 11 in which case we were going to give a fresh prophecy if the Lord set it up.

However we never were called to give any word of warning that may have resulted in being accosted in some way or other.

Other than the odd bomb observance we had the honour of witnessing, our trip overall remained rather safe from death's door. One bomb was right under our balcony where we ate every day. Another one was just at the bus stop down from the one we were waiting in.

One we saw left us with open mouths and shaking heads. It too was sitting under a bus stop bench. We watched as they sent a robot up to the bag to pick it up and here is where we shook our heads, open-mouthed. For the robot picked the bag up and believe it or not, s~h~o~o~k it wildly. Unbelievable!

Even our hitchhiking and camping on the shore of the Dead Sea under the stars was danger-wise uneventful. We had no place to stay, and dark was falling on us. It never ceases to amaze me that other parts of the world have sunsets that drop instantly. I was able to very quickly spot a few things in the dumpster.

I want to back up a bit here to inform you that we ended up tight for money to pay for food. The reason was that neither of us had let our banks know that we would be overseas and using our credit cards. The first time I was able to get money out of the ATM.

The second time around we were not so lucky. That left us scrounging. We learned to eat wisely, like at the Shwarma place where the guy gave us extra.

We discovered a way to get a bit of produce too. Some cultures believe in not picking up food if it falls on the market floor. I think it stems from a verse in the book of "Ruth" in the Bible. In "Ruth" during harvest, owners would instruct their workers to leave some behind for those less fortunate. In this case, that was the two of us.

Now back to the dumpster. My friend was somewhat taken aback at checking out garbage cans as a precaution and maybe for sustenance. So naturally, I easily spotted something that would help us camp that night on the shoreline.

There were several big cardboard boxes I had him help me drag out of the dumpster. In them were big huge bags full of large dinner buns. My friend was wondering what on earth I was hauling out all those buns for. After all we could probably only eat a couple for breakfast and keep a few more for lunch, so no way would we need all of them!

Oh yah! On that note, I filled him in on my plan. I figured we could lay the cardboard down and keep the buns in the plastic bags to use as mattresses and the smaller ones for pillows.

I made sure to keep ten or so for the next day to eat. Then as I prepared the beds, he gathered up enough kindling for the fire, for the night. You would not believe how cold it gets in Israel at night in January. Thanks to his fire and us each wearing all of our clothes at once, we did okay!

I told my friend I really was hoping somehow to soak in the famous Dead Sea Mud. How though, with it being very costly at the tourist resort spa up the road?

We arose to the most spectacular sunrise across the Dead Sea, coming up over Jordan. WOW, I can still see it! Off about 15 feet from us was a bucket sitting abandoned there all night long. With it being so dark the night before we had overlooked it. When I went to check it out, I just about did a jig right there on the beach. Surprise, surprise!

The bucket was full of MUD. YEAH! A gift from GOD! My very own bucket of mud, all for me-e-e! I am sure that amount at the spa would be a fortune to buy. I had plenty for each of us to cover ourselves from head to foot. I even had enough to share with others. Oh did it feel good! I have never felt anything so silky soft and nourishing for my body. If I lived there I think I would want to live within walking distance of that shore and swim every day!

For my friend it was astounding to see all the sights. For me I was encircled with sadness at how Christ was capitalized on. I make no apology for the sadness I experienced. I felt it had become a scene not any different from the one in the Bible where Jesus overturns the money tables in the courts of the synagogue.

We did make it home safe and sound but were red tagged for the flight. Apparently we looked suspicious. Understandably so, for we were so different in age. I in my 50's and he in his 30's plus all we had were backpacks and no souvenirs. We didn't look like typical tourists.

I think the rest of the world should take "profile training" from the Israelis instead of confiscating every nail clipper. If we got as good at spotting the suspicious people rather than treating everyone as a suspect, we would not only cut down on the costs and frustrations between passengers and airlines, but get the REAL culprits. After all, let's face it, a guy that wants to go out in a blast of glory is not going to be stopped by security going through all his stuff.

RINGING IN THE NEW YEAR WITH A BLAST

If you recall, the end of the world was to take place January 2012. What I said for the beginning of 2012 as my greeting to everyone on my emails for the New Year was:

MERRY CHRISTMAS! Cheers and blessings for you in this AMAZING NEW YEAR ahead! Full of all possibilities including the end of the world! Won't that be a blast! (Pun intended)! Which I do not believe for a minute because Jesus said when HE comes again that HE has no intention of letting us know the exact time and date (Mark 13:32).

GHANA

I began the New Year anticipating my trip to Ghana. Though it came on rather quickly, it seemed destined from the Lord.

I met a Golf Pro from Germany and he introduced me to a Pastor from Ghana that invited me to come. Which, I might add, is very interesting! For I had been thinking a lot about Ghana and the LORD had given me some very specific plans for Ghana even before this came into place. No one knew this but myself and the LORD.

This makes me think HE will accomplish great things over there. Another reason why I know this trip is from the LORD, is GOD again is paying for it! I have been invited to come back to both Mali and Ghana as well as India. So I wait for HIS answer to this invitation.

PROVISIONS OF ALL KINDS

I learned in all those trips that HE does provide. HE gives us what we need, when we need it! That occurred when I got my first condo. HE provided then too and ever since then for that matter. The list of provisions is constant and never-ending.

I didn't share with you what actually happened for me when I was moving into my condo. I had personal things that my ex-husband had me pick up from our home. Other than that I had no furniture to speak of. Once I got working I felt I should go out and buy a few things like an alarm clock. Up until then, I had relied on GOD to get me up on time.

HIS question to me was, why I would go buy an alarm clock when HE had been making sure I got up on time for work and so forth?

Then it hit me, that if I was to truly believe in HIM for all things, then I was to do just that. Hence my conclusion was that I would wait on HIM for my household needs and for the monies to travel on these crusades. To this day I have not bought an alarm clock nor do I ever intend to, nor furniture, etc.

When moving into my first condo, I was going to make a few pieces of furniture, with some paint left behind that I felt was a sign to make a couple of coffee tables and a sofa table. Totem had offered me scraps of lumber to build the pieces. Not long after though, neighbour friends insisted that I see if there was anything I might like, before their realtor hauled it all away. I got all of the furniture I wanted.

I got my first choice of condo out of the four I narrowed it down to. The person that sold me the condo was not a Christian, yet gave the place to me at my low offer because she could not help but feel that I should have that place.

CHAPTER 23:

WEIRD & MIRACULOUS

GOD can do anything, and in ways that we can never imagine or guess or request in our wildest dreams! These stories are not in any certain order but reveal answers to prayer in very unusual ways we can't imagine. And this isn't the half of it, only a sampling of the weird and miraculous!

MY GOAL

My purpose is fulfilled in those I have met and helped over the years. It is my hope that I can have a positive impact on those that continue to cross my path. I want to make a positive difference wherever I live or travel. I am trusting that I've achieved this and will continue to achieve it. I am glad I am glorifying HIM in the things I do.

More specifically, HE has asked me to bring other Christians into greater intimacy with HIM. He wants me to give words of encouragement and prophecy to others. All I have to do is let HIM set things up for me to continue making a difference in others' lives wherever I may be. And not baulk at how weird the happenings are or not.

WEIRD HAPPENINGS

Weird does not always mean miraculous or awesome in a wonderful way. Weird can be persecution or any kind of attack that is unsettling and out of place in some way. Sometimes weirdness hits from all angles through circumstances etcetera. Like every electrical or mechanical object in my condo or grade 3 classroom quitting and needing prayer to operate.

Or perhaps those persecuting me are stopped suddenly in mid-sentence to apologize for their condemnation. Or in spite of the fact I have been seriously injured in one way or another, I was spared excruciating pain. In one specific case the doctor even commented on how odd it was I wasn't wreathing in pain.

WEIRD ABILITY

Peter in the Bible can walk on water, and so did I! I didn't even scare the fish. Which I actually did, to get a teaching job. I welcomed the Superintendent to come with me down to Henderson Lake that winter to show him and to state I could do anything.

And that's not the weird part in which my ex-husband shot himself in the foot, so to speak. You see, the judge had declared that I was to pay alimony if I made over a certain amount in any job that I was able to obtain.

My ex telling the Superintendent that there was no one by my name living there (meaning, at our house), meant that I would miss out on getting a full-time teaching position in Lethbridge. I did not even know about the offer until months later.

I was down in Lethbridge in a store where I ran into the Superintendent. That is when he informed me of the offer and that he had been trying to contact me. According to what the Superintendent explained to me, my ex made like he didn't even know me.

Sad for sure because I may have had a full-time teaching job, be paying alimony and still been living in Lethbridge! Had my ex passed on my contact information (which he had of course) to the Superintendent that day, things would have played out entirely differently.

WEIRD FRIENDSHIP

We had some terrific times tubing down the river or snow covered hills. It didn't matter what time of year.

Even after he moved back to BC, we still had opportunities to visit. I remember us going to a birthday party and decorating our faces with icing. Or driving to the outside of Kamloops to watch the sunrise three different times in one morning and going skating on a lake where God created a natural Zamboni for us.

Then Bert's dog could pull us around on the ice. We twirled, we belly-flopped, we lay down and watched the sun come up again over the next set of mountains. Back in town we played in our favourite Tot Lot. We would go to the Feast and Vineyard church services Sundays. In the summer he climbed into the trunk of my (two-seater) car so others could join us, to go floating down the river.

We slept that summer on a trampoline in the backyard and even at his treehouse in Nelson BC. That's where I prayed for no dew! Thank you LORD! He even dressed up in one of my dresses and a wig of mine so that he could come to a bridal shower I was invited to.

Or the time he took me out and distracted me while everybody decorated his mom's place for my surprise birthday party! It was such a surprise to me, when we came into the house and I saw all the birthday decorations. I said, "Oh, does somebody have a birthday the same day as I do?"

In that same second everybody jumped out from behind the furniture and yelled, "Surprise! Happy birthday Karen!" WOW! I love fun surprises!

In winter we slept in front of the fireplace on the floor in the living room of his parents' home.

Our friendship was the very meaning of friendship. For anyone to think it was something more, they definitely were not observing nor knowing the facts. We were a weird match but a most beneficial one for both of us. We protected each other from any other attractions. Weird, maybe so, but truly a pure friendship, all above board.

WEIRD SOLUTIONS

When I was wrangling at the Pioneer Camps, young campers might get bruised in some way and would come crying for help. I would notice that the bruise was shaped like, maybe Mickey Mouse or Donald Duck or Winnie-the-Pooh. So then I would draw whatever figure around their bruise. That would instantly stop the crying and they would run off to show everybody their cute "cartoon" bruise.

One little boy could've gone away totally terrified of horses for the rest of his life. This was due to the traumatic experience he had in the corral one day when riding. He was riding Fat Albert, and Fat Albert always had a cold. Though he was a little Shetland pony, he was so fat, the little boy's leg stuck straight out in the saddle as if he was doing the splits. There was no way he could even get his little boots into the stirrups.

Then Fat Albert gave a big sneeze, Aaaaachooooh! The poor little guy slide right off onto the ground. It wasn't far to fall and get hurt. Nonetheless, this little boy thought he had been deliberately and traumatically bucked off. He immediately got up all tears and crying out at the horse for being so mean and vowed that he would not ever ride again!

Being the Wrangler in charge of this group, I couldn't have him or any of the others leave with a negative impression of horses. So I quickly ran to intervene to make sure he was okay.

I explained to him and the rest of the group that Fat Albert had a bad cold and that he had only sneezed; not meaning to hurt his rider. I said "Fat Albert really likes to give kids rides. He most likely thought you'd be okay and he couldn't warn you ahead of time, now could he?"

Once I had explained that horses can get colds, the kids saw the horse from a safe and different point of view. In fact the little boy turned his concern to Fat Albert to make sure he was okay and with a pat on his nose, wished him well in getting better. Ahhh!

Another time a boy a bit older had his dignity saved. We had just returned from a ride with a group of kids. This one boy dismounted as quickly as he could in order to squirm over to me all-a-wiggle wanting to know where the washroom was. No sooner had I pointed it out than he was bee-lining to the fence.

As he was climbing through to run to the outhouse by the barns, I could see something was wrong by the way he gave up and just stayed there planted between the two horizontal fence boards. So I tied up the horse I had and went over to him to find out what was wrong. I didn't have to ask, for I could tell what had him stuck on the fence like that. Embarrassed, he stood up in front of me without a word but his face spoke volumes.

He obviously was too late! The front of his pants was all wet.

I quickly jumped into action to save the day from being laughed at by his friends. I put my index finger up to my pursed mouth to indicate to be quiet because I had a secret plan. I motioned for him to come with me as I took his hand.

To the water fountain we went, but not for a drink. Instead, I started a water fight. While in the fight I got myself wet in the crotch and my shirt and pant legs.

Instantly he caught on to what I was doing and pitched in to get both of us wet. The changed expression on his face was priceless. He felt like he had a new lease on life. A total 180 from the look on his face when he wet his pants.

Now no one would ever know since both of us had wet pants! Before heading back to the group, I started laughing it up a bit over our water fight. That way the rest of the group would surely believe we had gotten wet from the water fight. Saved by a water fight!

WEIRD TEACHING VISIONS OR MOMENTS

As a therapist, counsellor, healer, and teacher I don't rule out "GOD things." I realize that baggage is something that we all have and need to manage as well as work on clearing it up in our lives.

I know keeping old baggage/old bad habits, will not serve me well. I get rid of them as soon as I can. I got rid of being a "pleaser" and trying to be perfect. Neither served me well in my marriage. In fact they probably were the reason I married the wrong guy.

I started off my new single life going to counsellors to seek to remove the unhealthy and damaging baggage I may have accumulated. In so doing I would periodically get the same vision.

The first vision the LORD gave me was of a huge pile of spilled, messy luggage. Some were open and the contents were spilling out all over. Some were nice pieces of luggage and others not so pretty.

Each time I saw this vision again the pile was getting smaller and neater looking. Then finally there came a day when HE showed me the pile again.

This time to my amazement, there was only one piece of luggage left! It was a great relief to see that the high messy pile was all gone. However, I was still not so sure about the one remaining piece of luggage.

It was a beautiful piece. One I would pick out to buy for myself. (Which I call a GOD THING.) For only HE would know what type of luggage I would like.

Interestingly it was the shape of a doctor's large medical bag. One like you would see in the movies when a doctor makes a house call. Only it was made out of a beautiful velvety rich tapestry of heavily embossed upholstery in very rich colours that gave it a very expensive look.

GOD knew I would be a bit disappointed in still seeing a bag remaining. However, HE knew I would like the piece of luggage HE chose for me to keep. HE reassured me to not worry. "You'll see. What I have stored in just the perfect piece I knew you would like to store precious resources in."

HE filled the bag with all my collected wisdom along with all my problem solving tips for people's issues to come in the future.

The doctor's bag held what I can pass on like medicine. I embraced that bag as my own treasure chest of valuable insights.

Since this glorious vision, years passed before a more recent one appeared. It was of me in my prayer closet, my sanctuary. There I was in my comfy wing-backed chair. Beside the chair was a beautiful antique floor lamp and beside it was my handsome medical bag! The closet itself was cozy, warm, colourful, bright, and clean!

There was no pile of baggage. I felt free and in power! In control of my life and in charge, regardless of who entered in.

Training means learning the rules in life.

Experience means learning the exceptions.

The latter is me!

CHAPTER 24:

WHERE I'M AT NOW

Once upon a time, I was asked to write something profound on a card that was going to be added to a number of others. The, "Something Profound" was concerning aging.

The card already began with the unfinished statement, "One thing younger people should know about aging is…" So I completed that statement with, "prepare effectively for major paradigm shifts in your life!"

I am not aging gently down the gradual slope that I had anticipated. Surprise! I am not capable of completing the same tasks at the same speed as before. Now it takes me two or three goes of my little one bedroom condo to vacuum or clean the place. Gone are the days of "multi-tasking." Heaven forbid I take on more than one thing at a time right now.

Being organized right now is not as good an idea as I use to think it was. In fact, the more I seem to organize the more the whole thing just falls apart. Things will even get lost when I go and reorganize because I am no longer familiar with where objects are placed. I am also discovering that out of sight means out of mind, so I leave things out in the open more and more. Consequently I no longer can keep my place uncluttered.

The older I get, the less I need to socialize. I find myself taking more time for myself, more alone time. Am I just doing so for cautionary reasons, or for circumstantial reasons, like financial and mobility reasons? I think it's all of the above. I do hope to maintain a balance at some point in the future.

Though I am not working anymore, my income was good enough as a Sub Teacher to pay for my little condo. My condo allows me to go swimming every day and soak in a hot tub afterwards. Or to go up to the theatre and watch a movie; better yet, to watch a curling game or the play-offs. Sounds pretty good to me. I could teach classes on how to economize.

I still have kept quite busy volunteering, though I am no longer on boards or committees, or teaching or socializing as much.

Though I am not dating right now, it has nothing to do with my change of heart and present desire to marry. I am actually tired of the dating scene. Can I get a second chance at this thing called marriage? That's up to GOD.

Of course the LORD knows my specifics and I have already asked HIM to please find for me the perfect husband for that second chance. As I said, this time I am leaving it entirely up to GOD to seek and set up for me to meet a man in my life.

For now I am satisfied with accomplishing this book and seeing where the LORD leads me next to speak and minister.

I recognize where I came from and where HE wants me to be as a new person in HIM! For HIS plans for me are nothing but fantastic. I would rather have GOD's plan for my life than let the enemy take over. For the enemy has access to us if we let him! Believe me it will only be for his evil purpose and not for your good.

I do not recall very much about my childhood visions of the future. It was more in my adult years that I remember specifics. I can confidently say that my visions are often true because some of those visions have come to pass and are still unfolding.

One in particular is the vision that I had before I was divorced. That I would see such a thing happening to me seemed impossible at the time. Yet it was and continues to be fulfilled.

It was a vision of me traveling so much that the planes were taking off and landing and taking off again and landing again and so on and so on. Since 1996 that is exactly what I have been doing. I have traveled on Mercy Ships in '96, to Mexico in '97 and '98.

I have been to Nicaragua, Guatemala, Nepal and Africa three times so far. The most recent trip for ministry was to Ghana in January of 2012. This of course only covers the destinations by air travel, not by other forms of travel.

I strongly suspect that my travels are not over.

NEWSFLASH

Newsflash, hot off the press! Here is something I found out this year in time to attach here. I'm a Grandmother of a two year old Grandson!

I am now officially a Grandmother as well as a Great Aunt five times over! That surely will add to my material for another book, in more ways than one.

PRAISE GOD!
"Joyously run forward into a learning curve great life of wonderful experiences!"
Karen McKenzieSmith